Retirement Planning for the Utterly Confused

Paul Petillo

New York   Chicago   San Francisco   Lisbon   London
Madrid   Mexico City   Milan   New Delhi   San Juan
Seoul   Singapore   Sydney   Toronto

To Bon,

Because you are what beautiful is

1 2 3 4 5 6 7 8 9 0   FGR/FGR   0 9 8 7

ISBN: 978-0-07-150868-1
MHID: 0-07-150868-6

This publication is designed to provide accurate and authoritative information in regard to the subject matter covered. It is sold with the understanding that the publisher is not engaged in rendering legal, accounting, or other professional service. If legal advice or other expert assistance is required, the services of a competent professional person should be sought.

—From a declaration of principles jointly adopted by a committee of the American Bar Association and a committee of publishers.

McGraw-Hill books are available at special quantity discounts to use as premiums and sales promotions, or for use in corporate training programs. For more information, please write to the Director of Special Sales, Professional Publishing, McGraw-Hill, Two Penn Plaza, New York, NY 10121-2298. Or contact your local bookstore.

Contents

Introduction

◆◆

By Any Other Name

In Spanish it is referred to as "jubilación." It is "avgång" in Swedish, "départ à la retraite" to the French, "Rückzug" among folks living in Germany, and "ritiro" in Italy. The Dutch have named it "teruggetrokkenheid," while their neighbors to the north in Denmark call it "tilbagetrukket."

A search for the English version of the word on Google reveals over 299 million references, and with good reason. It defies simple explanations, has a very recent history in America, and means many things to many people. The closer you get to it, it becomes an idea that is increasingly more difficult to wrap your mind around. By contrast, the farther removed from it you are, the less threatening it seems yet, as conundrums often are, it holds the most importance.

No newspaper or periodical that appeals to a wide audience can resist the lure of playing to their readers' concerns over the topic. No financial website overlooks the discussion, myself included (with over 880 references to date and growing). It is the fodder of water cooler conversations and the real reason we waste countless millions of dollars each week playing state and nationwide lotteries.

Almost every profession that orbits around the word finance has it at the center of their mission statement. Personal finance is designed to get to it with coffers filled to the brim. Financial planning is the act of getting there while financial planners are the guides—at least in theory.

We all know people who have experienced it and we have sought to improve upon their choices, discard their mistakes and hope that when we get to be "one of them" we will either be better off, as well-off, or able to survive longer at it than they did. We all know folks who have made mistakes, had life take a cruel and unforgiving turn, or been waylaid by their own bodies. We have seen plans disintegrate with the simplest twist of fate.

So we set goals. We dream dreams and make plans and hope beyond hope we can do better. Some of us have parents who successfully made the transition, while others have parents who have become financial obligations at a time when we are just freeing ourselves of our own children and focusing on our own future.

Famous people have mused about it. Simone de Beauvoir suggested that it "may be looked upon either as a prolonged holiday or as a rejection, as being thrown onto the scrap-heap." George Foreman was more concerned with the income than the age he may have picked. Chi Chi Rodriguez was quoted as saying that "my wife gets twice the husband but only half the income," while Jonathan Clements believes it "is like a long vacation in Las Vegas. The goal is to enjoy it to the fullest, but not so fully that you run out of money."

To offset some of the seriousness about the nature of the subject, we joke about the nature of the lifestyle. Humorists suggest that the greatest frustration will come with not being able to complete all the things you had planned to do that don't need to get done in the first place.

Some wise advisors suggest taking a week off to watch daytime television might cure the unnatural focus we have on it. Still other notable wise people, folks like George Bernard Shaw, call it the closest approximation to hell.

The *it* is retirement. The *it* looms large on the horizon for that well-publicized group about to enter the age when most of us consider retiring from active duty. Of course I speak of the Baby Boomers, the 78 million strong who were born between the years 1949 and 1964.

But this book isn't solely about *them*. It is about what retirement has become, an evolution that many are often willing to admit is not what they had hoped it would become. We can admit that with good reason. Retirement is continuing to change. Legislators are always eyeballing it. The financial community is dreaming up new products. Insurance people are crafting new policies. Lobbyists, the worker bees of these industries, are stepping up their activities. They want to help design the final product of this revolutionary event.

In the chapters ahead, we will take a look at this beast we call retirement. For lack of a better term, that is exactly what it has become, a poorly mannered nuisance that haunts those background thoughts we always have. It has all of the same traits that money has, which is why the two seem so inseparable, intertwined at the economic hip.

So retirement is essentially a financial discussion. Even if you view it in a philosophical way, money will enable those pristine thoughts to develop unencumbered. Perhaps you see retirement as spiritual fulfillment; the ability to financially support your efforts will make it easier to achieve the higher plane you seek. Perhaps you see retirement as a returning of favors, volunteer work designed to pay back what was gifted in the past. Retirement could be consultation, entrepreneurship or tinkering with a hobby.

The siren call might come from a desire to create. It might be a time to unleash your artistic prowess, challenge yourself in ways that were physically impossible while you earned a living. Perhaps it will be a time when each day adds a new page to that book.

Retirement is, with all of its possibilities, a recent development. America in the mid nineteenth century was still largely agricultural. As workers aged during that period, and it is important to note that those aging workers were probably family members, they were allowed to continue to work as long as they felt they were able. Their expertise was drawn upon more than their physical abilities, making them important in the success of the farm. They were the first semiretired consultants.

As America industrialized, that self-supporting community surrounding older workers slowly disappeared. Ironically, the one constant that remained as the shift from the farm to the city took place was the amount of men aged 65 or older who were still counted as working. Well over 60 percent of that age group was working as the country industrialized compared to 70 percent a half a century earlier.

But that was not bound to continue. Industrialization was becoming a corporate affair. Competition for jobs increased and ability to perform was suddenly scrutinized. A worker's productivity needed to keep pace with the increased demands of the job. Older workers were faced with a decision that no generation prior to them had to make: "If I can no longer work, how will I survive?"

There was no safety net in turn-of-the-century America. As families moved from rural areas to urban locales, elderly relatives became economic burdens on their families. There were no pensions, no government sponsored payments for food or shelter and, often, there was very little in the way of savings. Consequently, retirement was not really an option for nineteenth-century workers. And with the Panic of 1893, it looked to be much the same for twentieth-century laborers as well.

The Panic of 1893 will be remembered for the inability of economists to pin-point the actual causes. Generally speaking though, it was a run on the gold reserves. At the time, each note issued by the government was backed by gold held in reserve and if too many notes were redeemed, as was the case, the government, held by law to hold a certain gold reserve quota, simply stopped redeeming silver notes for gold.

Why, you may be asking about now, would the government allow citizens to redeem silver for gold? I'll tell you but only briefly. The Sherman Silver Purchase Act of 1890 increased the amount of silver the government purchased every month. Required by federal law to buy a regular amount of silver to cover the issuance of coins ($2 to $4 million as per the Bland-Allison Act of 1878), the new act increased that amount, forcing the Treasury to purchase an additional 4.5 million ounces of silver bullion every month.

People quickly found a loophole in the law (the notes could be redeemed for either silver or gold) and rushed to cash in. The Panic of 1893 ensued until President Grover Cleveland repealed the Act.

But that alone did not cause the panic. Businesses had gotten themselves into somewhat of a pickle. Workers were in great supply as the exodus from farm to city grew. That allowed them to increase production that, in turn, flooded the market with goods. In order to create those goods, businesses borrowed heavily from investors, giving them bonds in return.

In *Investing for the Utterly Confused*, I explained the way bonds work for investors and businesses, provided certain criteria were met. For instance, when a bond is issued to an investor, the investor becomes the lender and is awarded an interest rate in the form of a coupon. The borrower pays the investor in regular intervals based on the agreed upon rate. At the end of the loan, a maturity date is reached and the loan is paid in full.

What panicked investors in 1893 centered on a perfect economic storm. Businesses needed to pay high rates to attract too few investors. To pay those investors, businesses needed to produce goods. But the demand for those goods was not as high as the amount produced and prices fell. The result was collusion.

Collusion is an illegal activity. It happens when businesses group together to keep prices high. High prices and no customers are not good business policy. The next in a series of unfortunate events came with the bankruptcy of the Philadelphia and Reading Railroad. By the time the dust settled, the Panic had destroyed the economic landscape of the country. Over 15,000 companies had failed, along with 500 banks, with the western half of the nation taking the hardest hit.

Unemployment hit a high of 18 percent. Compare that with today's averages of around 4 percent and with the 3 percent rate in the year prior to the panic and you begin to understand the economy had shifted in a most unpredictable way. The Panic left families in financial ruins and those with elderly relatives were suffering the most.

While retirement was first enforced for elderly public officials around 1790, by the late 1800s retirement was something of an option of last resort. Once you left the workplace, you were more than likely to become impoverished. America in the nineteenth century was not the best time or place for the unemployed elderly.

Businesses began to see older workers as a burden to competition. In order to stay productive, they stopped hiring older workers and the ones in their employ were encouraged to leave. To entice them to leave the workforce, the pension was created. Railroads, now the backbone of the nineteenth century economy, needed an ever-younger workforce. Giving older workers a reason to leave helped with the problems faced with rapid growth and expansion.

The world had changed. The worker was now at the mercy of businesses and investors. Each ensuing disruption made their lives increasingly difficult. The Panic in 1893 was far from the only financial turmoil that caused investor worries and worker anguish.

The Panic of 1896 was caused by the lack of silver reserves. Five years later, the Panic of 1901 was the result of a financial power struggle over the Great Northern Railroad. The Federal Reserve System grew from the Panic of 1907. (This particular panic closed numerous banks and businesses and was largely the result of a credit crunch. A credit crunch can be described as too many borrowers and too few funds.)

And finally, the Panic of 1910–1911, while minor and often considered a much smaller panic than the previously mentioned disruptions, to this day draws criticisms for what it caused.

The Sherman Anti-Trust Act of 1890 (sometimes referred to as the Act of July 2, 1890, its formal name, or simply the Sherman Act) was, for the first time, an effort to keep monopolies from forming. It was this simple piece of legislation that changed the fate of the elder employee.

One of the most famous criticisms came from former Federal Reserve Chairman Alan Greenspan. His essay titled "Antitrust" pondered the loss of untold innovations and products as a result of forbidding companies to grow as large as they could. Competition, Greenspan argued, benefited consumerism. The Sherman Act *"was an attempt to remedy the economic distortions which prior government interventions had created, but which were blamed on the free market."* Mr. Greenspan believed that companies allowed to take their natural course would be far more beneficial for the overall economy.

(You can read the full essay at http://www.polyconomics.com/searchbase/ 06-12-98.html.)

If I disagree with that opinion I do so hesitantly. Many people believed in a classical definition of competition. The whole Austrian school of economics is built on this idea of no government intervention and free market activity.

Mr. Greenspan points this error in belief as the single defining mistake made by economists and businessmen of the early nineteenth century. They produced as much as possible while allowing market pricing to act as a natural force. Competition would, they believed, create the balance needed to keep the economy on an even keel.

Mr. Greenspan writes that businesses "aggressively attempted to affect the conditions of their markets by advertising, varying production rates, and bargaining on price with suppliers and customers."

The natural force Mr. Greenspan writes about starts with an industry that begins "with a few small firms; in time, many of them merge; this increases efficiency and augments profits. As the market expands, new firms enter the field, thus cutting down the share of the market held by the dominant firm." This created monopolized industries that, according to nineteenth-century thinking, stifled competition. Using the Sherman Act, they proceeded to dismantle industries that they viewed had shut out the natural forces of competition.

But, had there been no Sherman Act, there would have never been a single pension created for a single worker.

And, last, the final driving panic that created the post work social system we have now, in the form of pensions and Social Security and eventually 401(k) plans and similar self-directed retirement plans, came in the form of the Great Depression.

To this day, scholars are divided on the exact cause. In short, it may not have been the result of macroeconomic effects of money supply that is tied to production and consumption, or even the flip side of the coin, under-consumption and overinvestment (the latter of which creates an economic bubble), or even to the shady dealings of bankers and wealthy industrialists. It may have been the result of a cautious consumer who decided not to spend but to save. Each of these panics had the net effect of creating a discussion about a post-work life.

Retirement is an economic force to be reckoned with. You and I are encouraged to consume and to save but to do so in unequal and undetermined amounts. This book will help you reach a more equitable balance between what you need now and what you will need in the future.

We will look at the numerous ways to save now and in the future (that's right, we'll be doing the financial equivalent of reading the tea leaves) while pinpointing percentages and what investments would be best for you now and in the future.

I won't just look at the near retirees but the ones who cannot see that distant place because age removes their perspective. I will attempt to categorize this vast working force into three groups: the Early Bird, the Chaser, and the Relaxer.

The Early Bird is sort of self-explanatory. These are the youngest workers, the ones with the most potential to create great wealth with the simplest of moves. They are the same workers who pass up this opportunity time and again in favor of lifestyles that require a constant flow of cash. Often saddled with college loans, brand new paychecks, and credit debt, the opportunity is often squandered. Once lost, it cannot be regained.

The Chaser is often an Early Bird who failed to take advantage of *that* opportunity. While this is a harsh term, it befits the group who did not save anything during the prime years, when compounding coupled with time would have given them the head start they so desperately need.

Instead they bought a house, raised a family, and found the ability to borrow much more attractive than investing. Those that did invest most likely did not squirrel away nearly enough. Those that did invest probably did not utilize their retirement possibilities to the fullest. They are chasers in the great investment race and their anxiousness creates problems in themselves.

The Relaxer can see the end or is already there. Calling them Relaxers may be somewhat of a misnomer though. Many worry that they will outlive their money. Many worry that, after years of hard work, they may be still required to keep their jobs. To me, a return to the 70 percent employment rate for workers over the age of 65, as it was in 1890, does not sound so appealing.

Right now, it is estimated that 25 percent of the current workforce aged 55 will have to work past 65—not *want to*, as in electively choosing to stay active, gradually reducing their hours or becoming more like one of those nineteenth-century workers whose age is beneficial as a resident sage, but *have to*. As those Boomers take notice of the approaching benchmark and their generally acknowledged unpreparedness for it, that percentage is bound to increase.

So this discussion about retirement will be vast and important to each group. This, however, doesn't mean you can skip a few pages and move on to the financially appropriate section you assume you belong.

These three groups aren't age based. While there will be a short quiz at the beginning of the first chapter to help you determine which group you are in, chances are you probably already know. You sleep with the knowledge every night. You watch mutual fund companies implore you to save with them as you benignly watch your favorite sport on television. Women's magazines that fill pages with recipes and how-to-be-crafty now play to your financial sensibilities. You know exactly where you stand on this subject.

So the following pages are filled with suggestions on everything from debt to investments, to thinking about life while avoiding death.

Consider this short fable from Aesop. (This particular piece was translated by George Fyler Townsend.)

The Old Man and Death

AN OLD MAN was employed in cutting wood in the forest, and, in carrying the wood to the city for sale one day, became very wearied with his long journey. He sat down by the wayside and, throwing down his load, besought "Death" to come. "Death" immediately appeared in answer to his summons and asked for what reason he had called him. The Old Man hurriedly replied, "That, lifting up the load, you may place it again upon my shoulders."

PART ONE
Time

◆◆◆◆◆◆◆◆◆◆◆◆◆◆◆◆◆◆◆◆◆◆◆◆◆◆◆◆◆◆◆◆◆◆◆◆◆◆◆

Chiaroscuro is an Italian art term for the contrast between black and white. As we begin this discussion about retirement, it will pay to keep that rather obscure term in mind. "Why," you may ask, "should the way painters bring the focus of the eye to the brightest spot be important to the discussion about retirement planning?"

By creating the deep shadows, the artist gave the painting a three dimensional feel. It drew your eye to the brightest spot in the painting. Because of the intricate shadows, the details that surround the centerpiece of the work, the background was often ignored. But without it you would be left with a sense of loss, an emptiness.

As we begin this book on retirement planning, you must remember that retirement, or at least our current perception of what retirement will be like, is shaded differently for each of us. To that end, we will assume that "bright contrast" is how you may currently perceive retirement. But the plan you make must take into consideration all of those subtle shadows that surround an everyday life. Your plan depends on how well you see the whole picture, bright spots and soft shadows, foreground and back, light and dark.

Whatever your definition of retirement may be, and we will discuss many, it will be the time when your work life rewards your retirement life. It will be a time when you work if you want to rather than needing to. It will be a time to live dreams and pursue all of the glossy visions of "how it will be."

Our job presently is to get you to those options with as much money as possible.

CHAPTER 1
Calendars

◆◆

Why Retirement Focuses on Time

What the Experts Say

The result of this is, that old age is even more confident and courageous than youth. — Treatises on Friendship and Old Age by Marcus Tullius Cicero

Time is a measure. Since recorded history, people have sought to find a way to codify their existence with such abstractions and with good reason. Without knowing when to plant, when to harvest, when the rivers flooded, when the cold was coming, or when the migrations occurred, our ancestors would have been left to battle a brand new day without ability to plan for the future. Without some measure of time, life would have been happenstance and not well suited to our long-term survival.

Early peoples looked to the stars for some sort of understanding of these occurrences. In doing so, they were able to regulate their lives around these events. For us, calendars provide just such a measure of time over a wide expanse.

The ancient Egyptians are often credited with the first usable calendar based on the 365-day cycle that became known as a year. They were not, however, the first to try to bracket the world around us in a meaningful way. The earliest people looked to the sky for help. Because of the mystical nature of the events that unfolded in the night sky, many of the early astronomers were considered priests. Their power to predict left the average person in awe.

In Babylon, somewhere around the year 2500 BC, the Akkadians began keeping written astronomical records. In another part of the world, the Chinese recorded the first solar eclipse while the Polynesians were successfully navigating the uncharted oceans using the stars.

What is the Julian calendar? In the year 46 BC, the Greek Sosigenes convinced Julius Caesar to reform the Roman calendar to a more manageable form. At this time, Julius also changed the number of days in the months to achieve a 365-day year. In order to "catch up" with the seasons, Julius Caesar also added 90 days to the year 46 BC between November and February.

The calendar we use today was refined from the Julian calendar by Pope Gregory in 1582. This is the one based on 365 and a quarter days, which needs to be adjusted for that fourth day every four years, creating a Leap Year of 366 days. To this timetable we are forever locked.

Time Is Our Foil

It is impossible to have a discussion about the future without considering time. It is often thought of as "of the essence." Time can be given a wide variety of descriptions that it cannot possibly have. It "runs." It "flies." It "goes" by so quickly we often ask where it has gone.

As a father, the easiest way to measure time is through the growth of one's children. But one doesn't need children to feel the "march" of this abstract notion. For many of us time is framed by work weeks, deadlines, obligations to do certain things at a certain time, to be somewhere at a scheduled moment. It brackets our life yet it can seem distant and ethereal.

So how do we wrap ourselves around a future we cannot see let alone predict? How do we plan for the unknown when we have no idea how long we will live? And no matter how much we schedule and plan, each day holds a new foil.

Time is our foil.

Literature is resplendent with foils. Sherlock Homes had his Doctor Watson, St. John Rivers proved the foil of Rochester in Jane Eyre, Han Solo is Luke Skywalker's foil in *Star Wars*, Govinda acts the part as he travels with Siddhartha, Robin is Batman's, Squidward is Sponge Bob's, Venom is Spiderman's. For retirement, time is what acts against us and provides us with a ticking clock, a practical and obedient sidekick that never varies from its conviction to "fly-by," "march-on," or to simply "run."

We can, however, use this passing to our advantage. The essence of a plan, the whole idea behind the very concept, is based on preventing disaster by using what we know to offset what could possibly happen. In other words, we are simply trying to avoid disaster without letting the fear of the unknown grip us too tightly and, more importantly, without giving the appearance of simply shaking a Magic 8-Ball in the hope of the right answer.

Marcel Proust's million-word novel on memory, titled *Remembrance of Things Past*, was published in six volumes under the original title of *In Search of Lost Time*. Now published in seven volumes and under varying titles, the book wraps itself around a period of transition in France when technology was beginning to change life in significant ways and the world around the protagonist was upended by the advent of war. In it, the unnamed narrator simply dips a Madeleine in tea and unleashes a flood of memories, all designed to teach him that what he is now was shaped by the events of his life.

And this is what we bring to retirement planning. All of our past experiences, our attitudes about money, our concept of time and the simple act of opening this book—while not the work of Proust by any stretch of the imagination—will help us shape this discussion.

Because of the problems associated with the wide variety of experiences each of us has and the numerous influences that push and pull at our daily existence, I am forced to generalize a great deal. From each tidbit I will offer in the coming pages, you will have to form your own view of who you are and where you are headed. In other words, you will and should read yourself into it. And you should do so based on where you have been.

It is not as difficult as you might imagine. For the sake of discussion, we will assume that you fall—although probably not squarely—into one of three categories.

You are either just starting out, trying to catch up or are at a point where you are making plans to test your efforts. While no single age can be defined by these categories, it is generally hoped that starting out coincides with youth, catching up defines a middle age that was somewhat under anticipated and the final stage as the end of one's working career and the beginning of something entirely different.

Each type is important, using time as a foil or as an ally.

We will take a look at why we save so little. Even when we know that starting early will benefit us the most, we still put off until tomorrow what we can begin today. We will also begin the discussion on what risk is and how important it is in the effort to grow your retirement plan.

CHAPTER 2

How to Look at the Future through the Lens of Now: A Quiz

◆▬◆◆◆◆◆◆◆◆◆◆◆◆◆◆◆◆◆◆◆◆◆◆◆◆◆◆◆◆◆◆◆◆◆◆

This quiz is not really meant to pinpoint where you are in your plan, but instead it is designed to help you understand what you would like your retirement to be.

Do you agree or disagree with the following statements?:

1. Bernard M. Baruch, an American economist and adviser to US presidents, once said that, "Age is only a number, a cipher for the records. A man can't retire his experience. He must use it. Experience achieves more with less energy and time."

2. When George Burns died at age 100, he was still making the rounds plying the comedic trade he had worked at his entire life. He believed that "Retirement at 65 is ridiculous. When I was 65," he said, " I still had pimples."

3. George Foreman posited this thought: "The question isn't at what age I want to retire, it's at what income."

4. And, lastly, a friend of mine suggests that he has "enough money to retire as long as he lives for only a week."

If you are in greater agreement with the last two statements than the first two, you are certainly not alone. The amount of money the average American has saved for their futures is alarming—and not in a good way.

Table 1.1 represents a snapshot, provided by the Bureau of Labor Statistics, of the state of retirement planning in the US based on the latest available information.

Table 1.1

Variables	Percentage of population
Holding one or more retirement account	57.3%
Risk tolerance	
No financial risk	34.2%
Average financial risk	39.1%
Above average financial risk	21.2%
High risk	5.4%
Savers	78.5%
Time plan for saving less than a year	17.7%
Next year	11.3%
Next few years	26.2%
5 to 10 years	25.6%
Longer than 10 years	19.1%
Savings habits—past	
Spending more than income	19.1%
Spending equal to income	36.9%
Spending less than income	44.2%
Home ownership	56.0%
Financial assets	
Financial assets	$7,100 (median)
Retirement accounts	$49,944.82
Nonfinancial assets	$92,050 (median)

Japanese economist Albert Ando (1929–2001) and Italian-born economist Franco Modigliani (1918–2003), although not the first to develop the idea, helped to further explain exactly what Life cycle hypothesis is. It assumes that individuals consume a constant percentage of the present value of their life income. This is dictated by preferences and tastes and income.

Who Saves?

There are basically two schools of thought regarding savings: Life cycle hypothesis and the theory of planned behavior.

The *Life cycle hypothesis* is defined as savings that affects the population differently, depending on which age group you fall into. Economists suggest that there will always be a percentage of income consumed and not saved. What Life cycle hypothesis suggests is that, in order to purchase goods and services, younger people will borrow more against future earnings while older savers will spend down their savings. On the other hand, the middle-aged wage earner is likely to have higher income and therefore should be able to spend less with a higher ability to save.

The *Theory of Planned Behavior* is something quite different. This theory was developed by Icek Ajzen in 1985 and first appeared in an article titled "From Intentions to Actions: A Theory of Planned Behavior," which took his previously published work, "Theory of Reasoned Action," just a bit further. In the "Theory of Reasoned Action," Ajzen suggested that if someone thought their behavior would be perceived as positive by others, they would be more likely to act in such a way as to seek approval.

Intention, he believed, should drive the actual follow-though. Planned Behavior however is based on the theory of self-efficacy. So as not to burden you with a lot of theories, self-efficacy can be briefly explained as *the way we feel based on the success of our actions*. If we try something and fail, it affects any future effort and ultimately our likelihood to repeat the behavior.

Ajzen wrote that planned behavior comes with perceived gains. In a sense, we look for a certain outcome and plan our behavior around it. When it comes to savings, the idea that we can begin whenever we want and achieve whatever savings goal we set, opens us up to the same type of behavior as a smoker might exhibit, only in reverse.

Many of us know smoking is bad for us, yet we might say that quitting smoking is just a matter of stopping. Just as savings is just a matter of beginning, the results we may have experienced in the past may not have lived up to our expectations and, as a result, we stop trying.

Just as smokers often suggest how easy it would be to quit, modifying their behavior is not always that simple. Savers, who also have numerous tools to help them develop the behavioral controls that will help them save, often do not.

In a March 16, 2005 report, published on the Bureau of Labor Statistics website, Sharon A. DeVaney and Sophia T. Chiremba suggest that savers have "presented challenges for the American economy." Those closest to retirement, the Baby Boomers, born between 1946 and 1964, have had to deal with the repercussions associated with this sudden expansion of the population. Schools were built. Houses were in short supply. Competition for jobs increased. Increased pressure was put on the existing health systems.

Yet the Boomer generation, for all of its size and purported gains over previous generations and its appearance of prosperity, has had more difficulty with finances. Because of their monetary ineptitude, Boomers not only expect to work well into the age traditionally referred to as retirement but they will be more likely to file for bankruptcy than preceding generations. On the other hand, they will be remembered as the generation that was healthier, better educated and supposedly wealthier.

Those who are younger than these Boomers do not fare much better when it comes to saving. As I write this, the US has a negative savings rate. On the surface, this suggests that we are actually moving in the opposite direction of financial independence and retirement security. On the other hand, the calculation of the rate savings, like so many statistics, depends on how you interpret it.

When savings rates are reported, the income of current workers and the income retirees generate from "spending down" their savings are lumped together. This math *error* will increase as more workers retire, giving the savings rate a *negative* outlook for years to come.

If retirees were removed from the calculation—because they no longer save, and the savings rate included not just what was stashed away in retirement and savings accounts but the growth of those investments, the number would suddenly turn positive.

In the Real World...

The US Commerce Department is responsible for calculating the savings rate. By subtracting taxes and the amount of money spent by the entire population—current workers and retirees from total income (wages, salaries, interest, dividends, and numerous other sources of revenue but not

Continued

capital gains)—the savings rate attempts to determine the fiscal health of the nation. Many economists have additional problems with how the rate is calculated. Purchases of durable goods, even though many are financed over a period of time, are counted as spending against income. If you made $70,000 a year in income and bought a $30,000 automobile, the Commerce department would deduct the cost immediately, reducing your income in the year of the purchase to $40,000.

Instead of focusing on how our savings rate is calculated, Ms. DeVaney, who is a professor of Family and Consumer Economics, Department of Consumer Sciences and Retailing, Purdue University, and Ms. Chiremba, Ph.D. candidate, Department of Consumer Sciences and Retailing, Purdue University, co-authored a paper discussing how we save. The paper, "Comparing the Retirement Savings of the Baby Boomers and Other Cohorts" (full text can be found here: http://www.bls.gov/opub/cwc/cm20050114ar01p1.htm), split the population into four distinct groups called cohorts, a term that references similar experiences that generations can have.

Saving Across Generations

The Swing cohort was identified in their paper as those born between the years 1928–1945 and who have retired or are still working to supplement their incomes.

This group is often referred to as the "greatest" generation, a title that describes their quiet impact on the economy. They were frugal and seemingly self-sufficient, relying on employer's pension plans and Social Security to provide for them in retirement. These folks popularized the notion of the post-work era where leisure was the reward for years of toil. Many survived the Great Depression or grew up in households that suffered through those years.

 DeVaney and Chiremba noted the following statistics:

"There was at least one retirement account in 57 percent of the households. The average or mean amount in the retirement accounts was $49,944. The median amount held in retirement accounts was $2,000."

"About 34 percent of households preferred not to take any risk when saving or investing, while 39 percent would take average risk, and 27 percent would take above average or substantial risk.

"The Swing cohort was the smallest, representing just 14 percent of households.

"On average, respondents had completed about 13½ years of education. Forty-six percent of the households had children aged 18 years or younger living in the home. Thirteen percent of the heads of household were self-employed. The average or mean household income of the sample was $72,673; the median household income was $44,000.

"Forty-four percent claimed that they had spent less than their income in the previous year, while 19 percent indicated that they had spent more than their income, and 37 percent reported that they had spent an amount equal to their income."

The older Baby Boomers, born in the post-World War II era of 1946–1954, have been credited with attempting to be the opposite of their parents, choosing more idealistic paths and in doing so challenging the status quo. Think Magical Mystery Tour. In the prosperity that erupted following that war, Boomers learned how to spend.

Their offspring, sometimes called the younger Baby Boomers, were born between 1955 and 1964. This group sought the reward for any effort put forth, seeking self-gain and personal fulfillment as desirable objectives in their work and play. This group grew up with the threat of nuclear war and can tell their children of time spent hiding beneath school desks during practice drills for just such events. It was during times like this that these younger Boomers developed a near-term lifestyle and with it a propensity for debt.

Generations X and Y (born between 1965–1987), the last cohort mentioned in their study to fully enter into the workforce, has always had the benefit of technology to help them in their pursuits. According to the authors of the study, this group tends to be pessimistic, skeptical, and widely diverse. They have seen their planet shrink, and because of that they are able to embrace the dissolution of physical boundaries in an increasingly globalized world.

In the following table, the authors of the study break down the different categories:

Owns a Retirement Account

Born between 1928–1945	68.93%
Born between 1946–1954	72.92%
Born between 1955–1964	66.41%
Born between 1965–1987	45.3%

The Alliance of Risk and Time

A great many factors enter into who owns retirement accounts, chief among which is the tolerance for risk. While we will discuss risk a little further on, to define it is to understand its importance in an investment philosophy. Risk is not easily defined. In order to grow your money, you will need to take measured chances. The opportunities that are the safest, such as a passbook savings account insured up to $100,000 by the FDIC, are also considered the least risky. As the chances for gain and loss increase, so does the risk. Doing nothing with your money often implies no risk—although other forces such as inflation actually create losses which, in turn, create the *risk* that you might not have the same amount as you began with.

Risk allows a person to understand how investments and savings work over long periods of time and what savings can do over an extended period. It has also been reported as the single most important reason why the young people save the least for a future that seems too far away.

The inability to take chances (risk) with our savings at an early stage in our careers can limit the opportunities to grow that money. The earlier you begin to assume risk, the greater the ally time becomes. The longer you wait, the lower your tolerance for risk becomes and time becomes your foil.

There are additional groups who shun the idea of risk, and because of that are underinvested for their future. Nonwhite heads of households, single heads of households, and self-employed persons all tend to fall into this group, each with good reasons why they have failed to save.

What's next: There may be numerous reasons why you have failed to squirrel away any money for the future, none of which is very good. In the next chapter we will look at the wonder of financial and retirement planning and why, if you fail to take advantage of it, you will limit your options for the future.

CHAPTER 3

Understanding the Importance of Time

◆▬◆◆◆◆◆◆◆◆◆◆◆◆◆◆◆◆◆◆◆◆◆◆◆◆◆◆◆◆◆◆▬◆

E
arlier, I mentioned how the early calendars were designed to follow celestial movements across the sky. The ancients did this to regulate crop plantings and predict river flooding. What they were unaware of was the irony of what they were doing. To plan for the future they were looking into the past.

The Chinese recorded the first supernova in 1054. Danish astronomer Tycho Brahe studied an "extra star" in 1572 and in 1604, four years before the telescope was invented, Johannes Kepler extensively studied another burst of unexplained light. In 1987, Supernova 1987A exploded, coming suddenly and quite violently to the forefront of the Large Magellanic Cloud, a satellite galaxy of the Milky Way. The explosion was clearly seen in the southern hemisphere and was magnificently photographed by the Hubble Telescope.

But what few of us realize is that when we look up at the star filled sky we are looking at the past. When the light of SN1987A reached the surprised eyes of earth it had traveled for 163,000 years.

Saving has the same attributes only less astronomical. We get so caught up in the day-to-day existence that we have a difficult time projecting ourselves into the future. The younger you are, the more trouble you will have trying to see what some time in the distance will look like—and even harder, what your place in that distant time will be.

Saving is one way to ensure that at least one attribute of the future will be covered.

I understand the difficulty most of us have with seeing the future. Instead of wielding a crystal ball, what life tends to give us resembles a snow globe. Shake it up, as life often does, and you have much less clarity.

It doesn't need to be like that. If you have never picked up a financial book the following section will indeed be a revelation. Even if you have, the following information is at the foundation for all that follows and as such warrants more than a cursory review.

Compounding Interest

What is interest? Interest, no matter what side of the equation you are on, whether borrowing money or saving it, is a fee.

When you borrow money from a bank or lending institution, the cost of the loan is usually referred to as interest. (Yes, lenders do charge a whole hoard of additional fees but they are usually nonrecurring and are levied to cover paperwork and such.) On the other hand, when you save money, the interest is paid to you. Banks do this so they can, in turn, loan the money to borrowers. In essence, the interest they pay you is a borrower's fee.

Now, let's look at the terminology behind compounding interest: The principal is the money you deposit (or in the case of a loan, they money you borrow). In a math sentence—I did mention there would be math, didn't I?—it is represented as the letter **P**.

Interest rates are always represented as the letter **r** to signify the agreed-upon rate. Interest is usually expressed as a percentage. So far we have **P** (the principal) and **r** (the amount of interest you will earn).

The length of the loan determines how much money you will eventually pay for the right to borrow money. In a savings equation, the amount of time you save the money is represented by the letter **n**.

The result of money put in the bank initially (**P**) and the interest rate received (**r**), coupled with a certain time frame (**n**), results in what is called accumulated balance. This is shown as **A**.

Expressed as a math sentence, it would read:

$$A = P(1 + r)n$$

Suppose the interest rate is compounded more frequently than just once a year. Suppose it is done every quarter or even every month. The formula, for those that trust their math skills, and many of us sadly do not, the formula for quarterly compounding looks like this: $P(1 + r/4)4$ and the equation, should your money be compounded monthly would be: $P(1 + r/12)12$.

Here's how the math sentence plays out in terms of real numbers.

If **P** equals $1,000 and you will receive a 5 percent rate of interest, or **r**, and you plan on leaving the money untouched for 10 years or **n**, the amount of money you will have earned, even without any additional deposits will be $1,628 (**A**). This is based on a rate of interest that is compounded annually.

The simple fact everyone should grasp is the growth of a $1,000 left untouched over a decade. Let's, for the sake of our topic, assume that you are a 50-year-old worker who has saved very little for her or his retirement. Let's assume, for the sake of example, we use the savings of the average worker from the study done by Ms. DeVaney and Ms. Chiremba.

Suppose we use the interest rate mentioned in the example above as the rate payed to the average savings account. Five percent is a relatively high rate at the time of this writing but not unheard of. At the end of this section on compounding, I will give you a list of institutions and savings instruments that pay that or come very close.

So this wage earner has $49,944.82 and she or he holds on to it in an interest bearing account receiving an annual rate of interest of 5 percent and she or he leaves it there untouched for ten years.

$$A = P(\$49,944.82)(1 + r(0.05))n(10 \text{ years})$$

The cash in that account will have nearly doubled to $81,354.85. While the number of financial calculators online will allow you to play with different scenarios, we will run a few of them past you for the purpose of illustration.

Suppose that same worker added $100 a month over the same ten-year period. The amount that worker would have saved would climb to $97,202.99.

Suppose that same fifty-year-old worker puts away $2,000, the average tax return the IRS reports it sent to the average tax filer. Deposit that $2,000 annually and nothing else, your $49,944.82 will have grown to $107,768.42 over that time frame.

The average tax return sent to American taxpayers in 2006 is around $2,000. This is money not saved by you but instead held by the IRS for 12 months, which they refund without any interest. That amounts to $38 a week in unsaved cash. While depositing this amount at the end of the tax year is better than nothing, smart money would have made the cash work all year. Get with your employer and adjust your W-4 form to pay the IRS only what they have due—and not a penny more. You can find the form in your employer's personnel or human resource department or you can download it here: www.irs.gov/pub/irs-pdf/fw4.pdf.

To truly benefit from the magic of compounding, you need to start early. The younger you begin the greater your chances of growth with the least amount of money. Conversely, the older you begin the process of saving, the more you will need to save to gain the same benefit.

For example, a 25-year-old who puts that initial $1,000 away at 5 percent, leaves it untouched for 40 years, and doesn't add another dime over that time period, would have accumulated $7,039.99. While that doesn't seem like a lot at first glance, suppose this person added $1,000 every year, which is well below the maximum IRA contribution for that age group.

The money would be worth, at the time of their retirement, a cool $133,879.75 on just $46,000 worth of deposits.

 What is the maximum amount of an annual IRA contribution? Eligibility rules differ from person to person, but the simple answer is as follows:

- 2005–2007: $4,000
- 2008: $5,000
- After 2008: $500 increases in increments based on inflation

In contrast, a 35-year-old would have less time to save that amount but would have a better opportunity to save more. That thinking is based on average wage growth. I realize that, by the time you are thirty-five, you will have made more than a passing acquaintance with debt, probably become involved in a relationship, had kids, a mortgage and any number of additional financial responsibilities, but the ability to put away $20 a week (at least) should not create too much of a hardship.

That $20 a week added to your principal of $1,000 and held in an interest bearing account garnering 5 percent annual interest and held for 30 years will create a nest egg of $76,873.16.

There is money to be made using compounding.

Below is a list of places that will give you sizable rates for your savings. These rates change frequently, often daily. To get up-to-the-minute rates, bankrate.com is the best site available. All of these institutions are FDIC insured and many offer no "bricks and mortar" locations.

AmTrust Direct, Cleveland, OH. http://www.amtrustdirect.com/ 1.888.228.8146

5.36% with a minimum deposit of $1,000, no fees

BankUnited, Miami Lakes, FL. http://www.bankunited.com 1-877-779-2265
5.21% on a min. deposit of $5,000, fee on balance less than $300

---

iGObanking.com, Lake Success, NY. https://www.igobanking.com
1.88.432.5890

5.16% with a minimum deposit of $1, no fees

grandyielddirect.com, New York, NY. http://www.theapplebank.com/
1.800.588.5871

5.14% with a minimum deposit of $2,500, no fees

WTDirect, Baltimore, MD. http://www.wtdirect.com/
1.800.WTDIRECT

5.12% with a minimum deposit of $10,000, no fees

Why 75 Is the New 65

When you are 25, 65 seems so far off in the future that it achieves irrelevancy. Someone that age or younger understands that, whatever happens to them now, whether it be physical or financial, they will have a "lifetime or two" to recover from it. And while that might be just the placebo your brain needs to get through every day with each new event or obstacle, it is flawed thinking.

Just like that supernova I mentioned at the beginning of this chapter, the results of what happens today will be relevant 10, 20 or 30 years in the future. How will what you do now look in the future?

Merrill Lynch, in conjunction with Harris Interactive, surveyed Baby Boomer clients in order to delve into this particular group's thoughts about investing. The results revealed some facts that caught some investment types off guard.

First, more than 75 percent viewed retirement as a turning point, a moment in time when, at age 65, this group sees a world of opportunity in front of them. Many saw this as a time when they can change jobs or careers and continue to work into their seventies, well past the age at which they would typically begin to collect Social Security benefits. Recalculating the retirement age in such a manner will be done more often as normal life expectancies expand and the solvency of the benefit program comes into question.

Year of birth	Full retirement age
1937 or earlier	65
1938	65 and 2 months
1939	65 and 4 months
1940	65 and 6 months
1941	65 and 8 months
1942	65 and 10 months
1943–1954	66
1955	66 and 2 months
1956	66 and 4 months
1957	66 and 6 months
1958	66 and 8 months
1959	66 and 10 months
1960 and later	67

The earliest a person can start collecting
Social Security benefits will remain at
age 62—for now!

Merrill Lynch found that many who plan on retiring believe that they will still be economically viable well past traditional retirement age. While Merrill Lynch found that the vast majority of respondents will continue to work because they wish to stay mentally vibrant and physically motivated, over a third suggest the reason for continued employment will be due to the need for money.

 What the experts say: Do what you love. When you love your work, you become the best worker in the world.—Uri Geller

This means that age is no longer the determining factor for retirement. Instead financial preparedness has stepped to the forefront of a retiree's decision on when to quit work. And, with the few statistics we have uncovered so far, including average savings and the percentage of people who save, it appears that retirement may be very far away for far too many people.

You Will Live to Be ...

At the center of every debate about retirement, financial resources aside, is age. We are, almost begrudgingly, discovering that we will live to be much older

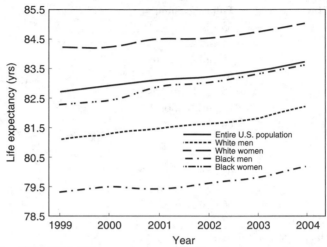

Figure 3.1 During 1999–2004, life expectancy at age 65 years increased by 1.0 year for the overall US population, 1.1 years for white men, 0.8 years for white women, 0.9 years for black men, and 1.3 years for black women.
Sources: CDC. United States life tables. Available at
http://www.cdc.gov/nchs/datawh/statab/unpubd/mortabs/lewk3_10.htm.

than most of us expected. Granted, this is a consideration many of us wish to ignore.

For many of us, we need to look at the longevity of our parents for clues to how long we can expect to live.

Social Security has its own life expectancy table (Table 3.1).

Table 3.1 Average remaining life expectancy for those surviving to age 65

The year they turn 65	Male	Female
1940	12.7	14.7
1950	13.1	16.2
1960	13.2	17.4
1970	13.8	18.6
1980	14.6	19.1
1990	15.3	19.6

In this graph, life expectancy is an actuarial notation. Because Social Security is, at its core, an insurance program and, if you think about it, retirement savings and planning for retirement is basically a home grown way of creating a financial insurance policy of your own. Determining how long we will live is not only important to companies and governments that provide benefits such as retirement payments, but it is also vital to the plans we make.

These are actuarial concerns.

Actuarial science applies mathematical and statistical methods to finance and insurance, particularly to risk assessment. Actuaries are professionals who are qualified in this field through examinations and experience.

Actuarial science includes a number of interrelating disciplines, including probability and statistics, finance, and economics.

Actuaries have two masters. The company they work for wants the best possible evaluation of how long you will live and, on the other side, actuaries live by the statistics that support their conclusions. For this, actuaries seem to be just short of erring on the side of you or I. In fact, I wrote once that an actuary is a person who, when he spies you drowning in a pool twenty feet away, throws you an eleven foot rope and claims they met you more than half way.

Dean P. Foster, Associate Professor of Statistics at the University of Pennsylvania Wharton School of Business, and his colleague Lyle H. Ungar, Associate Professor of Genomics and Computational Biology in the School of Medicine, also at the University of Pennsylvania, have assembled a life expectancy calculator.

Based on numerous statistics, they offer suggestions on how far a smoker would need to walk in order to offset the health consequences of smoking (a quarter mile a day per cigarette smoked) to not having been married (a 50 year-old single male will, according to their calculator, live three years less than their married counterpart). These stats also offer a way to offset each human foible with the simple act of walking.

The two professors have also teamed up with Chua Choon Tze, Assistant Professor of Finance at the Lee Kong Chian School of Business Singapore Management University to produce a much more detailed calculator.

(It can be found here: http://gosset.wharton.upenn.edu/mortality/perl/ CalcForm.html)

I found, based on the information I input into their tool, that I may live until I am 96. Not exactly comforting from a financial aspect! How long will you live, and how this will affect your retirement planning? We'll discuss these issues in the pages to come.

What factors enter into a long life? Professors now offer this list of stress-related issues that they feel will impact your health and longevity. While most of these are simply a consequence of being part of a family, each one can have adverse health effects. Ask yourself, do you have stress related to:

1. Serious illness in a family member (excluding death)
2. Serious concern about a family member (excluding illness)
3. Death of a family member
4. Divorce or separation
5. Forced to move from house
6. Forced to change job
7. Been made redundant
8. Feelings of insecurity at work
9. Serious financial trouble
10. Been legally prosecuted

Your Money Will Last until You Are ...

Preretirement surveys are sprouting up everywhere. They are asking about your lifestyle and what you plan on doing when you retire. And while the respondents to these questionnaires are mostly the ones who can see retirement as something that is close at hand, everyone should be asking the same thing—even young people.

Making it doubly difficult, even when retirement seems near enough to grasp, far too many variables enter into the equation to make the determination of "how much will I need" as easy as answering a few simple questions.

For the sake of this discussion, retirement will mean *the point when you draw solely on your retirement savings to help you with day-to-day expenses.* Granted, that is the drawn down version of what many feel retirement should be. But, in our case, we will also leave leisurely activities out of the equation.

Despite everyone's best efforts, the younger worker is not likely to prioritize retirement in their current spending/savings plans. Which is too bad. They will, and there is a good deal of evidence to back this claim, forfeit some of the best years for saving. With compounding and a long horizon in which the equity markets can grow (and falter and grow again, a cycle that has occurred numerous times over the last century), the younger investor will benefit over the one who begins late. But there are houses to buy and kids to raise.

Those late-to-the-game savers tend to try to catch up by socking away larger amounts in their middle years while taking greater risks with that savings. Although they may subscribe to the current thinking that we will work much longer than any previous generation, once you hit that benchmark age, retirement, or at least a significant and permanent retreat from a full week's work, begin to look increasingly attractive.

Pinpointing the Percentages

There have been numerous attempts at trying to define how much is enough. Planners and brokerage houses are rolling out new tools in the hope they can provide accurate measures of the far-off distant sum.

The most popular postwork guidelines suggest you will need anywhere from 70 to 85 percent of your preretirement income. I could easily suggest that you will have a need for 100 percent or more of what you are making now for later. And while all of these numbers are simply projections about a future full of unknowns, I would rather make the error of saving more than I may need. Not saving enough, on the other hand could be a very costly mistake.

The 70 percenters all believe that retirement will present fewer liabilities as we age. This group should be entering retirement with no mortgage, a home in relatively good repair, no debt or at least a manageable amount, affordable health insurance benefits, and limited travel ambitions. This plan also assumes that property taxes and insurance will remain stable based on preretirement levels. This group, in order to succeed, needs inflation to remain tame.

Inflation is incredibly difficult to predict. In the chart below, listing only the last ten years, it seems relatively stable but that can change.

2006	3.24%
2005	3.39%
2004	2.68%
2003	2.27%
2002	1.59%
2001	2.83%
2000	3.38%
1999	2.19%
1998	1.55%
1997	2.34%
1996	2.93%

During that time, prices on goods, excluding food and energy, increased 28.43 percent. The reason food and energy are removed from this calculation is due to their volatility. The Consumer Price Index uses inflation to calculate numerous payments on benefits paid by the government.

But taxes, insurance and inflation are not likely to be more affordable once your working income ceases. Health insurance, the conversation of choice among seniors I found out during a recent visit to a hospital-bound elderly relative, could also become a hot topic that has no monetary target. In other words, you cannot determine today what that coverage will cost in ten years. And this dire news does not account for possible changes to your coverage.

The 70 percenters would be wise to take advantage of every option available, including their IRA. A recent piece of legislation allows retirees to rollover their IRA in the newer enhanced HSA, a consumer driven health savings account we will discuss briefly when we look at the misunderstandings surrounding retirement and towards the end of the book when we will look at how they work. In short, an HSA permits savings to grow tax deferred and to be free of taxes once it is put into use for medical reasons. (Be aware of the stipulation that comes with such a rollover from an IRA to an HSA. That money, once it is moved, can only be withdrawn for medical reasons.)

But if that group was counting on that savings for income, what will they do now? You will find that the 70 percenters often make assumptions that are not based in reality.

Often, too often in fact, the 70 percenters will count their house as an asset (we will discuss this at length in Part Two, "The Seven Misunderstandings"). In the back of their minds, they look at the equity built up in the property as a sort of safety net. The two things they fail to understand with that thinking is that equity is equity until it is tapped; then it becomes additional debt.

 I've never lived in a building without my name on it. —Ivanka Trump

In many instances, the 70 percenters fail to recognize the cost of that debt in terms of interest rates and pay back periods. But, more importantly, will the lending institution lend you the money on your diminished income? Probably not. And, although you may trot out all of your accumulated savings as proof you can pay back the loan, why borrow only to accrue unnecessary interest?

The 70 percenters will often cite a pension as part of their plan. This added boost to their financial picture is only as good as the pension. If you have questions about your pension, the lion's share of which are under funded in this country, you have the right to ask if it is insured and, if you ask in writing, they must respond with your plan's funding condition.

The Pension Benefit Guaranty Corporation (PBGC) acts as an insurer, guaranteeing that pensioners will get something should the underlying plan fail. The shock for most people, who have accumulated the majority of their pension dollars in the later years of their career, comes when they realize that the PBGC has an income cap of $47,652 for retirees aged 65 in plans that terminated in 2006.

Fidelity Investments (http://www.fidelity.com) is suggesting that an 85 percent pretax retirement income is the best goal. The company feels that health insurance is the greatest risk to any retirement plan. That factor alone could impact savings more than many of us anticipate. Worried that a retiree's inability to pay for good health care coverage could have a devastating effect on a retirement income perceived to be adequate.

A First Look at Long-Term Insurance

After a recent appearance on a local television show, I was stopped and asked the same question most 50 year-olds seem to be asking these days: "Should I buy long-term care insurance?"

The daunting truth is probably yes. And the reality is probably no. If you consider the fact that you have a one in three chance of ending up in a nursing home, even briefly, as good odds, you probably shouldn't get it. But you should save for the possibility. Factor in an additional $100,000 above and beyond what you have set aside for retirement income. As mentioned earlier with the 70 percenters, rolling the balance of an IRA into a health savings plan at retirement is a good idea. (We will also discuss what to do and what not to do if that money is *not* in a tax-deferred account.)

While the premiums for long-term care insurance might seem considerably lower in your fifties than in your late sixties, you should also consider your resources. Is your home elder-friendly? Now would be a good time to rethink those stairs and discuss the possibility of not being able to use them. You will get to read more about this sobering topic a little further on.

Will you have your family to help you recover from some of old age's maladies? In many instances, a family member will step in and help. But you should consider this fact: one in twenty seniors aged 65 or older ends up in a nursing home for more than five years. (Look at your kids as they sit playing video games. Are these children your future caretakers?)

Perhaps a Little More Is Needed

People who believe that 85 percent of their income will be adequate can only really make that claim if they currently live on exactly that amount. These folks max-out 401(k) plans, hold investments outside of retirement accounts and realize that where you live is shelter foremost, with downsizing or reverse mortgaging as the last resort rather than part of the plan.

Determining what the industry calls an *income replacement ratio* can be difficult. Worksheets and calculations can be made at a wide variety of sites across the Internet. But how well they jive with your outlook is unknown and highly debatable.

The best thing to do would be to start the discussion now. Don't look at rainy Monday mornings as a good reason for retirement. But by all means, openly discuss with your spouse, your loved ones, or even your own reflection in the mirror, how you envision your post-work years. Can you afford it on your current take home pay? Remove your mortgage (but not your cost for taxes, insurance and upkeep) and ask yourself could you afford it now?

Factor in your health (and to a limited degree, the health of your parents) and try and determine those costs, which could rise almost 100 percent over the next ten to fifteen years.

Now determine your hopes, desires and aspirations. Is there enough money left over to do those special things right now? If not, after taking all of those other expenses into account, then you are not saving enough.

And, lastly, take the government out of the equation. While many count on something from Social Security, suppose it wasn't there. Could you face old age without Medicare or Medicaid?

Do your best to save as much as possible now. Ignore the percentage targets set by planners. No calculator can determine everything you will need—or not.

Do not plan on working later in life. There are only a select few who can or will try to do this because they want to. A far greater number of us would just as soon cease and desist from the workaday world.

People who have labored at trades or in service industries are among those who may not have enough energy left to keep on working. For other workers, the stress of everyday, even with its rewards, is reason enough to eyeball a no-work retirement.

If you think that working after retirement is a possibility, or even a necessity, you would be wise to start the job search today or begin the educational training you might need to make the transition as smoothly as possible. Be warned, the doors for late life job seekers are not as wide open as they were when you were 20.

Beginning to save as if you will need every dime of your current take home pay, possibly more, and doing it now, will make the future just a little less complicated.

After that rather sobering look at how long you will live and how much you will need, the conversation gets even a little more so. The temptation to skip parts that are unpleasant, such as the discussion on debt, should be avoided. There are some interesting ideas waiting ahead, including how family can affect your plans, how your house may not be what you believed it was, the reward of work, the high cost of health and what Washington and you should do, why insurance plays an important role, and the legacy you will leave.

In Part Two, "The Seven Misunderstandings," we will look at how you see your retirement through the lens of misinformation.

Sam Walter Foss (1858–1911) wrote a poem about how what we perceive to be true may be the result of one wrong turn repeated over and over again. In his poem, *The Calf Path*, he began:

> One day, through the primeval wood,
> A calf walked home, as good calves should;
> But made a trail all bent askew,
> A crooked trail, as all calves do.
>
> Since then three hundred years have fled,
> And, I infer, the calf is dead.
> But still he left behind his trail,
> And thereby hangs my moral tale.

As he looks at the history that path has seen, he concludes:

> For men are prone to go it blind
> Along the calf-paths of the mind,
> And work away from sun to sun
> To do what other men have done.
> They follow in the beaten track,
> And out and in, and forth and back,
> And still their devious course pursue,
> To keep the path that others do.

I hope to set the record straight, dispel some popular notions, and offer some encouragement where there seems to be little.

PART TWO
Seven Misunderstandings

◆◆◆◆◆◆◆◆◆◆◆◆◆◆◆◆◆◆◆◆◆◆◆◆◆◆◆◆◆◆◆

In July 2006, at the Chemical Heritage Foundation in Philadelphia, scientists gathered to discuss the role of alchemy in modern science. For those familiar with the term, the first image you might immediately conjure would be one of a darkened, shadowy laboratory, framed by books and ancient manuscripts, test tubes and assorted amblics, a hopeful yet slightly deranged looking man toiling under the weight of what could be a futile quest.

The image of the mad scientists, now believed to have occurred from too close a proximity to mercury, has kept the alchemists forever trapped in their own scientific poverty. We remember them, if at all, for their focused attention in trying to turn lead into gold and, in one famous Dutch court, the failed attempt to extract gold from silver. That unfortunate miscalculation led to the hanging of Hans Heinrich Nuschler in 1601.

Yet, alchemy, for all of its crackpot history, is considered the father of modern chemistry, pharmacology and medicine. The alchemist's attempt to reach a goal beyond their comprehension is very similar to our personal quest for retirement. To that end, debt might be considered by the alchemist as the lead in our quest for gold.

But now, it is time to set those failed notions straight, take what we have learned from the experience and move towards a more equitable end of our working careers.

CHAPTER 4

The First Misunderstanding: Debt

◆◆◆◆◆◆◆◆◆◆◆◆◆◆◆◆◆◆◆◆◆◆◆◆◆◆◆◆◆◆◆◆◆◆◆◆◆◆

The Negative Effects of Late-in-Life Debt

You will probably be surprised to hear this, but debt is something you will have in retirement no matter what you do. Debt, as a standalone concept, is actually a good thing. The ability to borrow money at a competitive rate is what fuels businesses, countries, and your personal finances. This is called liquidity. The more liquidity or money available, the better the interest rate and in reverse, when the interest rate is higher, there is usually less money available to lend to qualified borrowers. Business growth slows during times of lackluster liquidity, the stock market suffers and you have a more difficult time borrowing money when liquidity is low.

Debt may determine where you stand financially and if you are in good standing, credit is extended to you but liquidity determines how much that money will cost.

At the root of the term credit is the word credo, or "I believe." That belief is based on the trust that you will repay whatever was offered to you in good faith.

It is how that debt is maintained that makes all of the difference in your world.

I'll admit that I have taken the same view as many other writers before me have. We all preach from the same pulpit. Get out of debt now, we shout to the multitudes as often as possible. And we wonder why, in so many instances, it falls on deaf ears.

Stephen E. G. Lea, Paul Webley, and R. Mark Levine of the University of Exeter, Exeter, UK, published a paper in the *Journal of Economic Psychology* concerning the nature of indebtedness. The three men looked into socio-economic reasons—whether debt was more prevalent among the wealthy or those of lower economic status, whether religion had an affect, or perhaps how old they were. They found that the average debtor often had some religious belief with the non-Conformists, agnostics, and atheists among those least likely to be in serious trouble because of their indebtedness. The young, not surprisingly, tended to be the deepest in debt due to added factors such as student loans, just starting out, etc., and most interesting of all, they all knew other people with debt and did not assume they would be judged harshly because of their problem (from "The Economic Psychology of Consumer Debt" published February 1992).

The reason is simple. Those we preach to often wonder, in return, whether we have debt. They wonder, how can they live without it. We don't. We just handle it better. And that is key in the equation.

We may moralize about it—St. Paul even warned his listeners to "Owe no man anything." But how is that possible? In retirement, will we no longer be able to finance a car, use our credit cards to pay for a dinner or a hotel room, put a roof on the house if it needs one? Life doesn't stop just because we retire. Neither does debt. Debt is a fact of life and if used wisely, a handy little tool.

That's not so radical a thought as you might think. We are indebted to so many people throughout our lives that our life after work will, in all likelihood, be similar to the one you had before you retired. The question is, will you be able to afford the indebtedness?

Let's look at your debt now to gain some perspective. If you were to retire today, would you, with your current income, be able to pay for an emergency? Would you be able to pay the deductible on your home or cars insurance policy, should anything unfortunate happen to you or you loved ones?

If you are keenly aware of where you stand financially right now, you should be able to answer those questions. If you have debt, the calculation is much harder.

Upside Down: Your Car

There are basically three times in your life when you will be upside down. To be upside down in debt is a term that refers to a time when you owe more on something than the value of whatever it is that prompted you to borrow the money.

First we look at car loans. A vast majority of people who borrow money for automobiles will find themselves upside down in those loans in a relatively short time after the purchase.

Because people are fickle by nature, they tire of possessions long before they outlive their usefulness. It seems that about every four or five years carmakers make huge changes in their models and this is designed to catch our eye, to create a yearning for that new upgrade in safety or perhaps something as quirky as automatic parking.

When this happens, the owner of the car often seeks a trade-in only to find out that the car they have financed now exceeds the value of the car. These folks have focused on the car payment rather than length of time the loan exists. Cars quickly lose value but the amount of money financed seldom falls as quickly. Owing more on the car than the car is worth because you choose to finance the loan for 60 months or longer will find you upside down in the loan by month 48.

Remember we spoke about compounding earlier. It works the same way for debt as it does for saving—only in reverse. In the case of the car, which for most of us is numero uno on the list of upside down situations you are likely to face on the road to retirement, the solution is simple. But you need to understand why this happens.

You borrow money for a car. We all agree that cars are necessities and we can find ourselves making that same argument for any number of big-ticket items. The only problem is, the car you want or need has a sticker price that exceeds your budget. The key phrase in that sentence is *exceeds your budget*.

The very amiable dealer checks your credit and income again and offers you a different deal. This crafty salesman may offer you a longer finance period than the normal length of time most borrowers pay off their loans. For you, they will add months—and interest—just to accommodate your ability to pay.

Extending the loan beyond those first 48 months, in almost every instance, puts you upside down. Upside down is okay, a bad mistake you can live with and hopefully learn from as long as you keep the car until it is paid off.

As the car ages, you tire of it, begin to rationalize your ability and the affordability of keeping it maintained, or you simply outgrow it. Once that happens, you will no doubt catch yourself looking longingly at cars that are too expensive. You find yourself thinking about, even seriously considering the idea of, selling the car or trading it in.

Depreciation refers to the decline in the value of an asset. It is a noncash expense of what an asset is worth after it has outlived its usefulness over time.

Using our first brush with an upside down loan, you can see how depreciation works on a piece of property such as a car. Suppose, for the sake of the example, we bought a $30,000 car in June of 2007. Using a straight-line method of depreciation and depreciating the car over the course of a 60-month loan, we can estimate what a $30,000 purchase would be worth in five years. You will see it is worth zero, with each passing year stealing a little of its worth until the car is paid for in full. The figures below do not show the amount of interest paid over that five-year period.

(Add $4,799.04 to the loan amount at 6 percent interest to determine the total cost of the car. A 72-month loan at the same rate, which often is not the case when loans are extended this way, would add $5,797.44 to the total. A seven-year loan costs $6,813.56.)

Year end	Period depreciation	Accumulated depreciation
12/31/2007	$3,500.00	$3,500.00
12/31/2008	$6,000.00	$9,500.00
12/31/2009	$6,000.00	$15,500.00
12/31/2010	$6,000.00	$21,500.00
12/31/2011	$6,000.00	$27,500.00
12/31/2012	$2,500.00	$30,000.00

Often, this is our first brush with depreciation. The car may be worth more than the value of the trade-in. And in many instances, the car buyer, anxious to get rid of the car and faced with this new dilemma, will accept the cash rebate that may be offered to square the previous debt and then lock themselves into yet another spiraling (downward) loan.

The key to avoiding an upside down situation is to avoid the dealer turning lead into gold. They will offer you additional months to pay. You see, this is where the loan goes crazy. In the six-percent example above, the loan had a fixed payment of $579.98.

Sitting at the table with the dealer/loan officer/salesperson, you do the math and realize that factoring in insurance will put the car far out of reach. They offer six years (and often at a higher rate, but, for the sake of this example, we will use the 6 percent throughout) and the monthly payment falls further to $497.19. Seven years, a now-not-unheard-of-scenario, reduces the monthly loan payment even further to a much more manageable level—$438.26.

What you don't realize, even though by law they disclose it, is the total cost of the car. By the tenth month of the fourth year of ownership on that seven-year payment plan, you will have paid the total amount of interest as the buyer of the car on a 60-month loan!

With your eye on the target alone, you sign on the dotted line.

How do I get out of an upside down car loan? Hold on to the car until the loan is paid off and learn your lesson, refinance the loan at a lower rate and better terms or sell the car yourself. This last suggestion is not always the best solution for everyone but it often nets you the highest dollar value to car worth.

Upside Down: Your School Loans

The second instance of upside down debt comes with the college loan. This has been suggested as one of the good debts. And it may be. Yet the psychology of debt assumes that it will soon turn bad.

As I write this, the standard Stafford loan will charge a student 6.8 percent interest. On a $30,000 loan, the payment would be $198.58 for 360 months. On the surface, this does seem like a good deal. You enter the workforce with a much higher beginning salary than someone who did not attend college. But the total interest paid by the student over that 10-year period exceeds the total loan amount by $10,408.

According to the 2006 National Association of Colleges and Employers Survey of Salaries, the entry-level salaries of college graduates have steadily increased. Did they keep pace with the ability of these students to repay those loans? For some, yes. For others, such as those with degrees in liberal arts or who have chosen educational careers paying an average of $30,958 annually, it did not. Despite the fact that entry-level engineering graduates can earn more than $50,000 a year (business administration grads enter the workforce earning an average of $38,254, economics/finance students can expect to make $40,630, and those with degrees in accounting can start at $41,058) the cost of their education requires these newly minted workers to make some tough decisions concerning outstanding student loans.

So, faced with a $40,408 debt, graduating students often make the mistake of rationalizing the loan down. You have your first job and your first paycheck (averaging around $40,000 per year), and you are off to the spending races. At the very time when frugality would be your best friend, you befriend debt instead.

You buy a car. You rent an apartment. You rack up some credit card debt, all the while focused on your paycheck. But that $769 paycheck, about $560 after taxes, doesn't seem to be going very far. You consolidate.

 In the real world:

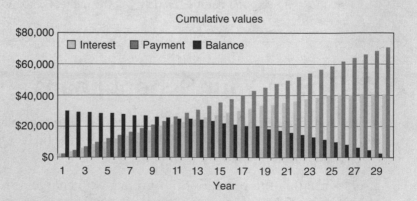

Loan amount $30,000; Annual interest rate 06.8%; term of loan: 360 months

Charted at http://finance.yahoo.com/

Your college loan is now upside down. Garnering additional interest over the life of the loan, a longer payback period, and coupled with higher rates paid on the credit card debt, you rationalize consolidation of all your loans, all of your trials with credit into one single loan as a cost effective solution to your debt. But your eyes are only on the monthly payment.

(Just a quick side note: This applies to all loans by anyone at any age when you wrap shorter-term loans into a longer-term debt simply to gain a monthly break on the payment.)

How do I handle a college payment? The answer might sound counterintuitive but the best thing to do is save. Take 10 percent from your paycheck and put it into your employer's retirement plan. Next, open a payroll deduction savings plan with your bank, taking that payment out each month. Then, ask your lender if you can save on the interest by making an automatic payment from that account. This will lower the monthly amount due the lender. Even a small savings of 0.6 percent in interest over the life of the loan can save you almost $4,000 in interest and lower the monthly payment by fifteen dollars. Your monthly salary after the funded retirement account and the automatic deduction for your college loan leaves you with $472 a week to spend. Not a lot, but not a bad paycheck to begin the rest of your spending either.

That upside down loan may not last for all college graduates but it has surfaced as a very real problem for those who choose careers outside the world of medicine, law and financial services. Teachers, social workers and other highly educated people are finding the rewards of their career choices are often not as monetarily satisfying as their chosen profession.

Parents who feel as though their obligation to their children extends to higher education may find themselves late in life saddled with student loans as well. In many instances this has come with a price. Too often, parents have sacrificed their own retirement funds; money that should have been directed towards their future was instead shifted to that of their children.

Upside Down: Mortgage

The last upside down moment in your life, barring the negative effects of divorce, is a home loan or refinance after the age of fifty. The temptation to keep your eye on the monthly mortgage payment is at its greatest once you hit this golden milestone.

For many of you, the assumption is that by age 50, all things being equal, your paycheck will have increased substantially and that added income will offset any additional loans. This thinking would be worthwhile if the mortgage was the only thing you had as expenditure.

For the younger readers, this might not even have crossed your mind. For older readers, this is something you want to put out of your mind.

Debt doesn't come just in the form of a mortgage payment. It comes with car payments (a $30,000 car at 6 percent is $579.98 a month or $1,159.96 for two, not counting insurance), saving for college (starting at age eight for one child attending a public university with a savings rate of 6 percent and the cost of college increasing at a 5 percent year-over-year rate, you need to save $532 a month), and insurance (rising on average 9 percent per year).

 According to CompuQuotes, an insurance aggregator, the average household pays the following:

Average cost of homeowners insurance	$1,000 per year
Average cost of auto insurance	$800 per year
Average cost of health insurance	$1,800 per year for adult individually
	$4,800 per year for a family
Average cost of life insurance	$500 per year

Refinancing at this age often includes the consolidation of all previous debt miscalculations into one neat and tidy loan *with* a manageable monthly payment. Unless you have signed up for a 15-year payback period, and even if you did, this is just not sound financing so close to retirement age. Worse, the average person is more likely to roll their credit card debt, their car loans, and their children's tuition into a 30-year loan. That is just not smart money.

 What should I do with all of life's large debt issues if I'm 50—or quickly approaching it? Get the refinance on your home but for only 15 years. Use any additional equity to fix what needs to be fixed in the home—if you plan

Continued

on staying or plan on selling, these improvements while you are working are about the only useful way to spend additional equity. But don't draw a dime extra otherwise. Talk facts with your kids about the cost of college as soon as they understand the value of a dollar. If you are behind on your retirement funding, you will need to step it up in a big way. The remainder of your debts should be manageable with a few simple techniques.

Three Simple Ways to Changing Course

Debt Reduction

Debt is simply the two steps backward for every one made forward.

At this point, it is important to understand that debt can be fixed once and for all. Two things are needed for this plan to succeed. The first is help and the second is the sliding scale. The help will be your financial partner, someone you can trust to mentor you in such a way that will keep you on track without forcing you to slip back into the bad habits you already have.

First, put your credit cards away in a safe place, out of easy access. Then get all of your credit bills in front of you.

The next step is to list all of your bills in order of smallest minimum payment to largest. For now, ignore the balances. We are concentrating on the minimum payments only.

Although there are numerous suggestions how to reduce those credit card bills, the sliding scale is among the easiest, causes the least day-to-day pain as you wrestle with the problem, and most importantly, actually works. And because of that, you will be more inclined to stay with it.

Consider these four monthly minimum credit card payments: $27, $46, $65, and $88—listed from least to most. Now it's time to perform a little sliding scale magic.

The sliding scale

$27

Double this $46
amount due until
the debt is paid, $65
then roll that amount
to the next minimum $88
on the slope.

Double the payment you will make for the smallest minimum bill only by making a $54 payment instead ($27 plus $27 equals $54). At the same time, continue to make the minimums on the remaining bills.

When you have paid off that bill, take that doubled minimum payment, in our example $27 plus $27 and adding that $54 to the minimum of the next debt which is $46. So instead of paying the minimum payment of $46, you are now making a $100 payment.

The sliding scale

$0

$46 + $54

The doubled $65
payment now rolls to
the next debt $88
on the slope.

When that is paid in full, take the sum of that payment, now $100, and add that to the next amount ($65 plus $100 equals $165). These gradual increases, which still have not exceeded the original $27, will eventually, painlessly eliminate your debt.

There are of course other ways to eliminate your debt and I would be remiss if I didn't mention them. A popular method is called snowballing or card hopping. This is a credit card game which involves switching balances for better interest payments in the short term. It buys time but does little if anything to pay the debt if you aren't making any effort to pay more than the minimum on each card.

Often, you will find yourself saddled with a credit card with high interest rates. A little comparison shopping will help you find a card with a lower fixed rate, which translates into a lower minimum monthly payment. The lower minimum is not the concern here, largely because you will be paying the minimum and then some. It is the interest that is accumulating while you pay the balance down. It is important to understand that, as you pay off these balances, interest is being charged on the money you owe. While you pay these cards off, you should help yourself to lower interest rates.

I mentioned the negative effect that debt can have on your financial goals. Here are some hard numbers. At Bankrate.com, the average for one-year certificate of deposit is around 4.83 percent at the time of this writing. The same site on the same day was posting credit card weekly fixed averages of 13.44 percent. The difference between the savings and the debt is 8.61 percent. This is the cost of your debt.

So how do you get out of debt if you lack the discipline to use the sliding scale method? There are several ways, none of which I recommend. Many of them involve borrowing, either from your personal savings, or from another source to pay the debt. Borrowing will not get you out of this mess but will instead simply spread out your existing debt over a longer period of time and land you a new creditor.

1. Borrowing against your life insurance can only be done on policies that have a cash value. Cash value is not usually associated with the less expensive term policies. You are, if you decide on this method, borrowing your own money; cash that will need to be repaid to the policy should you pass away before you have returned the money. Your beneficiaries will have the loan deducted from the amount of the policy if it hasn't been paid in full. The interest rates are usually lower than most commercial lenders, especially when you factor in the cost of paper work. You cannot borrow more than the worth of the policy so your beneficiaries won't be saddled with debt from this kind of borrowing. Think about it, won't that be a fun way to be remembered, your policy less your debt?

2. Borrowing from friends and relatives is probably easier for some than others. I make it a rule to keep money out of relationships with family and friends. It keeps the relationship on better footing. Besides, you might need them for a real emergency and not just for bailing you out of your foolish spending habits.

3. Borrowing from your 401(k) or other retirement pension plan depends on the difference between your interest rate for your debt and the return on the investment. *This is a patently bad idea.* If you have debt, reduce or suspend temporarily any percentage or lump sum contribution you are making to the retirement plan. Do this with one exception: If your employer is offering matching contributions, reduce yours, whether it be a whole dollar amount or a percentage, to the point where you can still get the match, but no more. You will learn more about these kinds of plans later on, but that matching contribution is free money. When the debt is handled, resume your normal contribution.

4. Contacting your creditors either personally or through some sort of counseling agency will result in your credit report being updated with the information that you are participating in a Debt Management Program (DMP). Using the DMP alternative avoids the longer-term (10 years) blemish that bankruptcy leaves on your credit report.

5. Bankruptcy is no longer a viable option. It doesn't create discipline; you'll need to stay out of debt. It doesn't solve any of the problems with the way you were using your credit. I understand that there are often some serious reasons why a person would consider such a course. Loss of employment, poor health and the bills they create, along with other extenuating circumstances, find people looking for relief from their bills. But if all you did was spend more than you could repay, bankruptcy should be your last resort.

Saving while Paying

If you are carrying credit cards from multiple companies, try to consolidate them to a single card, preferably one with the lowest interest rate. If you have paid your bills on time and are currently in good standing, contact your card company and ask for a better rate. It doesn't hurt to try. These companies know that your business is highly portable so they might be open to your request.

For people younger than 50, refinancing can reduce your monthly payments, freeing up additional cash that you can use to pay off other loans. Once again, I don't think its smart to roll short-term debt into long-term mortgages by taking money out when you refinance. But lowering your monthly payment is an excellent way to ease the burden and get those "ends" closer to meeting. The over 50 crowd should focus on creating a budget.

What is a budget? Budgets turn your financial world into a linear chain of events, forcing your money in the right direction. It involves some financial forecast such as placing a priority on debt reduction, starting with credit cards using a sliding scale, identifying upcoming expenses with the house, estimating the costs of possible major repairs, starting an allowance account to cover quarterly, semi-annual and annual obligations such as taxes, insurances, while making an evaluation on future spending on the family such as vacations, school expenses, and braces and, last but not least, developing a solid retirement plan that is both reasonable and attainable.

A Life Less Austere

Life is full of unexpected emergencies. These monetary bumps should not break a budget but should allow you to better absorb them. Budgets provide financial resiliency that would not exist without them. (See Appendix A—Budgets.)

Unmanaged debt can last a lifetime. To avoid a life of peanut butter sandwiches, there are several important things you need to never lose sight of.

Understanding the role of debt is extremely important.

If you are carrying debt, it has a negative effect on your financial plan. It is a subtraction of gains.

When something loses value it is called depreciation. It happens. Interest on the loan is now costing you more than the product's original value.

Using any method to control your debt takes a committed person with a supportive partner. Sometimes both of you may need help. In that case you should enlist a parent, ask a friend, or hire a counselor. There is nothing shameful about debt or asking for help.

The sliding scale method works incredibly efficiently but takes time and discipline. It builds character as well.

If all else fails, find a free service to help. If you do, you need to understand several things. Nothing is really free. And if that is true, be cautious of what they are selling. If they offer to restructure your loans, sell you insurance, or have the perfect annuity for you, run for the door.

A Poorly Reasoned Excuse

And lastly, before we move on to the second misunderstanding, think about why you *need* to go into debt. If it is a vacation, a must have toy, or even a remodel of your home, the cost of the loan (the length of time and the interest rate) can greatly diminish the worth of the purchase.

Try to plan some sort of advanced savings/payment plan (much like those quaint Christmas clubs the local bank sponsored for kids in days gone by) or take advantage of special free financing offers such as "twelve months same as cash deals" or "zero interest for the life of the loan." This last idea requires a little budgetary fortitude. If you plan on taking one of those deferred interest deals, keep in mind the following:

The interest continues to accrue. Each month that ticks past on the way to the 12-month target for pay-off has an interest calculation against it. In order to make this "special offer" work for you, you need to pay the bill—into a separate account you create for this purpose only—each month as if the company (the lender) was billing you. When the loan comes due, you should have the full amount saved and you simply write the check. If you fail this portion of the "special offer," all of the interest comes due at rates that are almost criminal.

> Always read any paperwork associated with any type of loan arrangement. Pay close attention to penalties for prepayment or delinquency and any conditions that need to be followed. And most importantly, how much that loan is going to cost you over time—not how much it costs you each month.

Controlling debt is the first step in completing a successful retirement plan. Misuse of debt can often derail, albeit temporarily, those plans. And if we remember that time is our foil, our retirement plan's antihero, those missteps can add up to valuable dollars unearned. The next misunderstood fact in the retirement plan is your family—and not just the wife and kids. Now, more than ever, your parents are a consideration.

CHAPTER 5

The Second Misunderstanding: The Family

◆◆◆

I f you think about it, the idea of family as a unit that sticks together through thick and thin, sickness and health, rich and poor was a fact of life a little more than a century ago. During those preindustrial times, this tight knit enterprise known as family was a birth to death experience. But times change and when huge migrations of people left the hardship of rural life to pursue job opportunities and the promise of a better life in the city, the whole economy of the family changed as well.

While those times brought distinctive changes in how we saw family, they have quietly changed back again. With extended life spans now considered as something we should plan for, the family has returned to those days when elderly family members, who may have outlived their usefulness on the farm, could retire to the front porch as the next generation repaid its debt with long-term care.

Few people focus on the economic reality of what it takes to raise a family before they begin. They enter into a relationship that is usually awash in soft hucs and warm edges. For the newly married or recently committed, this is a time of life when familiarity is something you will learn as time goes past.

The equation often means children. And children cost money. But they are often easy to plan for despite those unknown expenditures. The chart below shows some of the costs of growing a child in the United States. Many of those numbers are largely ignored by new parents and are often dealt with in an almost "in-stride" temperament, a "can-do" attitude that is at the core of family life.

And who can blame them or us? When you do the math, as it is laid out by the USDA, it offers us scary projections of costs up until the age of majority, and if you factor in the simple pleasures that life can afford, you can understand why some people choose to remain childless and you can also embrace the reasons why people do.

In the Real World...

Age of Child	Total	Housing	Food	Transportation	Clothing	Health care	And education	Miscellaneous
Before-tax income: Less than $44,500 (Average = $27,800)								
0-2	$7,580	$2,880	$1,030	$910	$350	$570	$1,150	$690
3-5	7,750	2,840	1,140	880	340	540	1,300	710
6-8	7,780	2,750	1,470	1,030	380	630	770	750
9-11	7,710	2,480	1,780	1,120	420	680	470	780
12-14	8,570	2,780	1,850	1,280	700	690	330	980
15-17	8,540	2,230	2,000	1,690	620	730	550	720
Total	$143,790	$47,820	$27,750	$20,670	$8,430	$11,520	$13,710	$13,890
Before-tax income: $44,500 to $74,900 (Average = $59,300)								
0-2	$10,600	$3,890	$1,230	$1,360	$410	$750	$1,890	$1,070
3-5	10,910	3,860	1,420	1,330	400	720	2,090	1,090
6-8	10,780	3,760	1,810	1,480	440	820	1,340	1,130
9-11	10,610	3,490	2,130	1,570	490	890	880	1,160
12-14	11,340	3,780	2,140	1,710	820	890	640	1,360
15-17	11,660	3,240	2,380	2,160	730	940	1,110	1,100
Total	$197,700	$88,060	$33,330	$28,830	$9,870	$15,030	$23,850	$20,730
Before-tax income: More than $74,900 (Average = $112,200)								
0-2	$15,760	$6,180	$1,630	$1,910	$540	$860	$2,850	$1,790
3-5	16,140	6,150	1,840	1,870	530	830	3,110	1,810
6-8	15,790	6,050	2,220	2,020	570	940	2,140	1,850
9-11	15,490	5,790	2,580	2,110	620	1,020	1,490	1,880
12-14	16,310	6,070	2,710	2,250	1,040	1,020	1,140	2,080
15-17	16,970	5,540	2,850	2,730	940	1,080	2,010	1,820
Total	$299,380	$107,340	$41,490	$38,670	$12,720	$17,250	$38,220	$33,690

http://www.cnpp.usda.gov

There are several key elements to understanding the financial structure of a family without losing sight of the greater goal—your retirement. We have already looked at some of the basic aspects of any good financial plan. Delving into the ideas of savings and debt are important first steps in the discovery of how we can manipulate money for our own purposes. Yet the underlying problem, as I refer to it in the first chapter as our "foil," is time.

 Time is not money. If anything, it is more important than money. The time we have to care for one another, especially for our children and our elderly, is more precious to us than anything else in the world. Yet we have more experience accounting for money than we do for time. —Nancy Folbre, Department of Economics, Thompson Hall, University of Massachusetts, Amherst, MA

A Question of Balance

Adam Smith wrote that an invisible hand—the self-interested quest for wealth that he mentions in Book IV of "The Wealth of Nations" —is what drives the economy, a sort of balancing mechanism that, while benefiting the individual, also benefits the community at large. Nancy Folbre, economist and author of "The Invisible Heart," objects.

While Smith offers his idea in a compelling metaphor: "It is not from the benevolence of the butcher, the brewer or the baker that we expect our dinner, but from their regard to their own interest. We address ourselves not to their humanity but to their self-love, and never talk to them of our necessities but of their advantages. Nobody but a beggar chooses to depend chiefly upon the benevolence of their fellow-citizens." To the contrary, Ms. Folbre suggests that it is the family that is at the foundation of all economics and values.

The Daily Reality

For many of us, faced with the day-to-day costs of running a household, the roles that many couples and singles must play during the course of their daily family lives can seem overwhelming.

But there are two simple things you can do to make whatever comes your way much easier on your finances. The first is to finance your retirement, beginning as soon as you can. The first gift a newly joined couple can give each other is the effort to fund their retirement. Once it is set in place as a fact of life, it is much easier to absorb many of the additional financial blows that life, without a doubt, will toss your way.

The second is the 50 percent mark. I mention this in the appendix (the section on debt) about the necessity of a budget. The worksheet provided is only partially inclusive. It cannot hope to address all of the roadblocks you may encounter along the way. What it should provide is an open dialogue between the planners.

Business adopts the same guidelines with their own financial plans, revisiting them periodically, setting long-range and short-term goals, and using the information of the past to set a course for the future. And because those futures are unknown, educated guesses are needed in order to succeed.

What to Ask? What is debt service? Simply, it is the cash required over a given period for the repayment of interest and principal on a debt.

The 50 percent mark is simply a debt goal. No more than half of the income entering into the household should go towards the service of debt. Keeping your eye on this target will allow you enormous amounts of wiggle room in your budget for those children and create a comfortable cushion for the second greatest concern a family can have—an issue that should be at the center of your welfare as you grow older: aging parents.

Parents Cost More Than You Think

By now you have heard the term "sandwich generation." It was coined to describe the growth in elder care that is delivered by grown children. It is estimated that over 20 million people in the US care for one parent or relative in their home. The economic effect of this on a household can be overwhelming.

In many instances, one spouse's career is put on hold or greatly reduced. Families can be uprooted from familiar surroundings to take care of a distant relative or, in a growing number of cases, the family absorbs the new member of the family into the household.

This can come with costs. Long-term elderly care can average more than $70,000 a year, a discussion we will have at length further along in the book. These older members of the family come with medical conditions and special needs and often with financial concerns that will need to be managed by the caregiver.

The following resources offer much more detail about the challenges facing families with aging parents:

THE AMERICAN ASSOCIATION OF HOMES AND SERVICES FOR THE AGING (www.aahsa.org or 202-783-2242) publishes free brochures on how to choose a nursing home or assisted-living facility, a directory of continuing-care retirement communities, and information on long-term care insurance.

FAMILY CAREGIVER ALLIANCE (www.caregiver.org; 415-434-3388) offers information for caregiver concerns, newsletters (English, Spanish, and Chinese), and an online support group.

THE NATIONAL ALLIANCE FOR CAREGIVING (www.caregiving.org; 301-718-8444) is a national resource center that provides information on elder-care conferences, books, and training for professionals.

NATIONAL ASSOCIATION OF AREA AGENCIES ON AGING (www.n4a.org; 202-872-0888), an advocacy group for local aging agencies, offers The Eldercare Locator (800-677-1116) or www.eldercare.gov, a service that puts you in touch with a local resource-and-referral organization, which, in turn, will recommend home health care aides.

Not all aging parents come with economic hardships. Many have planned for this time in their lives and are in a financial position to help themselves. But it is important for the children of older parents to understand how their financial plan will work.

If they are healthy, they may be able to stay in their own homes or move into a managed care facility that allows them to rent or own their own apartment with access to nursing facilities should they be needed. Some may need additional in-home care either on a part-time or full-time basis.

Understanding the costs of a nursing home requires a plan as well. The best way to determine these costs on both your finances and your aging relative is to begin the research early. The best facilities often have long waiting lists.

And because this is a financial book, the costs are the primary concern. Who will pay and how much is as important as the familial obligation to give this older generation the best care at the most affordable prices.

There is financial help available but it is usually short term. Medicare will only pay for brief nursing care stays, while Medicaid are primarily designed to help the low income members of society with limited assets. For instance, Medicaid will not allow the family home to stay in the family if the asset can be sold. Savings and investments must be divested before Medicaid can kick-in and, often, the payments are not enough to provide top notch care. The average nursing home now costs $6,175 a month.

When elderly relatives move into your house, their finances become your problem. Maintaining a conservative approach to protecting whatever wealth they have accumulated is important but may not be the best fit for all situations. As we look at your investment portfolio further along, it may be important to reconsider how your newest charge has invested their money as well. Perhaps you might need to offset inflation if your parents are in good health, allowing their investments to grow to keep pace.

Risks and Rewards

Elderly parents present additional problems for caregivers. According to the National Alliance of Caregivers and AARP, there are surprising amounts of work place risks taken by people who care for an older relative. Considerations that should be taken into account involve possible early retirements to provide full time care when needed and the fact that over 30 percent of those surveyed in 2004 either quit work entirely or switched to part-time employment. Additionally, promotions are often no longer part of the caregiver's equation and over 40 percent of employees thrust into the position of primary caregiver take a leave of absence.

By far the riskiest workplace result of this type of family generosity shows over 80 percent of the people arriving late, leaving early, or simply taking additional time off during the day. This not only jeopardizes the family's finances by jeopardizing the caregiver's employment, but detracts from the caregiver's own retirement savings — especially if their plan's contribution is withdrawn on a percentage of pay basis.

While the rewards of taking care of a close aging relative are worth the risk, employers are not willing to add it to the list of benefits that might attract workers. The Society for Human Resource Management has found that fewer than 6 percent of the companies they surveyed as recently as 2003 offer anything in the way of written assistance for their employees. While many have adopted proactive childcare help, the often-sporadic needs of geriatric relatives are not considered an economically feasible benefit. The group does suggest that the vast majority of businesses do help their employees on a case-by-case basis.

People who find themselves in this position grapple with two thoughts: How long can this last *and* how can I prevent the same situation from affecting my children? While we will work on the later question further along, the first question needs to be answered with some urgency.

First, you need to examine the health of your parents right now. While many of us look to them for answers concerning our own longevity, their time is the greatest unknown in a family's financial outlook.

Second, the family needs to discuss with these aging relatives where they are financially. Older folks are not often open about this subject but your insistence will show you care about their well being and not their inheritable property.

Last, if you are an only child, try to incorporate your household finances around theirs. If you have siblings, begin the conversation with the possibility of jointly purchasing a long-term policy. Determine who will be the executor of the estate and hire an attorney to review all of the legal options that are available. This might incur some initial costs but, in the long run, it will provide you with a much clearer, less emotionally charged picture of the future.

What's Next ▶ So far we have looked at the negative effects of debt on your plan. If you skipped that chapter, we'll wait while you go back and add this important piece of information to your retirement plan. I haven't actually called one debt worse than the other for two reasons. First, debt is a fact of life and, second, our skill

Continued

at managing it determines whether it is good or bad. Poor management leads to multiple and often cascading problems. Well-managed debt can actually work to your advantage by not having a negative or lasting impact on your retirement plan. Then we added a look at the role your family plays in this theater we call life. And with that, we now have some idea how your family puts pressure on the best laid plans. About 14 percent of married couples choose not to have children and, while there are numerous reasons why, chief among them is the financial pressure. This number is expected to grow to 20 percent by the next decade.

I'll agree, these initial two looks at retirement planning you did not consider are a bit sobering. Clearer explanations tend to be like that. But many things we quite possibly thought of differently have some unintended consequences. The next five topics are not any less difficult to wrap your mind around. Let's take a look at housing, one of the biggest pieces in your retirement plan that shouldn't be.

CHAPTER 6

The Third Misunderstanding: Your House

Living in Your Retirement Plan

I magine living in the time of Aristotle, if only for a moment. He proposed that the earth was the center of the universe. By doing so, he suggested that everything in the heavens moved around us. His thinking on this subject actually prompted the addition of a fifth element to the mix. Where there was once only fire, water, earth and air, there was now the stuff of the heavens, the quintessential.

Fast forward 1,500 years to Copernicus, who understood the religious implications of disagreeing with such earth-centric thinking, admitting on his deathbed that this was not true. He essentially demoted the earth to an object that moved around the sun, which he believed was stationary. We were no longer *the* world or even *the* earth but instead part of something much more cosmically larger.

We now knew we were part of a greater whole and not in fact the center of the universe. Turns out, there were thousands upon thousands of other universes with numerous suns and now numerous planets that may be just like earth in the vastness of space.

Perhaps what I am about to tell you, while not as profound as some of these notions, but just as likely to be as upsetting, involves the center of many of our individual universes—our homes.

What the Experts Say

I have been very happy with my homes, but homes really are no more than the people who live in them.—Nancy Reagan

For those of you who are just beginning this journey, the first house you buy is, in many instances, your last. As of 2005, the rate of home ownership in the US stood at 68.9 percent, just five percentage points higher than 15 years earlier.

In the Real World...

Age of Householder	2005
Less than 35 years	43.0%
35 to 44 years	69.3%
45 to 54 years	76.6%
55 to 64 years	81.2%
65 years or over	80.6%
Type of household	
All households	68.9%
Married couple/families	84.2%
Male householder family, no wife present	59.1%
Female householder family, no husband present	51.0%
One-person household, male householder	50.3%
One-person household, female householder	59.6%

How many of these people consider their homes part of their retirement plans is unknown but you can rest assured that far too many people calculate the relative worth of their homes into their retirement equation.

Why Some Consider the Nest an Egg

The Spectrum Group, a consulting firm based in Chicago, has found that home ownership is more than just a roof over your head, a place to customize and improve, raise families in, and host festive holiday get-togethers. Their research has turned up what may not be news to you at all: your home is part of your retirement plan.

While we all look at our property as an important part of our lives, a place of sanctuary and peacefulness, we also calculate the value of the structure giving it a monetary value. That value is often added to the total asset amount we have accumulated.

Is that wrong headed thinking? Quite possibly so and the result of it can add more anxiety to our plan if the property is not living up to our expectations. But suppose it is. Suppose we have gained enormous amounts of equity in the home due to those improvements, changes in the neighborhood or just simply a good economic tailwind at our backs.

The first home we purchase, if we buy it according to our income, should be something we can grow out of over time. In that case, the starter home is usually too small to raise a family but large enough to give us a sense of ownership, how the credit markets work, and what this type of investment can do to your taxes.

The use of the word *investment* is common even among personal finance writers and advisers. They will often say that a house is a great investment, or a must-have investment, but when the term is applied to home ownership, they make a serious miscalculation. An investment is usually described as something you put money into and watch it grow (hopefully) through any number of market forces such as compounding or asset appreciation, but, as we will find out soon, it is not the best word to describe your involvement in your own house.

Careers often force the selling of this first home almost as often as does the arrival of your first child. The cramped quarters that made your home right-sized often do not deliver the same satisfaction. If you have taken care of the property, acted as good stewards and not borrowed against the property for anything other than improvements, you should be able to get what you paid for it plus a dividend. Not a profit but a dividend.

The typical family may move again for any number of reasons, but the vast majority stop right there. They will, if they have shopped for a home in a neighborhood that has all of the amenities they seek, stay put, quite possibly until the nest is empty, and beyond.

You will tackle improvements, tweaking and rebuilding kitchens and bathrooms, landscaping and roofing and you will, over time, watch the property value increase. Many homeowners will do some simple math at this point and this is where most get into trouble.

Some academic economists believe that your home's net worth—the difference between what you owe and what it might sell of today—should also be considered when you tally your assets. It is important to think of assets in terms of their immediate liquidity—the ability to get cash when sold—rather than its *possible* worth. It makes for a fun parlor game and may let you sleep a little better at night, but unless you plan on living outdoors, selling your home requires reinvestment of that cash into another type of shelter.

How much is your home worth? In recent years, numerous Web sites have cropped up to estimate your home value. While many provide an accurate comparison of properties in your neighborhood based on what has sold recently, the true value of your home will be unknown without a physical inspection of the property. Only an appraiser, whose services can run upward of $500 depending on where you live, can give you an accurate number. Real estate agents, even friends in that business, will be focused on market value—what they can move it for fast rather than actual value. Be prepared to deduct your emotional attachment.

The Emotional Attachment

Often that simplistic calculation leads us to overvalue the worth of the property by failing to deduct the costs of numerous repairs over the years, the relative inflation and what we often overlook, the emotional value. If you have only used your equity for remodeling, the equation becomes much easier.

Adding any add-on loans to the original purchase price and comparing it to similarly sized homes nearby can give you a good estimate of what you would take away from the house should you sell.

When you are 30, the plan to downsize once the kids move out, move to a warmer clime, possibly closer to the activities you enjoy the most, seems like a good plan. But as the kids get older and move out, the comfort level you experience usually increases in conjunction with your age.

 A man travels the world over in search of what he needs and returns home to find it.—George Moore (1852–1933)

Yet that same span of time may have hobbled us, leaving us unwilling to take those flights of stairs. We may have found that the cost of upkeep has grown too great and the taxes have become too prohibitive. So we decide to sell.

But, before we do that, we need to fix a worth on the property. First thing to correct: your home is not and never has been an investment.

Fixing Our Thinking

Repeat: your home is not an investment. The true definition of investment is the use of money for the purpose of making a profit, gain income, increase capital or sometimes a combination of all three. While you may be able to rationalize your homeownership plan cum retirement plan as something you paid money for, lived in and hope to profit from, it is not.

Investments often require only the initial outlay of cash. Investments, as we will discuss later in the book, require research into potential growth, past measures of performance, and an optimistic belief that the investment will grow over time based on those educated decisions/guesses.

Homes, on the other hand, demand upkeep, reinvestments, protection in the form of insurances, along with levies on the home's worth such as taxes, the effects of neighborhoods, growth within the city boundaries and often the city itself, all of which eat away at what the typical homeowner views as profit.

Happiness is someone to love, something to do, and something to hope for.
—Chinese proverb

The best example of just such a miscalculation involves interest payments. Let's assume that you have a $200,000 mortgage at 7 percent for 30 years. The first mistake is the belief that the interest payments on that mortgage are spread evenly out over the remaining years of the loan. For those of you who may have overlooked this fact when signing those reams of paperwork at your home's closing, the total interest on a mortgage like this is $279, 017.80 if you owned the home for the full term of the mortgage.

After just five years and 60 months of payments totaling $1330.60 (not including taxes, insurance, etc.) you would have paid $69,197.68 in interest. In that short span, your so-called profit must exceed your original price of the home by almost 35 percent. Most markets, even at their recent peaks, failed to generate that kind of return. None has done so consistently. Own it for 10 years and the cost in interest alone has now exceeded $144,159.09.

Here is an abbreviated amortized payment schedule on a $200,000 home with a 30-year mortgage of 7 percent.

Year	Payment	Interest Paid	Principal Paid
2007	$1,330.60	$116.67	$163.94
2012	$1,330.60	$69,197.68	$11,962.22
2017	$1,330.60	$132,298.51	$28,704.69
2022	$1,330.60	$188,410.18	$52,429.32
2027	$1,330.60	$234,613.86	$86,061.95
2032	$1,330.60	$266,771.69	$145,440.14
2037	$1,330.60	$279,017.80	$200,000.00

The first conclusion you might draw from just such a table is "why buy?" Renting might seem so much cheaper with so many more advantages. And, depending on when you buy, it just might be.

Whenever newscasters speak of a seller's market, the price of owning a home has made it much more profitable for the seller, who can demand a higher price because the inventory of homes available for purchase is low and the people looking to buy is high. The reverse is true with a buyer's market when there are numerous homes on the market and not nearly as many potential buyers competing for the same homes.

If we continue to look at the process as an investment, then yes, the renter would come out ahead of the buyer, provided they saved the initial upfront costs of buying a home. The actual transaction can cost the buyer thousands of dollars upfront and are often added to the mortgage. If a renter invested those dollars in the stock market or, even more conservatively, in a 30-year Treasury, they would do far better than the homeowner.

The average cost of closing a home is $3,305.

A Good Faith Estimate, or GFE, is just that, an estimate of the costs to sign the papers and take control of the home. In 2006, Bankrate.com commissioned a survey asking over one thousand homebuyers about their GFEs. They found the GFE ranging anywhere from the total to the lender had quoted to as much as three times higher. Obviously, these instances were the most memorable in the minds of these borrowers. GFE usually includes appraisal fees, title insurance, lender fees, fees and taxes that might be levied by third parties, and in many instances, fees the buyer may not have anticipated: association fees, property taxes, insurance, and even mortgage interest. A HUD-1 statement attempts to list these fees within 24 hours of signing, itemizing them as accurately as possible.

Upkeep, Insurance and Taxes—Oh My!

If the renter had taken that $3,305 and invested in a mutual fund returning 6 percent a year over 30 years, they would be ahead of the buyer by a considerable amount.

Will I make more money renting than buying? Table 6.1 offers a look at what the average closing cost, invested for 30 years, would net the renter. The table does not account for taxes or inflation, or even reinvested dividends, that the fund might make over the course of that time period and it offers only a modest example of the potential gains that such an investment can net.

Your investment of $3,305, earning a rate of 6 percent annually for 30 years, would grow to $19,905, before taxes. This assumes that you do not withdraw investment earnings or make any additional contributions.

Table 6.1

Year	Future Value (without additional contributions)
1	$3,509
5	$4,458
10	$6,013
15	$8,111
20	$10,940
30	$19,905

The renter versus buyer argument ebbs and flows with each marketplace swing, from a buyer's advantage to a seller's. Several distinct factors need to be considered.

First, your length of stay in the home. This is extremely important for older buyers who are downsizing from previous homes that may or may not be paid for. Taking that equity, or as some like to refer to the amount we often view as profit, the rebate from that house and rolling it over into a smaller domain has its advantages. But not many. For older Americans looking to retire, their stay in their newer, downsized abode may be more limited than they anticipate. Health concerns and related issues may come into play and some of that rebate may have to be used to buy a long-term insurance policy (more on that later) or using it to invest in a health savings account (once again, more later).

Nonetheless, if you plan on staying in the home more than 10 years, you might be better off buying. Recent studies have shown that, as we age, those plans of moving become less important. Keep that in mind if you are younger than 50. Chances are, the home you buy when you are between 30 and 50 will probably be the last one you purchase.

Property values come into play as well. Here the ebb and flow plays itself out in a different way. Often, when money is inexpensive to borrow and buyers can access it rather easily, rents tend to stabilize and sometimes even fall. Landlords are concerned with a renter's exodus and attempt to sway them from making the "big move."

Conversely, when money becomes expensive and the buyer has a tougher time qualifying for a loan, the landlord might see the advantage of raising their rates, making renting less economically attractive but, with limited options, the renter must pay.

The often-touted tax deduction that comes with a home only benefits the buyer in the early years. Older buyers might be drawn by this just as younger buyers are. But the more money you put down on the property can offset this tax gain quickly. The older we get, the less likely we will want or will qualify for a long-term mortgage.

Older buyers will want to consider the higher costs associated with buying very carefully. Maintenance, insurance, and taxes all need to be factored into the monthly budget and because of the shorter time frame of the mortgage, this could prove very costly indeed. Younger buyers should look at making an additional year's payment in an attempt to reduce the principal as quickly as possible, saving both interest and time.

What to Ask?

Which is the best mortgage? Hands down, the 30-year mortgage is—for those under 40. It can be improved upon without any additional costs and shortened, often without any monthly budget constraints. A buyer who makes an additional thirteenth month payment (payment divided by 12) can reduce their mortgage by almost seven years.

Using the previous $200,000 mortgage example, a buyer who made a payment of $1,441.48 ($1,330.60 divided by 12 = $110.88 plus $1,330.60 = $1,441.48) would save $68,281.32 ($279,017.80 less $210,736.48 = $68,281.32).

Make a fourteenth month payment—adding $221.76 to your monthly mortgage payment would reduce the length of your mortgage by 10 years. This move would save you $107,370.74 in interest. While that seems like a lot, the same $221.76 invested at 7 percent return over that same 20 years would net you $214,950.

While older buyers eyeing retirement often see their accumulated savings as a hedge against unforeseen problems that can crop up, younger buyers often have additional expenditures that can put pressure on a monthly budget.

Add all of these factors in and the older you are, the less likely you will have time to travel extensively or simply be more mobile. Younger buyers tend to accept these realities.

Sell or Sell Out

If you have been calculating your home as part of your retirement plan, don't worry. The strategy isn't necessarily a bad one if three things exist: You have been in the house for more than 20 years and have not refinanced it for anything other than to capture lower interest rates; you have kept the house in relatively good shape and any improvements you made were done with an eye towards resale (subdued, less custom improvements are the best) or to accommodate an older you; your plans do not seem outsized for the amount of money you will walk away with at closing.

The harsh realities I have just spelled out do dampen the psychological benefits of your simple calculation of selling price less what is owed on the mortgage. The harshest reality comes with finding a new place to live. Remember, the inflated cost of your home is usually relative to the area you live in.

That downsized home you have always dreamed about is going to be more expensive if you choose to stay in the general area of where you live now. Ask yourself now, are you willing to move away from friends and family, activities you have come to enjoy and a climate you are comfortable with, for a home with one known factor: you will either have to wait for visitors to come to you or add the expense of travel to your plans to visit them.

 For a good deal of you, the idea of wiping your home off the list of retirement assets is very harsh medicine indeed. Sorry about that. But the younger you wrap yourself around the idea, the easier it will be to appreciate your home for what it is: shelter. It is in our natures to want to make it as livable as possible but don't do it thinking you will be able to capture those dollars as profit. That's not to say a short-term homeowner who happens to be in a rapidly

Continued

accelerating housing market can't walk away with a staggering amount of cash but most of us don't do that. We stay put. So enjoy your home for what it is and refocus your attention on building a real retirement plan.

We have mentioned the word "work" numerous times already. Sometimes we have used it in the context of something we have done and didn't want to do any longer. Our work, however, is part of what makes us who we are, what shapes our destinies and greatly affects our plans for retirement. And if you think your viability will exceed well beyond the common benchmarks for retirement, you need to develop your plan much earlier than you may have thought.

Our fourth misunderstanding is work.

CHAPTER 7

The Fourth Misunderstanding: Work

◆◆◆◆◆◆◆◆◆◆◆◆◆◆◆◆◆◆◆◆◆◆◆◆◆◆◆◆◆◆◆◆◆◆◆◆

Another Rainy Monday

Let's take a minute and review where we are. We have just covered three of the eight misunderstandings about retirement planning. Debt, we have found, has a negative effect on your plans, acting as a sort of reverse savings. The drag it applies so subtly does not allow you to get as far ahead of the game as you would like. (No, this is not a *game* but the willingness to keep score suggests it might be some self-absorbing competition.) Some debt is good; some is not.

We have looked at the cherubic faces of our children and the timeworn appearance of the elderly and realized that the people we love come with more than an emotional cost. We may not have actually thought of these loved ones in economic terms but they do exact a price tag and we willingly pay. Having these people in our lives makes us what we are and they, as the well-used phrase suggests, are priceless. Squeezing our own retirement into that family portrait takes more effort than we may have previously realized but, nonetheless, it is definitely doable.

Your Job and Inflation

Our fourth misunderstanding about retirement is work. The goal of retirement planning is to create enough wealth so that we will not need to work when we decide to part ways with our "day job." But many factors, many unknown and beyond our direct control, affect our ability to quit working when we want to.

For most of you, the career path you have chosen is based on your level of education. How much schooling you have is the lynchpin in a successful pursuit for a retirement without work. If you are under 30, the return on investment in additional education is easy to equate. The more you have learned in a formal setting will directly translate into a higher income.

Once you reach the middle of your career, the return on education may not be as obvious but is, without a doubt, beneficial. Toward the end of your working career, training can be more specific, centered on interests rather than the search for a new career. Those among us who cannot envision ourselves doing the same job for 40-plus years are those that have not increased their educational worth.

But the reasons for more education are much more noble than just for the sake of having more money. In order to create a retirement, you must first fund it with work.

It is relatively easy to make a correlation between income and lifestyle. If you are living within your wages, you probably already understand what it will take to retire with exactly the same lifestyle.

But who among us takes inflation into consideration when we make those future lifestyle estimates? Inflation acts much like a tax. Kept low, inflation can be planned for and treated like just another fact of life. But if inflation begins to outpace the income gains we so studiously educated ourselves in anticipation of receiving, it becomes more than a nuisance. It becomes a negative weight against all we have done and are attempting to do as we plan for retirement.

Inflation is always in the news. The Federal Reserve is always looking at a "comfortable inflation range" and adjusts short-term overnight rates they lend to the biggest banks in an attempt to control the economy. The economy reacts to the cost of borrowing by slowing down when money is expensive and speeding up when it is inexpensive to borrow. The 10-year Treasury bond can act like an inflation signal. The higher the yield, the greater the likelihood the economy is expecting inflation to rear its ugly head. You will

Continued

often hear it called a "flight to quality," a place where investors who have become skittish about the activity in equities (stocks) can park their money until the pressure inflation is putting on the market ceases.

You may be counting on wage increases steadily over the course of a career. Labor unions calculate them into their contracts—referred to as cost of living adjustments (COLA). Many of us expect our annual salaries to keep pace with our own notion of living expenses. Yet wage earners rarely factor inflation into their retirement plan even though it affects them in a direct and very real way. Inflation can wreck havoc on that hard-earned paycheck.

We often suffer a real disconnect between how inflation affects the building of our nest eggs and what that savings will buy 10, 20, even 30 years down the road. Inflation is rarely static or predictable and, because of that, including it in your estimates requires you assume the worst.

When the Federal Reserve focuses on inflation, they target a range where they believe the economy would be comfortable. They do this to allow for economic growth. If businesses can sell products at an equitable price, then they will keep workers employed and any pay increases they might receive would be reasonable. Keeping inflation in the 2 percent range achieves this complicated goal. Put in better perspective, each dollar you earn is worth only 98 cents in spendable income—and the top bankers are okay with this.

Retirement poses a different challenge. The estimates we make involve life on a fixed income. Suppose we use a nice round $30,000 annual income to illustrate how inflation impacts your idea of retirement. That figure may seem modest but it is probably closer to what many people will actually settle down with in their post-employment years.

If inflation held steady for 10 years, that modest income would have to increase to $37,293.24. By 2027—in a world of modest inflation, your income will need to have increased from the original $30,000 by two thirds. Remember, your retirement income is a *draw down* of saved income. Where at age 80 will you find another $20,000 a year in retirement income?

The point is, once you understand how inflation can wreck havoc on your paycheck, you can begin to imagine the destruction it can wage on your fixed income.

The Reward for a Job Well Done

The single easiest way to fix this problem *after* increasing your education level is to save your pay increases and bonuses. These incremental and often regular paycheck increases create two unique opportunities.

First, *your* overall savings rate would climb.

The second thing that would happen would be much more subtle. It would provide you with a safe glimpse of how life on a diminished income might be. Saving each pay increase and yearly bonuses is perhaps one of the least painful and most instructive methods to adjust your thinking for life beyond the daily grind. Think of it as a dividend reinvested. (In the last section of this book, we will discuss how to structure your investments in order to best overcome inflation and its evil twin, taxes.)

Saving this *in addition to* any retirement plan available to you, either at work or on your own, will put you comfortably ahead of your estimates and a little closer to your dream. It is your opportunity to develop a mindset that will refocus your present with the inevitabilities of the future.

The next two topics in our discussion about retirement misunderstandings will focus on your health and insurance. These are hot button topics and decisions you make today can have an impact on how much you need to save. Spoiler alert: the discussion can be quite sobering.

When it comes to your health, we will look at some of the things you do to undermine all of your efforts at creating a future and a stream of wealth you can count on and the industry that wants to place the bet on how well you might do.

CHAPTER 8

The Fifth Misunderstanding: Health

Planning while Living Dangerously

I have to admit that when I read about major league baseball pitchers plying their trade well into their 40s, I am encouraged. Pitchers like Nolan Ryan (no-hitter at 43—number six—then another at 44), Warren Spahn (21-game winner at the beginning of his fourth decade, at 42 he won 23), Tommy John (pitched until 46), Phil Neikro (hurling the baseball until he was 48), and a slew of still-pitching athletes like Roger Clemens, Randy Johnson, Tom Glavine, and Jamie Moyer are poster boys for good health and longevity in a sport that can consume your game after a long career, one which likely started in little league.

Now there are naysayers to this notion that middle-aged pitchers are something worthy of note. Frank DeFord, senior editor at *Sports Illustrated*, recently bemoaned the strategy of allowing pitchers to throw no more than 100 pitches a game. "Save the arm when they are in Little League," he cried. Not when they are adults! It doesn't matter whether it is 100 pitches or six innings, we can learn something from not only the pitchers, but plenty of other unmentioned athletes who have given their respective sports a go long after the average age of injury and retirement.

Your health is no small consideration when planning for retirement. We cannot predict the future but our state of well-being when we arrive at that unknown place can be helped along by the lifestyle we choose. Athletes and their coaches understand this. But it seems to be a moot point when it comes to the retirement plan of everyday workers.

The Cost of Health

Rather than turn this conversation about retirement planning into one about health, which we could easily do, we will instead focus on the costs of risk, the second most common usage of the word outside of investment and insurance.

Risk in many instances carries some reward. Except when it comes to health. Insurance folks measure numerous aspects about who and what you are with an eye on your physical well-being. The insurance industry will offer discounts to those who appear healthier than the average of the group. Never having smoked or gained weight beyond your peer group's range allow the insurance industry to offer some attractively priced policies. Your savings can be a source of additional funds that can be directed to those investment opportunities we will be talking about soon.

As the saying goes, an ounce of prevention is worth a pound of cure. When health is the topic of discussion, risk is about the only thing you can control. Risky behavior, as outlined by the Harvard Center for Cancer Prevention (http://www.yourdiseaserisk.harvard.edu/), include the following: unhealthy weight, poor diet and lack of vitamins, lack of physical activity, sun exposure, tobacco, alcohol and drug use, sexually transmitted infections, lack of screening with regard to family health history and genetics. With the exception of family history and genetics, all are within our control.

Continued

The HCCP believes that most of the risk of disease can be eliminated with nine simple steps. Maintain a healthy weight, exercise, don't smoke, eat healthy, drink alcohol in moderation, take a multivitamin with folate, use sunscreen, protect yourself from sexually transmitted disease and, as you age, get yourself screened.

Census data about health insurance in this country has been increasingly depressing as the nation's health progressively deteriorates. The saddest side of these numbers is the alarming number of children who do not have access to preventive care. With 46.6 million uninsured Americans, 8.3 million of which are under the age of 18, the best many of us can hope for is a little luck in the journey from birth to young adulthood. (For the full text of the report: http://www.cbpp.org/8-29-06health.htm)

But the more youthful we are, the more risks we take with our health and that type of behavior can have lasting financial consequences should that "luck" run out. Jonathan Gruber edited a book of collected essays about the economic impact of risky behavior among youths. While numerous contributors focused on teen problems, the issues they raise often last well into adulthood.

Consider the issue of smoking. In an essay coauthored with Jonathan Zinman, the MIT professor writes that "younger smokers clearly underestimate the likelihood that they will still be smoking in their early twenties and beyond." The economic impact of smoking has been well documented. What the authors discovered in their research suggested that those who did smoke after high school tended to smoke more.

The 2001 publication touches on numerous carry-over habits developed during the teen years that can have a negative effect on our financial well-being.

Mid-life Misadventures

Those carry-over habits seem to gain a whole new meaning as the toll of those foibles begin to catch up to us. And then the reality hits. We might lose our insurance coverage at the exact moment we might be more inclined to use it. No amount of prodding from me can get you to change the path you are on better than the idea that midlife can signal the greatest possible risk to your retirement plans, both in higher insurance premiums and potentially higher health costs once you have reached retirement.

This is the point we begin searching the volumes of medical data for placebos. A new report surfaces suggesting that a drink or two after dinner is beneficial. You rationalize that information and make it your own.

But midlife has its own set of risk factors. Weight gain is often the result of just these sort of rationalizations; ignoring the diseases lurking in the background is another. Normal life changes such as menopause can disrupt a normal person's health, but when coupled with the numerous other controllable risks we pile on can make the transition doubly difficult. Diabetes is often the result of unchecked weight gain. And while it is endured by almost 10 percent of the population, many of whom have no idea they have it, and although it is only the *sixth* leading cause of death, the long-term disabilities related to this disease make it a financial minefield.

The list below was prepared by the National Center for Health Statistics and gives the leading causes of death for 2005, the latest data available:

Heart disease	654,092
Cancer	550,270
Stroke (cerebrovascular diseases)	150,147
Chronic lower respiratory diseases	123,884
Accidents (unintentional injuries)	108,694
Diabetes	72,815
Alzheimer's disease	65,829
Influenza/pneumonia	61,472
Nephritis, nephrotic syndrome, and nephrosis	42,762
Septicemia	33,464

Midlife is also the time when we are faced with the realities of the rising costs of health coverage. An increasingly large portion of the middle-aged population will be forced to shop for health insurance. While the reasons vary widely from job loss to early retirement before the Social Security mandated age, insurance is rarely if ever budgeted.

And insurance is rarely fair to the consumer. A recent study by the Harvard Medical School found that those costs will be passed on to women at a much higher rate than men. The report suggests that women will be penalized almost $1,000 more in the popular high deductible plans that are correctly being discussed as a possible solution for health coverage across the US.

These high deductible plans are being tested in Massachusetts. They are designed to make consumers more cost conscious by offering a deductible that falls between $1,500 and $5,000 a year. Co-pays kick in after out-of-pocket limits are reached and sometimes there is an additional coinsurance payment as well. While the plans offer a glimpse at the cost-effective possibilities of these plans, what they uncovered was a disparity of who pays more.

According to the study, which was published in the July 2007 issue of the *Journal of General Internal Medicine*, the average man paid only $847 in expenses in 2006. Women, on the other hand, are seemingly penalized by the industry for their ability to bear children and the potential medical maladies associated with that. They are forced to shell out an average of $1,844.

 High-deductible health insurance penalizes anyone who's sick. Even common, mild problems like arthritis and high blood pressure make you a loser in a high-deductible plan. And these financial penalties keep people from getting the routine care they need to prevent disastrous illness later on. —Dr. David U. Himmelstein, study coauthor and a Harvard Medical School associate professor

http://pnhp.org/PDF_files/CDHC_Unwise.pdf

The Expenditures of Old Age

In Shel Silverstein's elegant seven-line poem, "Woulda, Coulda, Shoulda," he points out the simple notion of *did*.

Did is the opening for numerous questions from the curious minds we encounter each day. *Did* begins the process that pushes the memory of what happened to the forefront of what is now. *Did* you bring home the milk? *Did* you go to college? *Did* you ever call that girl/boy/repairman/restaurant/hotel?

Did you know? Why *did* the chicken cross the road? And my favorite, *did* you or *didn't* you?

At the heart of old age and the health expenditures that may face many people as they age lies the word *did*. What you do know will help you answer the question of "what did you do?" I have mentioned that one of the primary causes of increased costs at any age is obesity and poor health maintenance during a period of time when you have the most control. Smoking, excessive drinking, lack of sleep, and poor dietary habits all manifest themselves in unique ways once we reach "old age."

The percentage of the population in the US that is considered old will increase dramatically in the coming decades. Below is a chart published in the 2005 Annual Report of the Board of Trustees of the Federal Old-Age and Survivors Insurance and Disability Insurance Trust Funds.

Projected rise in aged population

	2005	2025	2045	2065	2080
Number of aged (in millions)	37	62	79	89	96
Share of total population	12%	18%	21%	22%	23%

This has the government worried for several reasons. This segment of the population will have the same needs as previous generations of elderly (nursing and institutional care) but with higher costs and this portion of the population is likely to live longer.

While the conversation usually turns to the cost of this increased care placed on the tax burden of the working population, generally considered to be narrowing as the old get older, the price can be greatly offset with some simple steps taken before you reach the age of old.

As I suggested in the very first paragraph of Chapter 1, Chiaroscuro, the art term for light and dark, comes into play when we talk about the expenditures associated with old age. It is not what we focus on, the bright part of how we envision retirement, but what is hidden in the shadows that frame that life changing event.

Several years back, a local television show in Portland, Oregon, asked me to profile the financial futures of several people. This involved long conversations about the subject's personal and financial histories. One of the people I profiled was young, just finishing an internship, and just beginning her career in television. The other woman was middle-aged, divorced with custody of two teenaged daughters. She was also supporting her parents.

Her parents, recently retired, had dreamed of a life on the road, traveling self-sufficiently in their RV from one roadside attraction to the next. They had worked hard their entire lives and shared this vision of the future together. They sold all they had with the understanding that pensions and savings and the equity they would reap from the sale of their modest home would provide for them as they began their sojourn across the country. Aimless travelers letting the road take its course. But life took its course first.

This has since turned into a financial horror story for their daughter. Her mother developed an illness that was not planned for in their dream retirement. They would, they assumed, be as healthy as the day they punched the clock for the last time. They returned to their starting point, sold the RV, rented a small apartment, and watched their savings disappear to medical costs. Without a home address, they were forced through numerous paperwork hoops to gain any coverage for the stricken spouse. The daughter now gives them several hundred dollars in cash each month along with additional help with groceries and utilities. This story is just one example of why people must consider their health when planning their retirement.

In 1962, nearly half—46 percent—of health care spending was financed by individuals out of their own pockets. The remaining 54 percent was financed by a combination of private health insurance and public programs. By 2002, the amount of health care spending financed by individuals out of their own pockets was estimated to have dropped to 14 percent.—David M. Walker, Comptroller General of the United States

Sanford Bennett wrote a book discussing his old body called *Old Age—Its Cause and Prevention: The Story of an Old Body and Face Made Young*. He began his journey at 50 with an assessment of who he was physically. He described his business career as too active, his wrinkles, his baldness, his sunken cheeks hanging on a drawn and haggard face, his body suffering from atrophied muscles and "30 years of chronic dyspepsia." The book is copyrighted 1912 and is in no way a recommendation. Yet, the subject matter should be of great interest to those of us concerned with the cost of old age.

So, take these lessons to heart. When planning for retirement, you must consider the very real fact that you will not always remain as healthy as you have always been. You must plan your savings to address this situation.

There are some grim facts of life that face those of us who fail to maintain good health as early as possible and do so throughout our lives. The misunderstanding about how we will enter this time of life can be extremely costly. In the next chapter on insurance, we will take a look at the debate that is shaping up as we head into the 2008 elections—and how it will continue well beyond that fateful day in November, how the vital programs sponsored by the government are facing financial difficulties in the coming years and the politics surrounding those programs is affected by you and we will take our first look at long-term health coverage and its connections to the financial futures of not only you but your parents and your children.

CHAPTER 9

The Sixth Misunderstanding: Insurance

◆◆

O ne thing is for certain, other than the old adages about death and taxes, we need to find a way to survive, not only physically but financially. What role does insurance play? Is it a cure-all for the unknown, or simply a panacea for what we have failed to prepare for when we had the chance? Insurance may, or may not, be the answer.

 The selective advantage of intelligence is clearly high. Other things being equal, if you can figure the world out, you have a better chance of survival. —Carl Sagan (1934—1996) Gifford Lectures, 1985

The Current Conversation

Health care is shaping up to be a major topic on the political stage in the next several years. Leading up to the election in 2008 candidates will be stumping their plans to the American public with great conviction. They will hire teams of analysts to examine the problem; they will scour the opinion polls and survey their constituents. They will try to put their finger on the collective pulse of the voters and look for plausible and affordable ways to address the number of people who lack insurance in this country.

This debate will continue after the nation makes its choice and the new president takes the oath of office. In the meantime, the more than 44 million uninsured people in the United States will be paying close attention and so will those who have insurance. At the heart of the conversation will be cost.

At the time of this writing, the candidates have yet to spell out each minute detail of their plans to the general public. Even if they did, they would still be facing some serious issues once they reached Washington. The political headwinds facing this kind of reform will be sizable to say the least.

What the Experts Say

Can you match the candidates to their pledges on health care?

"There are three parts to my approach. First, lowering costs for everyone. Second, improving quality for everyone. Third, insuring everyone."

"Health insurance should become like homeowners insurance or like car insurance."

"It's a plan that lets the uninsured buy insurance that's similar to the kind members of Congress give themselves."

"I'm going to have a plan that every American can take advantage of and afford."

"Let insurance companies offer true market-based products."

"It's based on the concept of shared responsibility."

(In order: Hillary R. Clinton D–NY, Rudolph Giuliani R–NY, Barack Obama D–IL, John McCain D–AZ, Mitt Romney R–MA, John Edwards D–NC)

These candidates all have experience with some sort of health issue. Candidates also declaring their intent to run for president at the time of this writing who have also suffered some brush with the insurance industry, although within the protections that members of Congress provide for themselves, are Sen. Joseph R. Biden Jr. (D–DE), who had two brain aneurysms in 1988 and former Sen. Fred Thompson's (R–TN) lymphoma. While each candidate attempts to connect with the general population, the costs of what they have encountered have varied widely. Mr. Obama's mother worried about her legacy, wondering if she did survive her fatal bout with ovarian cancer, what would she have left for herself and her heirs. Mr. Obama's battles with the insurance carrier over exactly when his mother's cancer manifested itself is at the heart of the problem with private carriers. Seeking to deny coverage as a pre-existing condition forces him to use words like "stranglehold" when describing the strength of the current industry on not only patients seeking care but the legislation that seeks to change it.

Mr. Edwards well documented dealings with his wife's breast cancer forced him to formulate a plan that would focus on preventative care, mental health, and a simplified funding that would make employers and the government responsible for making health a priority.

Senator Clinton draws her experiences with her husband, former President Bill Clinton, as she promotes her plans to streamline the system, removing antiquated accounting procedures that would, she believes, make the whole system more cost efficient, and in the end, more affordable.

Mr. Giuliani's approach is not so much political commentary but merely an observation, as when he suggests that ownership of a health insurance plan should resemble other types of insurance. Homeowners' insurance or car insurance operate under a different set of actuarial principles. Based on concrete evidence, those types of insurers can make relatively experienced estimates about how well your house will survive a natural disaster, what prevention you have done to avoid fires, what traffic patterns and driving habits of a local municipality will enter into your chances of having an accident, and how old or new is that car that you operate. That is not such an easy calculation when it comes to the human body. As you have seen from examples earlier in this book, how long you live is based on a number of factors. But how healthy you will be depends on so many unknowns that the true cost of insurance, delivered like your automobile policy, might be double its current cost.

Mr. Giuliani's battle with prostate cancer cost him a run at the New York senate seat, now occupied by Mrs. Clinton, and the marriage to his wife at the time, Donna Hanover.

According to a *Los Angeles Times* report on John McCain in May 2007, his ability to survive a presidency with a war ravaged and surgery-riddled body was brought into question. The article cited the fact that "McCain has twice developed melanoma, a potentially deadly form of skin cancer. He had four surgeries between 1993 and 2002: two to remove melanomas, one to remove skin lesions, and one to treat an enlarged prostate."

Mr. Romney was instrumental in developing a plan for his state of Massachusetts, although he has made clear that the plan he instituted there, one that requires individuals to obtain health insurance, would not work on a national level. Such an action would fly in the face of how Republicans generally feel about increasing the role and, by default, the size of government.

Could the Massachusetts plan for mandatory health coverage work for the nation? The simple answer is not to be had—at least in a simplified form. Making the Massachusetts plan national requires a number of hurdles not faced by residents of that state. The number of uninsured on a percentage basis is much smaller (10 percent compared to 18 percent nationwide), the costs of funding the plan require a simple diversion of already existing funds, and the decidedly liberal bias made the program's passage much easier. There is little likelihood that businesses with more than 100 employees will ante up the required sum for each employee ($295 per employee) under a similarly mandated nationwide program.

President Bush has advocated repeatedly for the strengthening of health savings accounts. With the focus of this discussion on retirement planning misconceptions and misunderstandings, health savings accounts, or HSAs, have a prominent role, almost as much as our next subjects: Medicare and Medicaid.

This is how they are designed to work. Signed into law in 2003, HSAs plans are designed to work as self-directed savings plan used for current health care expenses. You must have a high-deductible health insurance plan to qualify. This type of policy is considered the most cost-effective policy because it forces you to pay higher out-of-pocket expenses before coverage kicks in. In theory, the HSA-saved funds will offset those medical deductions and any coverage your plan does not cover.

According to the Treasury Department, HSA accounts limit the types of insurance you can have while employing an HSA. "You are only allowed to have automobile, dental, vision, disability, and long-term care insurance at the same time as a high-deductible health plan or HDHP. You may also have coverage for a specific disease or illness as long as it pays a specific dollar amount when the policy is triggered. Wellness programs offered by your employer are also permitted if they do not pay significant medical benefits." The key to the program is the high-deductible policy.

Medicare recipients may not have an HSA. Uninsured persons may not contribute. Veterans who have used the VA for services, current military personnel, many people who have Flexible Spending Arrangements (FSA) and numerous Health Reimbursement Arrangements (HRA) plans where they work are also ineligible. So too are the unemployed—provided they do not have a high deductible health policy. (There is more on HSAs, FSAs, and HRAs toward the end of the book.)

What to Say!

HSA contributions have set limits. For 2007 and forward, your maximum annual HSA contribution is based on the statutory limit for your type of coverage. For 2007, if you have self-only HDHP coverage, your contribution limit is $2,850; $5,650 if family HDHP, no matter what your HDHP deductible is. If you are older than 55 years of age you may make catch-up payments in addition to the regular deductible for the following amounts: 2007—$800, 2008—$900, 2009 and after—$1,000 (To receive more specific answers, check

http://www.treas.gov/offices/public-affairs/hsa/)

There are tax advantages to HSAs as well. Often, your employer can make contributions to your plan pre-tax. The IRS also has additional information on how these plans work and what is covered (see publication 502 for a list of maladies covered by your HSA for which you can withdraw funds tax-free to pay for).

Because of these above-mentioned restrictions, this type of plan has barely penetrated the marketplace for health coverage. With only a 5 percent adoption rate among companies nationwide, the plan, no matter how advantageous it may seem on the surface, still lends itself to the higher wage earning family who can afford insurance coverage outside of what is offered by their employers. In fact, the conservative group at the Cato Institute has lobbied to have the annual deductible tripled from current levels. This would remove dollars from the current tax base while adding to the tax-free accounts of the few. There is legislation on the table to remove some of the inequities in these plans but they are mainly focused on veterans and military personnel.

The Politics of Old Age: Medicare

Many people ask, "Will Medicare and Medicaid last?" The naysayers say no while the hopefuls suggest that there are ways of fixing these social programs without too much pain—read: new taxes. But first we need to look at what these plans are and how much of a role they might play in your retirement plan. Because I chose to put this discussion under the topic of "Seven Misunderstandings" and not in another part of the book, we need to examine how these plans are referred to on the public stage.

Today, Medicare provides health insurance to about 40 million seniors and disabled individuals each year. The number is only expected to grow as the baby boomers begin retiring.—Jim Bunning D–KY

Medicare consists of four parts:

Part A involves inpatient hospital care, skilled nursing care, hospice, and certain home health services. At age 65 you are automatically enrolled. Coverage is free providing you paid into the plan for 40 or more quarters in Medicare-covered employment. You are still able to "buy-in" if you or your spouse does not meet that work history requirement.

The premiums can run as low as $226 (30–39 quarters of covered employment) to a high of $410 (less than 30 quarters). All eligible Part A insured pay a deductible for hospital stay of around $992. Ninety-nine percent of those enrolled in Part A pay nothing out of pocket.

It is this portion of the program that is financed by that deduction that you see on your paycheck. At the time this system was set up, there were far more workers than Medicare recipients, so a pay-as-you-go system of financing was actually attractive. But times have changed.

Although costs for care have been rising, often dramatically, the number of people paying into the system as a ratio of those who use the program has been altered, with even greater impact. Fearing that the future holds the possibility of higher payroll taxes to offset this growing disparity in available dollars needed with those that are withheld, the alarms for reform have been ringing with regularity.

The second part of Medicare, Part B, is funded in a wholly different way. This part of Medicare is optional with monthly premiums for coverage. The premiums are usually reasonable. The monthly premium for Part B coverage is $93.50 in 2007, an increase of $5 or 5.6 percent from the previous year. According to the Health and Human Services, one of the main drivers for these increased premium costs is the growth in the traditional fee-for-service spending. (Additional information can be found at http://www.cms.hhs.gov/)

Those premiums, which for numerous additional reasons are capped from further increases, will leave the Part B balance sheet somewhat disrupted. A premium increase of a $1.50 would add an additional $2.8 billion to the plan. Otherwise, they warn, doctor and health care providers will see a 5 percent decrease in payments.

The Part B premiums paid by those that visit physicians and outpatient facilities are added to funding referred to as general revenues, all of which are used to offset any difficulties on this side of the ledger.

What are general revenues? They are budget surpluses and additional miscellaneous revenues collected from a variety of sources. For many, the point of contention is the ability of Congress to take money from various trust accounts, such as Social Security—which is paid for with payroll taxes and is currently in a surplus, write the fund an IOU and use the money as general revenues. To answer the question, it depends on whom you ask in Washington.

According to a General Accounting Office report dated April 2003, "SMI, or supplementary medical insurance, also known as Part B, is financed through general revenues and beneficiary premiums. The history of SMI financing illustrates the difficulties of maintaining fiscal discipline. Originally the Part B premium was set at a level to finance 50 percent of SMI program costs. However, less than 10 years later, the method for setting the SMI premium was tied to changes in the cost of living, resulting in premiums dropping below 25 percent of program costs. Under current law, the premium is now set at 25 percent of program costs, with general revenues paying the remaining 75 percent."

Organizations such as the American Association of Retired Persons (AARP) have issued financial health statements on Medicare of their own. Many have focused on the HI (Part A) side of the plan projecting payroll tax revenues out into the future. They predict a 3.12 percent deficit in this side of the program in 75 years. This is of course given the median range between the best and worst case scenario. Added to that projection is the even more frightening possibility of the reduction of benefits, by some estimates of more than 45 percent of current levels.

On the SMI (Part B) side of Medicare's balance sheet, any reduction in general revenues and premiums will begin to rise. Unfortunately, it may be a foregone conclusion. Spending was estimated at lower levels than reality. Because Part B does take from general revenues, it can be calculated as a portion of the Gross Domestic Product or GDP. In terms of actual percentages, the current Plan B funding amounts to 1.2 percent of GDP. Seventy years from now it will be eating up a 5 percent portion of what this country produces. This means it is likely you will have to pay more in the future.

 In a report on the financial health of Medicare, AARP noted that, "combined expenditures are projected to rise to 7.7 percent of GDP by 2035 and to 13.8 percent by 2078."—"The Status of the Medicare Part A and Part B Trust Funds: The Trustees' 2004 Annual Report Research Report" by Craig Caplan, AARP Public Policy Institute, and Ryan Cool, AARP Public Policy Institute

http://www.aarp.org/research/medicare/financing/the_status_of_the_medicare_part_a_and_part_b_trust.html

The Sum of Its Parts

Understanding how Medicare works can have important financial ramifications for you as you approach retirement age or for your parents as they approach 65. Because Medicare is a branch of Social Security, registering within seven months of turning 65 (beginning three months prior to the fateful birthday and ending four months after) can save you, in many cases, time and trouble and sometimes money.

Suppose you fail to register with Medicare Part B during that seven-month period, what's the worst that could happen? You could end up paying for it for the rest of your life. Almost like acting in reverse of Social Security benefits, failure to enroll in Medicare within those seven months will cause you to be penalized 10 percent on each month's premium based on 12 months increments. If you delay enrollment until you are 68 and three 12-month periods have passed since you were initially eligible, you will be paying 30 percent more than you would have had you enrolled during the seven-month period surrounding your birthday. The penalty for delaying enrollment in Part D is much more severe.

Part C operates a little differently than Parts A and B. You will need to be enrolled in both A and B to be eligible for Part C. These are plans offered by private health insurers and because of that, they can require prescreening of most applicants. By registering within that tight time frame at age 65, whether you are working or not will qualify you for coverage under Part C without any medical exam or any obligation to participate in it. Waiting, however, will force you to take a complete medical evaluation, which, if you have an existing medical condition, could be a reason to be denied benefits and coverage.

Coverage under these plans is already paid for by Medicare as an enrollee in both Part A, which no premium is paid for qualified participants and Part B, where you are already paying a premium.

Because Part C of Medicare offers access to private insurers who often contract with the program, it is important to understand the terminology associated with health care.

HMO plans, also called Health Maintenance Organization plans, are self-contained plans that usually emphasize preventive care offering services generally available within the HMO network. POS plans, or Point-of-Service Plans, offer services outside of a preferred network. These types of plans offer the participant a network of preferred providers, often at a reduced rate, much like HMO plans do. Unlike an HMO, these plans can involve multiple visits for the same condition because they typically require a referral from a network primary care physician to gain access to a network specialist. The upside of

Continued

these plans is they sometimes offer drug benefits. You will find that, if you have such a provision in your plan, you may save money and avoid the addition of Part D to your coverage. Regionally Expanded Preferred Provider Organization (PPO) plans saved the more rural enrollee from unnecessarily higher cost because of their location. A PPO is similar to POS plans in that they generally do not require a referral from a network primary care physician to access network specialists, another cost saving for the participant. PSO plans (Provider-Sponsored Organizations) are similar to the POS plans but are usually organized with physicians that practice in a regional or community hospital. There may or may not be coverage for providers or facilities outside the PSO network, depending upon the plan designs offered. They may require a referral from a network primary care physician to access network specialists. The latest addition to the group is Medical Savings Accounts. MSAs work differently than Health Savings Accounts (HSA). These plans are usually set up in conjunction with private fee-for-service plans, providing at least the same benefit coverage levels as Medicare Parts A and B or some additional high-deductible coverage. The money deposited in the account comes directly from Medicare but only after the high deductible (not to exceed $6,000) is met.

Before we move on to Part D, the last part of the Medicare puzzle, there is often a gap in coverage. Generally, most folks who are eligible for a Part C plan (enrolled in both Parts A and B), will find the need for **Medigap**, a private insurance often referred to as Medicare Supplemental Insurance, unnecessary.

Insured but Uncovered

In southeastern Iran, the first pair of dice was created 5,000 years ago. Dice were originally made from the ankle bones of oxen, hence the name among those who roll these common six-sided objects to play games of chance are often referred to as bones. Is Medigap a simple roll of the dice, a journey into the mathematical world of probability? Like most types of insurance, the answer is yes.

First let's outline how Medigap works and why it is necessary for some people. By the time we reach middle age, some of what the insurance actuaries refer to as "preexisting conditions" that we might have are already known to us. If you know certain ailments will continue into your retirement years and possibly become worse, a policy that covers those conditions above and beyond what Medicare might pay, after deductibles, might be in order.

The hardest part is not knowing whether you might need it. The plans currently come in twelve flavors, all of which offer a different level of benefit coverage.

Based on the coverage offered by either Medicare Part A or part B, you may find insurance gaps in the following areas:

PART A COVERAGE GAPS

Medicare pays for your hospital stay for the first 60 days after you pay your deductible. This is based on a "per spell of illness" basis. For lengthier stays beyond those initial 60 days, the Medicare Part A participant would need to co-pay his continued stay at $248 per day—these are 2007 figures and are expected to rise. Should you need to stay longer than an additional 30 days, you enact the lifetime reserve days in your coverage, which begins a co-pay of $496, also in 2007 for a stay extending between 91 and 150 days—also per spell of illness.

If you need hospital services beyond 150 days ("per spell of illness"), which require the services of a skilled nursing facility (Medicare covers the first 20 days in full; the daily coinsurance payment for days 21 to 100 is $124 per day in 2007) or need that nursing facility beyond 100 days, you will experience a gap in coverage and out-of-pocket expenses.

A Medigap policy will help if you need home health aide services on a more regular basis than provided by your Medicare coverage. Part A usually covers you on a part-time or intermittent basis.

PART B COVERAGE GAPS

While Part B covers many items such as durable medical equipment, prosthetic devices, supplies incident to physician's services, and ambulance transportation, the annual deductible of $131, in 2007, must be met before Medicare will make payment for covered services but it stops short in many cases of full coverage. Depending on the services and items provided to you as part of the outpatient experience, Medicare will cover 80 percent of the charges. The 20 percent "gap" as a Part B coinsurance payment, however, is not covered.

A Medigap policy will help with balance billing. Because Medicare has a list of approved charges, the actual bill you receive from many physicians and providers will exceed what Medicare will pay.

Listed A through L, the plans, in their simplest forms, all have what is called a core benefit. Each additional plan offers you something in addition to this basic set of coverages.

Here are some important things to consider when buying a Medigap policy. The law requires that the insurer cannot question your insurability if you begin the Medigap policy within six months of your sixty-fifth birthday. The additional coverage offered beyond the core policy, which comes with the lowest premium, may not be necessary. These policies often cover out-of-pocket expenses such as normal deductibles and depending upon the type of policy, which part of Medicare you chose to cover. Some folks, who plan on making foreign travel an aspect of their postwork years, might consider a gap policy that covers travel emergency care, which, depending on the amount of traveling they do, could be a much less expensive purchase than travel insurance, with additional medical coverage based on a per trip basis.

The Brief but Turbulent History of Part D

For many of us, drugs are a fact of life. Affording them, however, has become one of the greatest anomalies of capitalism. We often hear terms such as "market forces" used when describing the cost of drugs. Research and development of new and more targeted medications are at the mercy of these forces. Recovery of those dollars, the high cost of testing and the lengthy approval process, along with the marketing surrounding the product, all push drug prices higher.

Without coverage of some sort, the high cost of those pharmaceuticals would be impossible. Medicare Part D coverage was born amidst great controversy and under the guise that market forces would help the consumer. Only the most fervent optimist would agree.

With over 60 options available in the new Part D plan and the future of yet another premium stacked on top of the premiums they may already be paying for Part B ($88.50 per month) and in a Medigap policy, of which some carry some drug coverage, Part D looked, at least on the surface, as yet another out-of-pocket cost that might not be necessary. It became another roll of the dice.

Part D can be obtained in several ways. It could be added to your Medicare plan as a separate prescription drug plan, known as PDP. Each state offers numerous plans, all with varying degrees of cost, prescription medications available under the plan and the defining factor in the overall cost of any insurance product, how much you are willing to commit in the form of a deductible.

How do you find a prescription drug plan? Each state has numerous options. California, for example, has 48 different PDPs available for its residents. To sort through many of the options, Medicare.gov has provided a state-by-state aggregator at this address:

http://www.medicare.gov/MPDPF/Public/Include/DataSection/Questions/SearchOptions.asp

So Many Choices

Unlike buying houses, where we tend to bite off more debt than we can afford, drug plans force us to cut every possible corner to save money. There are numerous things you should focus on when looking at prescription drug coverage. Staying focused on the premium is not always enough. That premium is determined by the deductible—like all insurance policies. If you opt for a deductible less than $250, your premium will rise.

Ask yourself about your current drug use. Do you take more or less than $250 worth of medication during the normal calendar year? For unusual spikes in drug medication, Medicare can cover a lot. But, if you have some specific ailments and require a regime of medicines that will last you a lifetime and continually exceed the deductible, signing up for a PDP might, *might*, save you money.

If I am 35 and planning for retirement, or even 50 and planning to take my leave from the workplace, why is this discussion about drug coverage important to me now? As we look at what those post-retirement dollars will actually buy, we seldom take into consideration the cost of health insurance and, to a much lesser degree, the cost of prescriptions. Even fewer plan for the gap in coverage referred to as the donut hole. Medicare will cover the first $2,250 of your drug bill in a given year, paying 75 percent of the costs. If your prescription costs exceed that amount, you fall into the hole, a place where drug coverage ceases

Continued

to exist until you make up the difference in the deductible. Once you reach the $5,100 mark, Medicare begins to pay again, covering 95 percent of the costs. Let's do the math really quickly for all of you who have failed to calculate this expense into your retirement plan. Suppose, in the spirit of worst-case scenario, you pay out 25 percent of the first $2,250 ($2,250 ÷ 0.25 = $562, or $46 a month). But your medication runs over that amount. The hole or gap in payments is yours to pay. That can add an additional $250 to your monthly costs. To top it all off, many if not all PDPs come with a standard $250 deductible before they pay anything. Add that $296 to the cost of Part B ($88.50), the deductible need for Part A ($997) and any Medigap policy you might have and you could be faced with a monthly medical budget of $600 or more. This needs to be factored into your retirement plan. Remember, these figures represent the 2007 costs for a retiree on Medicare. It would not be unreasonable to add 3 percent for every year until you retire to get an even closer view of how much you need to save. To reach Medicare, call 1.800.633.4227.

Finally, as if that grim news wasn't enough, the Employment Benefit Research Institute, or EBRI, has estimated that a couple age 65 *today* can expect to spend $295,000 out-of-pocket expenses on premiums and medical care (but not long-term care—which we will get to in the next chapter) should they live a normal lifespan (82 for men and 85 for women). This means that Medicare will pay only half of what you will need.

The Politics of Old Age: Medicaid

So it goes on. Most people believe that Medicaid is generally available for them after a certain age. And, if the plan you have built for retirement fails you in a catastrophic way, you might be one of the eligible.

I don't believe one grows older. I think that what happens early on in life is that at a certain age one stands still and stagnates. —T. S. Eliot

Eligibility for Medicaid assistance covers a broad range of people. It is everyone's hope that they are not in a position to tap this insurance program. Unlike Medicare, which primarily provides insurance for those that are 65 or older, Medicaid is for low-income people who are unable to pay medical or long-term care costs. The program's well-defined categories have extended a helping hand to more than just the individuals it was originally designed to help.

Certain statistics stand out when we begin a conversation about poverty. As I mentioned earlier, every plan in of itself has at its core a disaster we are hoping to avoid. Being poor in our later years of life seems like a good disaster to avoid. Unfortunately, many of us are unwittingly and sometimes unfortunately being sucked into the lower portion of the income levels in this country.

Some have achieved this status with the unnecessary burden of credit debt and overextended mortgages. Living paycheck-to-paycheck does not however qualify you for Medicaid assistance. But an unforeseen injury, job loss, or otherwise catastrophic medical event, could leave you well positioned to access this program.

As of 2006, there were over 50 million people in the United States who qualified as poor based on the federal poverty level (FPL). This amounted to 17 percent of the total population. An additional 19 percent of the nation finds their household income at the near-poverty level.

The US Department of Health and Human Services (HHS) considers the term "federal poverty level" to be "ambiguous," preferring to break the term into poverty thresholds and guidelines. Mollie Orshanky, who worked as a statistician at the Social Security Administration, conceived the idea of defining poverty with threshold measures. She used the cost of feeding a family based on the nutritional guidelines laid out by the Food and Drug Administration as her source. The following chart illustrates the latest threshold levels measured by the Census Bureau in 2006.

Number of related children under 18 years

	None	One	Two	Three	Four
One person					
Under 65 years	10,488				
65 years and over	9,669				
Two persons					

Continued

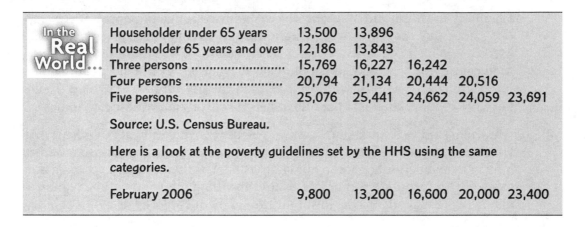

Householder under 65 years	13,500	13,896			
Householder 65 years and over	12,186	13,843			
Three persons	15,769	16,227	16,242		
Four persons	20,794	21,134	20,444	20,516	
Five persons...........................	25,076	25,441	24,662	24,059	23,691

Source: U.S. Census Bureau.

Here is a look at the poverty guidelines set by the HHS using the same categories.

February 2006	9,800	13,200	16,600	20,000	23,400

The qualifications for receiving Medicaid are based on federal and state guidelines, giving the states some leeway in the administration of the funds. It is important to clarify several terms used in determining your, your spouse's, or your parent's eligibility.

Income is defined as any money you might receive in the form of payment for job, pensions, or other accounts such as IRAs, Social Security, etc. Resources can include savings accounts and invested interests and just about anything that can be sold for cash. Excluded from the calculation is your home and one car.

To obtain the PDF file for download, go to:
http://www.cms.hhs.gov/MedicaidEligibility/downloads/MedGlance05.pdf

From Doughnut Holes to Loopholes: Medicaid Math

As nineteenth-century physician Oliver Wendell Holmes once said, "The young man knows the rules but the old man knows the exceptions." When it comes to Medicaid, and this is equally as important in your retirement planning as it is in that of your parents, a lawyer is your best asset. We are talking about a legal squabble over assets, who owns what and is it countable under the ever shifting regulations of government?

Assets of married couples are considered as one even if only one is headed towards a nursing home. The relative value of cars, prepaid funeral plans, savings accounts, furniture, clothing, and jewelry must all be examined and estimated under the law. The Deficit Reduction Act of 2005 put unfair pressure on seniors and their spouses. Seniors with equity in their homes exceeding $500,000 must spend that equity down to the limits set by Medicaid before they will pay for any nursing home bills.

Lawyers can help with the transfer of rights to joint property and readjust wills so that the surviving spouse in the nursing facility is not the beneficiary. These legal eagles can also protect nursing home residents from disruptions in their Medicaid payments by working with inheritances between siblings and other relatives.

Lawyers can also help with a durable power of attorney. Everyone older than 35 who is married with kids should put this important document in a safe deposit box. Your parents should have one and you should state who will assume power of attorney if you become incapacitated.

Among the other helpful things an attorney can do for someone facing an application for Medicaid assistance is help in restructuring assets, protecting against unwarranted or overestimated liens, reverse mortgage rules, and how to spend down assets legally.

The look-back period, probably the most devastating addition to the law, requires that people look back five years when considering assets. In other words, if you have been giving gifts to your children or grandchildren, Medicaid will focus on these assets as real and consider them to still be part of what you are worth.

With our focus on retirement planning, can you expect to save enough to offset five years worth of (potential) nursing home coverage, which can cost upwards of $70,000 a year before Medicaid kicks in? Possibly and it is as simple as a loophole.

There is almost no way to determine exactly what old age is going to cost. The topic we have just covered lays out some serious considerations for every age group about how to finance ourselves in the future. Doing the right things now to protect your health offset the unknown financial burdens that might lie ahead. Knowing what you might possibly face greatly increases your ability to plan. If an ex-marathoner like Alberto Salazar can have a heart attack, so can you.

In the next chapter, we will discuss the policy most asked about by middle-aged people planning for retirement: the long-term care policy.

CHAPTER 10

The Seventh Misunderstanding: Long-Term Care

Insuring Yourself Against Age

Mark Meiners, director of the Center for Health Policy, Research and Ethics in the College of Nursing and Health Science at George Mason University, says "Unfortunately, many Americans falsely believe that their long-term care costs will be covered by Medicaid, but this is true only after they've spent themselves into impoverishment."

So much time and effort spent planning for retirement focuses on how well our investments perform. Calculating how much of that future income succumbs to pressures from medical and health issues is an equally important exercise. Unfortunately, we can only guess at the costs. That said, the insurance industry has created a solution to these fears.

Long-Term Care insurance (LTC) is not the end-all-to-be-all it is often portrayed as being. Insurers will tell you that Social Security and Medicare will not pay for your long-term care. That is true. Also true is the push by Medicaid, with Congressional support, to get you to pay more and more of the long-term care bill that they currently assume.

LTC policies have numerous shortcomings that are often overlooked and undermentioned when the policy is offered. In the last chapter, I mentioned the way Medicaid utilizes a *look back* period of five years and the necessity of retaining a lawyer to navigate these rules. This period gives Medicaid the opportunity to tally your assets back to that point when they determine your level of benefits.

LTC policies usually cover you for only three years. This two-year gap can be financially devastating. How do you strategize your retirement plan for yet another unknown cost? Even as a recent AARP survey found out that over 90 percent of us have no clue what a nursing home stay might cost in today's dollars, we can do something to help estimate those costs and the viability of these plans.

There is still a lack of competition among LTC policies that makes them hard to compare. The insurance industry understands your confusion and has launched a concerted effort to sell more of these policies to people who are considering them.

Here is the most recent price index for long-term care insurance compiled by LTCI Partners LLC:

2007 National Long-Term Care Insurance Price Index

If you purchase a policy at age 55 with a premium of $665 per year, it will get you a $100 daily benefit for three years. Shop for that policy at age 65 and the premium will be, under the best of circumstances, $1,292 per year, with the same $100 daily benefit for three years.

What It Is and What It Is Not

The mention of "nursing home" probably makes you bristle. You have specific ideas of what nursing homes are, who goes there, and why you would never put a loved one there. LTC is not necessarily nursing home insurance care. Consider it as more of a caretaker policy for some unknown but likely ailment that you might have a history of in your family, that you might be susceptible to because of lifestyle, or because you know the odds and determine them to be tipped unfairly in the direction of less vibrant health.

Most insurance companies use a fairly straightforward criterion when making the decision to pay the insured for their claim. The insurer will require a certified and licensed health provider to do a determination of "chronically ill."

What is chronically ill? Generally this refers to someone who is incapable of performing at least two daily activities of living such as feeding themselves, bathing and toiletry activities, or someone who requires substantial supervision. This is often referred to as an ADL or Activity of Daily Living.

Sounds simple enough, but insurance companies rarely have fixed guidelines when it comes to triggering the policy. Policies can be written to cover a variety of care situations and you must determine this at the time of policy execution. Problem is, how do you know what you will need. Will your policy need to cover a nursing home stay, of which a portion of the total is reimbursed over a preset time period?

Or, perhaps, your chronic illness will require assisted living residency or in-home care. Will your insurer cover custodial care or informal care? What about Alzheimer's care and the facilities generally set aside for treatment and care of that specific illness? Hospice care is also a distinct possibility. Will the policy cover a family member who has decided to take care of you in your or their home?

Long-term care insurance can cover a variety of home and community-based services and therapies. Often, the policy can be used for physical and/or occupational therapy, as well as some speech rehabilitation. Home health aides and sometimes visiting nurses are often considered by the insurer as benefit worthy.

In the jumble of definitions that often accompany anything as vaguely written, at least in your eyes, as an LTC policy, words such as *skilled* and *intermediate* and *custodial* carry added weight.

Skilled is often associated with registered nursing and most often with round-the-clock care, usually under a doctor's supervision. This would be the most costly form of coverage for the insurer.

Intermediate simply means occasional. It may refer to nursing home care and supervision where the care may be rehabilitative and can be done in a facility where the medical care is done by skilled personnel. Custodial care is a more personalized approach to caregiving, providing assistance in some of those daily activities that can no longer be done without help (eating, bathing, etc.).

What these policies are not is the end-all-to-be-all financial product that many assume they are. As we take a closer and albeit more skeptical look at these types of products, you will find that they vary widely, not only among insurers but also in how they pay out when the policy is executed.

How Do You Know What You Will Want Then?

Determining the policy needs is often difficult. We have only a vague notion of what our health will be like in the future and most of our anxiety over that is based on fear.

In the Real World...

Just because you want it doesn't necessarily mean they will cover it. Determining what is generally insurable is much easier (and is a much shorter list that what is *not covered*).

1. AIDS
2. Untreated alcoholism
3. Alzheimer's disease
4. ALS/Lou Gehrig's disease
5. Unstable angina—cardiac workup is underway
6. Severe osteoarthritis or rheumatoid arthritis (with continual steroid use, surgery recommended or multiple joint replacements)
7. Severe chronic pulmonary disease (including asthma, chronic bronchitis and emphysema with use of oxygen; more than two hospitalizations in last year; evidence of congestive heart failure; and functional limitations)
8. Ataxia (unstable gait)
9. Some types of cancer (depending on history)
10. Cardiomyopathy with symptoms or with congestive heart failure
11. Cerebral palsy
12. Cirrhosis of the liver with appearance of jaundice
13. Congestive heart failure (chronic, uncontrollable, or accompanied by diabetes)

Continued

14. Dementia
15. Demyelinating disease
16. Diabetes
    (with elevated blood pressure, neuropathy, retinopathy, nephropathy, skin ulcers, or morbid obesity)
17. Dialysis
18. Seizure disorder/epilepsy (uncontrolled and of unknown etiology)
19. Esophageal varices
20. Osteoporosis (with a history of multiple falls or fractures)
21. Fibromyalgia (with limitations of daily functioning)
22. Hepatitis B, C, E, F, G
23. Incontinence (complete or with use of a catheter)
24. Chronic kidney failure
25. Hairy cell leukemia
26. Systemic lupus
27. Macular degeneration (with vision loss in both eyes)
28. Multiple myeloma
29. Multiple sclerosis
30. Muscular dystrophy
31. Myasthenia gravis
32. Neuropathy (due to diabetes, alcoholism or polio)
33. Organ transplant (except corneal)
34. Organic brain syndrome
35. Osteomyelitis (chronic or active)
36. Pancreatitis (chronic with liver inflammation)
37. Paralysis
38. Parkinson's disease
39. Peripheral vascular disease
    (with regular claudication, poor exercise tolerance, continued smoking or history of skin ulcers)
40. Polycystic kidney disease
41. Renal insufficiency or failure
42. Schizophrenia
43. Scleroderma
44. Syncope (multiple episodes with unknown cause)
45. Stroke (multiple episodes, with certain other conditions)
46. Transient Ischemic attacks (TIA) (multiple episodes)
47. Tremors
    (with unknown cause or neurological workup in progress)
48. Tuberculosis (active)
49. Ulcers of skin (due to disease processes)

At the time you apply for insurance you must be able to meet the companies' criteria. You must be able to show competence at completing the Activities of Daily Life, you must be able to exhibit some intellectual skills such as orientation, attention, memory, judgment and comprehension, and you must be within a certain predetermined height and weight range. Each of these components will come into play when making a policy determination.

Although you do not have access to the companies that rate the long-term care insurers, a good rating by these companies is often a selling feature.

What to Ask?

What is my insurer rating? Insurance companies are rated on a variety of components. Why your insurer received that rating is often the most confusing aspect of any rating system. You should, as a rule of thumb, pick a company that is financially sound. Many of the ratings companies will rate your insurer on the basis of creditworthiness and this is often seen as an implicit endorsement of quality. Most people do not look any further. Letter designations is one of the common grading systems used among the industry. Here is a brief list of the top ratings given by the most well known among the investment rating companies:

A. M. BEST:

A++ or A+ = Superior.
A or A– = Excellent.
B++ or B+ = Very good.
B or B– = Adequate.

STANDARD & POOR'S:

AAA = Superior financial security
AA = Excellent financial security
A = Good financial security, but capacity to meet policyholder obligations is
      somewhat susceptible to adverse economic and underwriting conditions
BBB = Adequate financial security

MOODY'S INVESTORS SERVICES:

AAA = Exceptional financial security
AA = Excellent financial security
A = Good financial security, but there may be possible problems in the future
BAA = Adequate financial security

The High Cost of Home Care

Aside from the emotional drain home care can have on a family, the cost in terms of dollars and the stress involved in planning for those outlays can be enough to trigger a health problem in and of itself. It is estimated that almost $29 billion is lost by businesses in terms of worker productivity.

Not surprisingly, the average caregiver is female, in her late forties, and possesses some college education. Even more surprising are the estimated number of these caregivers providing services for family members. According to AARP, the number may exceed 44 million at any one time with 17 percent of these people working at it for 40 hours or more per week.

According to a Rice University study, poverty is prevalent among those who care for family members at home. Compared to their noncaregiving cohorts, women who give care are 2.5 times more likely to be in poverty, five time more likely to receive some of their income from Social Security, and deal with lower median incomes.

Not surprisingly, these family members are often spouses, but what is more alarming is the number of 8 to 18 year olds (1.4 million) faced with giving some health care to a family member.

Tax Benefits of LTC Policies

If you are an employer or are self-employed, you will find a favorable tax environment for obtaining a long-term care policy. For the majority of us, we are required to list the premiums paid on our tax return if our health expense deduction exceeds 7.5 percent of your adjusted gross income. HSAs offer additional tax benefits, which we will address a little further along.

As a sole proprietor, a partner, or an owner of an S corporation or LLC, including just about any small business endeavor, you can eliminate that 7.5 percent threshold and instead deduct premiums up to a certain maximum that increases with age.

The real savings come for the employer using a C-corporation, where premiums are fully deductible. It remains to be seen whether Congress will change this law.

Some Things Never Change

The reason you should be as skeptical as I am of this particular corner of the insurance industry has less to do with its relative newness as a product but rather with its aggressive selling by the industry. When a product comes to market, it is always promoted to the widest audience available. It is not different with insurance.

The trouble is, we only come face-to-face with an agent who represents a company and a product and that product is something we might not need in the near future. Long-term care insurance is bought on good faith, research and soul-searching. We pay the premiums diligently and when the time comes to execute it, we expect it to perform flawlessly.

Why then was one out of every four policies filed in the state of California denied in 2005? Companies gave numerous reasons why, which prompted a Congressional investigation into the practices of these insurers.

A large number of the claims the companies denied were due to paperwork not filled out properly or the right forms not submitted. They also cited that denial of claims was a result of the facilities the clients chose for care not being appropriate or acceptable for nursing care—although all of the people who had filed complaints had used state licensed facilities.

This is cause for concern among current and future policyholders. If Congress can offer incentives such as tax breaks to the industry to encourage people to buy the product, federal oversight may be necessary. This would take the industry's current overseer, the state, out of the regulation game.

Even as states begin their own market investigations into the practice of long-term care, it adds another layer of concern about whether this industry is too young to be an important part of your retirement planning.

Congress is right in worrying about this industry. There is a push under way to make LTC policies available for purchase through pretax dollars, penalty-free from 401(k) dollars. While Sen. John Thune (R–SD) has his heart in the right place, there are far too many questions about the industry that need to be addressed.

The Community Living Assistance Services and Supports Act offers another alternative by establishing a voluntary long-term-care insurance pool. Sens.

Edward Kennedy (D–MA) and Tom Harkin (D–IA), who are sponsoring the bill, suggest that those who paid a monthly premium would be eligible for monetary benefits if they became disabled. They would also be allowed to choose from a menu of services.

 Only one in four paid caregivers receives any formal instruction, and even that training is often minimal. People are given handbooks and told to read them. —Dr. Larry Wright, codirector of the Caregiving Project for Older Americans, who also oversees the Schmieding Center for Senior Health and Education in Springdale, Ark

How to Fix the Problem

Policies need to have a certain amount of consistency. All of them need to offer inflation protection. They need to offer a fixed rate on all policies, dropping the low introductory rate that is raised beyond many senior's budgets further down the road.

The terminology needs to be clear. When a policy is called "guaranteed renewable," it needs to clearly state that unless you miss a payment, the insurer cannot drop your coverage. What is often left out of that terminology is the right for the insurer to raise the premium.

Non-cancelable, something that Congress should insist be de rigueur for every policy issued by LTC companies, does not allow the premium to increase during the life of the policy and the policy can only be cancelled if a payment is missed. Congress could also work to make the cancellation policy more like that of the credit card industry. A financial slap on the hand if the payment is missed would suffice for most policyholders.

Legislation could also make the chance of denial of claims harder with a simple front-end underwriting clause. A potential customer would simply submit a health statement provided by their physician with the application. Having this on file with the insurer and possibly the state regulator would make the claims process more seamless.

Congress could also act on two very important aspects of the long-term health care issue. First, it could allow for a graduated level of care. Perhaps you will need a nursing home but not directly following a hospital stay.

You should be able to execute your policy at that point for both nursing home care and skilled at home care.

The second but certainly not the least, our lawmakers could make the fate of the home care workers a top priority. We are facing a staggering shortage of workers in the health care industry that could forebode trouble in the near future. Shortages among doctors (24,000 will be needed over the next fifteen years), nurses (one million short), and home care workers (three million) have health care officials worried.

A recent Supreme Court ruling about the pay home care workers receive should prompt Congress to act as well. The Court did not think that home care workers were subject to the same rules under the current federal minimum wage and overtime laws. This is an easy fix for an industry that employs largely middle-aged women.

One final note before we move on and it is a very important one. If you are asking yourself whether you need long-term care insurance, the answer is probably no. There are several reasons why.

In the course of good retirement planning, you can save enough to create the wealth you need that will more than offset your need for an LTC policy. If you have considerable assets — in excess if $500,000 equity in your home, or you want to leave an inheritance that you will not be forced to spend down to get Medicaid benefits, you should consider a policy.

If however, you only believe you want to leave money and assets for your heirs and your estate is much less — right now — much of the information in the remainder of this book will assist you in creating enough wealth to offset the need for this type of protection.

If you are looking to protect an elderly parent, the cost of the premium can be shared amongst all of the siblings. But set it up so that each sibling pays automatically in the event that there is a familial fallout down the road. Once again, a considerable amount of assets need to be worth protecting for future generations for you to purchase a policy — at a considerable expense depending on the age of the relative and the ability for the elderly relative to spend down their own assets is limited.

In the next chapter, we will take a look at those much touted and largely misunderstood percentages again.

CHAPTER 11

The Eighth Misunderstanding: How Much Will You Need

◆◆

Mirror, Mirror on the Wall...

The late Kurt Vonnegut began Chapter Six of his novel *Galapagos* with the following observation: "This financial crisis, which could never happen today," the narrator, Leon Trout, a ghost from the future, tells us, "was simply the latest in a series of murderous twentieth-century catastrophes which had originated entirely in human brains." At the heart of every financial book is the search for a way, a method, the right turn of phrase that will alter what happens in the human brain when we talk about money.

The Emotional Tug-of-War

We are at the last of our misunderstandings about retirement planning: how much do we need. We have discussed debt looking to identify some of the various ways you might justify your use of credit. The discussion about what is good debt and bad debt is individual with each person. It is all in how you look at it. And, most importantly, what you tell yourself in that brain of yours.

Taking more than a sideways glance at your kids and parents, we examined what your heart demands of you and the impact those emotional ties have on your financial way of thinking. We are social animals that tend to adopt the problems of the group we are closest to: family, friends, churches, charities, etc. Often, we fail to do the math on these commitments and understand how they can impact where we will be 20, 30, of 40 years down the road. Readjusting your thinking without changing your devotion to your cause may not be easy but is definitely something within the realm of possibilities.

Looking at housing, your house in particular, as less of an investment than you had previously thought it was may be the hardest medicine to swallow for most folks. Accounting for the roof over your head as something it is not has gotten more of us into trouble than the statistics have revealed of late. The mortgage crisis that is building a good head of steam as I write this will not go away soon. Why? Because we have yet to wrap our big brains around exactly where a house fits into our overall retirement plan.

What the Experts Say Think enough and you won't know anything.—Kenneth Patchen, American poet, 1911–1972

More mental calisthenics are played imagining life without work than probably work gets done in this country. The exercise we give our brains thinking about that postwork lifetime is an enormous untapped energy source, which, if it could be harnessed, would probably make the world a greener place. Every age group does it as they strive for better positions in a company, better pay packages and even better benefits. Each one of those things enables us to siphon off—at least in theory—additional cash to ensure a better retirement.

Unfortunately, the same things that pull us hardest to do the best are also part of our undoing. We can become physically and emotionally drained, which derails all of those plans. We fail to think beyond where we are in the moment and that is a flaw in any plan. Remember, every plan is merely a way to dodge an impending disaster. If our work, our careers and our ambitions were aligned, you would see some startling things about the plan you have developed—if you had a plan at all.

The ever-growing hole in many of our plans was looked at in our discussion in Chapter Eight about health. We don't think about health when we are doing well. But each day has the net effect of adding days to our overall lifetimes.

In this chapter, we will discuss some of the key misunderstandings of those plans, but they are all for naught if you do not arrive at retirement in a condition that will allow you to enjoy them. Most important, we fail to see the monetary impact of all of our hard work should our health turn sour. While we cannot predict the future, we certainly can skew it in our favor.

The fate of social programs in this country has reached a point of uncertainty. In 2006, San Francisco Federal Reserve president Janet Yellen suggested in a speech about income inequality in the US that policy makers are caught between what might be good for everyone, equity, and what might be best for the nation, efficiency. The subject of social programs always seems to enter the discussion and not in the way most of us hope. She is quoted as saying: "Heeding this lesson, some European countries have recently taken steps to reduce the distortions associated with generous social insurance programs and employment protections," suggesting that further erosions of our social network is inevitable. Brigitte Madrian of Harvard University, along with coauthors Gary Burtless and Jonathan Gruber, identified this change in policy in a Brookings paper published in 1994. Their worry has been expressed numerous times in recent years. Group policies, while providing low cost insurance, often were accused of providing low quality insurance as well. Not only does it inhibit job mobility but it is not spread evenly across the entire business population.

The cold hard truth about Medicare and Medicaid was detailed and, with any luck, clarified. Its role in your retirement plan is limited to your ability to arrive at retirement relatively healthy, be able to stay healthy, and in doing so, take advantage of the lowered premiums offered to those with better physical well being. These programs may have newsworthy problems facing them in the future and it's worth considering what your postretirement life would be like without including them in your overall plan.

With the huge push towards a sort of universal acceptance of long-term care insurance, it became the standalone topic of Chapter Ten. This type of insurance is still in its infancy and has many problems to sort through before it is given my seal of goodness. It is a huge misconception and it seems, wherever I go, the hottest topic on the minds of the 40-plus crowd, many of whom are worrying about what they might leave their own children or what will be left of their parents' estates should they face a nursing home or home-care situation.

These are all good concerns, but I'm not seeing LTC as the end-all-to-be-all to allay those fears. True, there is some, almost too many insurances involved in life and in your retirement plans but, for the vast majority of us, long-term care insurance is not yet the product it purports itself to be.

How Much?

Gary Foreman, a colleague at TheDollarStretcher.com, recently answered a budgeting question from a visitor to his site. In it, she asked where she could find a single software tool that "allows me to input my annual income, regular monthly bills (utilities, mortgage, vehicle insurance, etc.), and other "self-inflicted" debt such as credit cards and loans (other than mortgage), then calculates what I should budget for particular items based upon my income and the monthly expenses mentioned above." Gary began his answer with a question: "Without a benchmark, how do you know if you're spending too much?"

He outlined some "after-tax" spending benchmarks that might surprise you as we begin to formulate your plan for retirement. He suggested that the writer of the query determine where she is right now based on these percentages and try and adjust her lifestyle accordingly.

Gary wrote that a good daily budget should look something like this, dispersing your take home pay in the following manner:

Housing	34%
Food	16%
Auto	15%
Insurance	5%
Debt repayment	5%
Entertainment	7%
Clothing	4%
Savings	5%
Medical	5%
Everything else	4%

All of the above figures seem to be attainable and realistic but I believe that many of you are asking yourselves, *on what planet*? Many of you are living well beyond your housing allocation right now, which I assume contains its own calculation for insurance, taxes and upkeep and few of us are willing to scale down our current living arrangements to slice a few percentage points from our budgets.

Few of us manage only a 15 percent allocation of funds for transportation, a number that increases exponentially if we live in the suburbs and make regular commutes to our place of employment. Which means, in order to allocate your take home pay to serve your "big brain," you must find the money somewhere. The writer calls her little solution to the problem "self-inflicted."

In our big brains, it is all self-inflicted. We make conscious decisions daily and even if we make a no-decision, deciding to do nothing as the saying goes, we still made a decision. Our conversation in this chapter is about how to accumulate enough so that those budgets do not go haywire once we decide to retire. Which means we need to adjust our thinking just a bit.

The Traditional Approach

Generally, a retirement plan has numerous components. It is how you use each of those that makes the difference between a working plan and a plan that is over, or worse, under used. The importance of pinpointing that balance is the key in correcting our misunderstanding about savings. And it helps identify the benchmark best suited for each of us.

There are five symptoms of this kind of misunderstanding, the first comes from the belief that your day to day, paycheck-to-paycheck existence is something you will grow out of, earn your way out of, or even better, inherit your way out of. Where you are right now on your financial balance sheet makes a huge difference in where you will be in 10, 20, or 30 years.

 What is a financial balance sheet? For the sake of simplicity, we will call your financial balance sheet the difference between income and all bills (pick the last month and gather every receipt from every purchase—or the itemized bills from any credit or debit purchase and use that total, regardless of what you spent it on) lumped into one file called outlays. How close to your benchmark depends on how close you are to zero. In other words, you may find that, after the tallying is complete, what is left may be very close to what is going out.

$5,000 (income) − $3,700 (outlays/bills) = $1,700 $1,700 ÷ $5,000 = 0.34 or 34%.

Any amount left is divided into your total income—yes, before taxes, and you will have a decimal that relates to the portion of your income left over after everything is paid. Be sure to include surprise incidentals such as a car repair, a quarterly insurance bill you weren't expecting, or the cost of sending your child on some field trip. This number represents where you are after one month. Is the number positive? Or is it negative?

If you find that your one-month snapshot is troubling, then you will not likely grow your way out of your debt. "Malarkey" you might utter on both counts. I should never pass judgment on anyone's finances just looking at a single month's tally. But how different is one month from the next. If it's not Christmas it's spring break vacation or a new water heater or family reunion or a bill for gasoline you never really budgeted for or one thing after another. They all become financial blurs and so do the stopgap measures we employ to fix the leaks. One month is plenty of time to get a cold, calculated feel for how you allocate available cash.

And we begin using them as part of the regular cycle of give and take, work and reward. This is the hardest habit to break. Which means that if you have fallen into this habit, any shift in lifestyle will seem like a change for the austere. You probably fall well within the current statistics. Among those, current as of June 2007 and not likely to change dramatically anytime soon, are the following numbers that relate to your life.

You carry at least three credit cards. The national average is four; one out of 10 people have 10 cards on their person at any given moment. The reasons vary but you can bet that a number of them were associated with that extra 10 percent off the department stores offer for opening an account at the time of checkout or to gain points/airline miles/cashback incentives for spending with one card or another.

If you have a negative savings number as the percentage represents, you probably have used those credit cards for medical emergencies. A full third of those who were classified as low to middle income cardholders did just that.

Experian reported that half of the credit card accounts received the minimum payment on the bill while a third of us pay the bill off in full each month.

So how do I reverse my spending and turn it into savings? In the pantheon of financial publications, there must be a million answers. Not to say that I don't have a few to add to the discourse but many an economist has debated how to change the way we save. In a paper written in 2000 dealing with the behavior of people and savings, Andrew Caplin and John Leahy of the New York University and National Bureau of Economic Research wrote: "Yet the challenge is in many ways even deeper, since our ignorance about the psychology of savings is so comprehensive. To what extent is it stressful to contemplate being poor and sick in retirement, and how does this stress influence savings behavior? Is it stressful to learn how to save and invest, and if so does this cause complete withdrawal from the process? Is it stressful to have a savings portfolio that fluctuates in value, and if so does this account for low holding of risky assets?"

Somewhat flummoxed as to what to do, they add that the second challenge should not be based on just data but should look at why the "data reveal simply that many people save practically nothing, and end up with low consumption in retirement. If low consumption in retirement is a matter of deliberative planning and leaves households overjoyed, there is no policy issue. Otherwise policy makers may want to know why so many end up in such dire straits, to help determine what to do about it."

And it would not be complete unless I told you about the one in 50 households in this country that carry $20,000 plus in credit card debt, one in 20 owes $8,000 with the average across the industry at $2,000 or less. The average rate assessed on these cards according to the Federal Reserve Web site is 13.46 percent. Consumers now carry almost $904 billion of credit card debt with them to work each day, tucked in their wallets when they pause to watch their children play and, not surprisingly this burden slips into bed with them at night.

As Misters Caplan and Leahy suggest, we have backed ourselves into a corner and we are more or less okay with it. So all we can do from here is suggest that you stop saying you will change.

Stop saying that when Aunt Millie passes away you will pay off the bills and be on easy street. Stop promising yourself that you will begin to save your raises or the extra money from your bonus or promotion. If you haven't developed that culture by now, there is little likelihood that I, or anyone else for that matter, will be able to change that.

Unless, of course, we do it on the sly. Like before you begin spending.

I Have a Good Plan

The majority of people who make these kinds of claims are planning on receiving some sort of defined benefit pension. Now a defined benefit plan was formulated by businesses to attract workers, keep them and pay them for their loyalty. The result was a plan that was good for the company and good for the employee.

Quite possibly the hardest thing to accept about the promise of a defined benefit pension is the simple fact that it is only as good as the company making the promise. The health of the corporation and the reasons the pensions were created all play important roles in the success of the plan. But, like many plans, especially those with long-range promises that span years, sometimes generations, they need to be revised and revisited often.

 Oft expectation fails, and most oft where most it promises; and oft it hits where hope is coldest; and despair most sits. —William Shakespeare (1564–1616)

There is a problem with the way defined benefit plans currently operate. The promises made to employees were often done during better times—and by better I mean periods of time when the company was flush with hope and the business horizon seemed to be all blue sky and green lights.

Companies, and more important, the environments they operate in, change. Those shifts in operations from a local to a global scale are often done seamlessly by most of the company. The one exception to this shift in how business is done is concerning the pension obligation.

As I said, companies promised pensions to employees as a way of retaining skilled help. The employees took that promise, the one that stated that when they no longer worked they would be compensated for their loyalty to the business to mean exactly that: they would be taken care of first.

What the promise failed to state was the nature of businesses to go through distinct stages. They all begin full of hope and promise, having found a niche in the market that they believe they can provide products to fill that need.

In the beginning, it is all about growth. Employees are often asked to wait until profitability before asking for long-range benefits such as pensions. As the company grows and the workers become more skilled, their value to the success of the company becomes important. To retain these employees, companies make promises of future pay outs that sometimes go well beyond a pension check to include hard-to-estimate, health benefits.

What is the difference between defined contribution plans and defined benefit plans? For the last three decades, the line in the tax code—401(k) and its lesser-used sister, 403(b)—that permits you to save money before taxes were withdrawn from your paycheck has become synonymous with retirement planning. This is a defined contribution, referring to a decision by you to make a contribution to your plan. A defined contribution plan or pension builds in value with each year worked and under many circumstances with each increase in pay. This type of plan rewards the worker who stays on until the end. Unlike defined contribution plans, pensions are not portable. If you leave your job, often you forfeit your pension as well.

David McCarthy of Oxford University see pensions as possessing a life cycle. In a paper published in the Journal of Pension Economics and Finance, he suggests that when you first begin your working career you are in possession of human capital and are less likely to willingly suffer income shocks. Pensions provide financial capital later in a worker's life when their human capital is on the wane. Pensions, he feels, lessen a worker's investment risks much in the way mutual funds do for investors. Because pensions have a more conservative approach, they prevent adverse investment selection at a time when it could do the most harm.

These promises tend to doom a company's accounting, especially if they underestimate or fail to have a good fixed income offering to peg their estimates on.

When President Bush did away with the 30-year long bond on Halloween of 2001, he basically doomed a good deal of this country's pensions plans, many of whom were still reeling from the sudden and dramatic demise of the stock market, a sudden and vicious tumble that had been progressing for over a year. (In January 2000 the Dow Jones Industrial Average hit a high of 11,908.34; in November 2001 it hit a low point of 8659.90.)

Many plan administrators, seeking some way to fix the enormous losses and stem any future mistakes, needed something tangible and fixed—and long range. The move to do away with that bond wasn't the sole reason for the problem, although, without alternatives, it did exacerbate the issue.

The plans gambled during the heyday of the NASDAQ and paid dearly when those stocks fell, leaving an incredible source of revenue suddenly no longer on the books. Companies flush with stock market gains had been skimming surpluses from their pension plans and accounting for them as profits.

Once that cash was no longer available, the company sought to make profits the old fashioned way: raising prices and cutting help. The raising of prices proved to be difficult in the post 9/11 environment and the subsequent recession. As companies trimmed their workforces, businesses were left with fewer opportunities to grow shareholder value, and with little room to grow and fewer bodies to produce the growth, pensions were the next best cost-cutting target.

The harsh reality is that many of the still existing company-run pension plans are currently under funded and will likely remain so for the near future.

What to Say! Pensions are not an obligation by law. The promises that were made to employees are not legally binding. This lack of property rights left many pensioners without anything when a company dissolves itself into bankruptcy, merges with another company or, worse, falls into the hands of private equity and is no longer a publicly traded entity. In fact, the bankruptcy courts do not take those pension obligations into consideration when making their ruling. Without property rights, those promises mean nothing.

It seemed we watched in some sort of detached wonder as airlines battle with their workers over pension promises they made, then Detroit with its workers, so by now everyone should know the precarious position many companies are in. We all believe that when a company makes a promise to its employees, they are bound by ethics to make promises that they can keep.

There is a conundrum in place. The law does not allow the company to make fraudulent promises beyond the laws that govern these types of plans. But, ironically, it is those same laws that encourage the promises to be made, even if the company knows it may not be able to make the obligation true.

One of the most problematic issues facing private and public pensions is the $400 billion shortfall currently reported by the Pension Benefit Guaranty Corporation or the PBGC.

How does the PBGC work? It is intended to act as a pension insurance policy that collects premiums from companies so that, if a pension plan fails, the retired worker will get a portion of what they previously had coming. In terms of payout, the design is somewhat flawed. The premiums PBGC collect act as a buffer, so if member companies, should they run into trouble, declare bankruptcy and/or dissolve, their employees and retirees will not lose their entire pension. The PBGC usually is able to pay low-end workers what they have been promised. Upper-end pensioners do not receive the full amount; sometimes those reductions in benefits can be as much as 50 percent of what they believed they should have been paid.

Those shortfalls in funding will continue to grow as company after company lines up for help, all blaming poor actuarial guesses. The problem lies in the inability of the PBGC to reach full funding through premium levels. They act as a tax on the business, making profitability and full funding of their own private plans even more difficult. Taxpayers will be too busy bailing out state and local plans that are underfunded or will face future underfunding of their own to worry about the state of private pension problems and funding of the PBGC. There is little likelihood that we can tax our way out of this problem.

A speculator is a man who observes the future, and acts before it occurs.— Bernard Baruch

What people who have believed that their pensions were all they needed should know is that the solution to this problem, as usual, falls squarely on the shoulders of the worker.

Pensioned employees should do three things. The first two begin with reining in those runaway spending habits and rethinking their refinanced and/or long term mortgage obligations. The last relies on an increase in personal retirement savings.

Inflation Will Not Matter—Much

Most of us know that we possess two kinds of memories: short-term, the kind that allows us to recall a phone number or a person's name we were introduced to recently, and long-term, the memories that help us recall the past in vivid detail. No one is sure how this process takes place or why it can happen as rapidly as it does. One thing is evident as researchers study that particular organ, one with more neurons than stars in the sky, is the brief moment when we do pull a particular memory from our vast and subcategorized storage, we risk erasure. In an instant, what we were trying to remember can be wiped out in pieces or in whole.

Which is why we so often act as if we had no past memories of what happened a month, a year, or a decade ago, with even less chance of recall if the event did not directly affect us. Even as we work harder to get ahead, some things are pulling us back.

Inflation works against savings the same way as debt does. It acts as a drag against growth. Even if you predicted a modest level of inflation, you could be broke before you reach the average age of retirement. Consider the following calculations: You are 40 years old with a target date for retirement being the same one Social Security allows right now, around 67 years old. For the sake of calculations we will assume you have the median US income ($43,200), with the average amount of money put away for retirement ($56,878, according to the Employee Benefit Research Institute. Average individual retirement account balances for people 50 and older is $80,000, even as savings rates have continued to drop with US households spending $41.6 billion more than they earned). The amount of pretax contributions has also dropped steadily since 1999 to 6.1 percent of salaries. That may be due in part to the demise of a bull market in 2000. And speaking of salaries, they have been decreasing in terms of overall historic measures of household income.

So, for the sake of argument, we will assume that 25 years from now you will be earning roughly the same as you are now—I hope not, but for this discussion it is possible. We will also make a modest assumption for growth in that investment both while you work and when you retire. (We will discuss growth and how to make it work for you in the next section.) And because we are focusing on how much will be enough, we will make our withdrawal rate at 75 percent of our preretirement income.

By age 79 you would be broke.

Your plan could, with all things being equal and the markets having not experienced any long-term downturns, provide $364,205 when you retire. This is based on retirement expenditures of $32,400 in your first year of retirement (75 percent of your last year's income of $43,200). This plan also includes $21,577 per year from Social Security starting at age 65, which is good considering you will only have that income for the rest of your life. That number will not keep pace with inflation. If it did, your estimated Social Security income for the year when your savings runs out would need to be well over $63,000!

Age	Interest and savings	Retirement account withdrawals	Ending retirement balance
41	$6,048	$0	$62,926
50	$10,218	$0	$136,594
60	$18,298	$0	$279,353
65	$21,852	$32,400	$353,657
70	$17,625	$37,743	$273,637
75	$10,053	$43,967	$133,631
76	$8,018	$45,330	$96,319
77	$5,779	$46,736	$55,362
78	$3,322	$48,185	$10,499
79	$630	$11,129	$0

My Tax Bracket Will Be Lower

Let's put those same numbers in and look at just taxes. The topic will also be discussed at length in the next section, but here, as we dispel notions and myths about retirement savings, we will look at the effect of taxes on what you have amassed if you were the subject of our example.

If you calculated a 25 percent federal tax rate, the lower bracket that your projected retirement income would place you in, your money would run out after 12 years.

What is my tax bracket? According to the IRS Web site for 2007, Schedule X or Single filers would pay:

If taxable income is over	But not over	The tax is:
$0	$7,825	10% of the amount over $0
$7,825	$31,850	$782.50 plus 15% of the amount over 7,825
$31,850	$77,100	$4,386.25 plus 25% of the amount over 31,850
$77,100	$160,850	$15,698.75 plus 28% of the amount over 77,100
$160,850	$349,700	$39,148.75 plus 33% of the amount over 160,850
$349,700	no limit	$101,469.25 plus 35% of the amount over 349,700

Schedule Y.1 or Married Filing Jointly or Qualified Widow(er)

$0	$15,650	10% of the amount over $0
$15,650	$63,700	$1,565.00 plus 15% of the amount over 15,650
$63,700	$128,500	$8,772.50 plus 25% of the amount over 63,700
$128,500	$195,850	$24,972.50 plus 28% of the amount over 128,500
$195,850	$349,700	$43,830.50 plus 33% of the amount over 195,850
$349,700	no limit	$94,601.00 plus 35% of the amount over

Schedule Y.2 or Married Filing Separately

$0	$7,825	10% of the amount over $0
$7,825	$31,850	$782.50 plus 15% of the amount over 7,825
$31,850	$64,250	$4,386.25 plus 25% of the amount over 31,850
$64,250	$97,925	$12,486.25 plus 28% of the amount over 64,250
$97,925	$174,850	$21,915.25 plus 33% of the amount over 97,925
$174,850	no limit	$47,300.50 plus 35% of the amount over 174,850

Continued

Schedule Z – Head of Household		
$0	$11,200	10% of the amount over $0
$11,200	$42,650	$1,120.00 plus 15% of the amount over 11,200
$42,650	$110,100	$5,837.50 plus 25% of the amount over 42,650
$110,100	$178,350	$22,700.00 plus 28% of the amount over 110,100
$178,350	$349,700	$41,810.00 plus 33% of the amount over 178,350
$349,700	no limit	$98,355.50 plus 35% of the amount over 349,700

This idea that taxes on a state and federal level will strip a good deal of what you had planned to spend seems wrong. But the agreement many of us made deferred those taxes until this moment, when we made the assumption that the benevolence of the federal government would lower those rates. The truth is, according to a recent Congressional Budget Office report, the government seems to be downright giddy at the positive tax revenue that will be generated by the large number of us that will be retiring in the coming years.

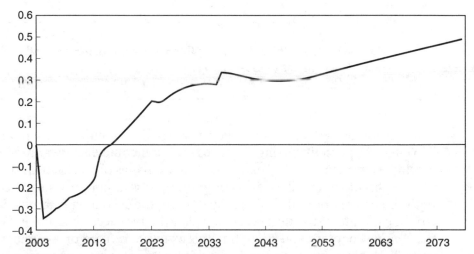

Figure 11.1 The effects of tax-deferred retirement plans on income tax receipts, 2003 to 2078
Source: Congressional Budget Office.
Notes: Data are normalized to zero in 2003.
The initial dip in revenues is associated with restoring pension plans to a fully funded status and has no effect on the long-term results.

Counting their pennies before they are collected, the CBO wonders if this increase in tax receipts will make a difference had there been no tax deferral system of investment in place. Some believe that, in the absence of a tax-deferred system like IRAs and 401(k)s, but not plans designated as Roth IRAs or Roth 401(k)s where after taxed dollars are invested, less money would have been saved but that money would nonetheless have been invested.

But the benefit of tax-deferred savings does tend to outweigh some of the disadvantages (more on that comparison later). It helps first to understand how these two types of tax treatments work.

Our taxpayer in the above example is in a 25 percent federal and an 8 percent state tax bracket. At age 40, she deposits $1,000 into a tax-deferred account. It stays there until age 65 when she begins withdrawal. That money has grown at 6 percent (same as the example) and is now $4,291.87. If we adjusted that total for inflation, the real value of that savings is $2,004.20—but that is, unfortunately, not how you will be taxed. It is this figure that will be subject to the 25/8 tax rate, leaving you with a tax bill of a little less than a $100 to the state. Calculating just the percentages though, you would have an after tax income of $3,219 or a tax bill of $1,073.

 Diligence is a good thing, but taking things easy is much more restful. —Mark Twain quotes (1835–1910)

But had you placed that same $1,000 in a taxable account and tried saving it for 25 years at 6 percent, paying the taxes on the income each year as it grew, you would be left with $3,005. This amounts to a savings of $214. (In any calculation such as this, done for illustration only, numerous assumptions can be made by both the calculator and you and, by default, me. The idea is to give you some sort of estimate of the difference between the two accounts, albeit roughly. In the coming chapters, you might find this example refuted on a number of levels as we look at growing our savings and investments and strategizing to achieve the best favorable tax environment.)

Taxes have their own veil of misconception and the effect of taxes on your plan is, for lack of a better word, huge. It plays into every decision you make, affects your returns and your future returns on investments and hinders your thinking and focus.

I'm just going to spend a moment or two more clearing some of the misconceptions about taxes before we move on to the last in our five misunderstandings about how much you will need. Tax brackets and earnings are not necessarily married to each other. You can maintain a tax bracket on your earned income as long as you do not earn more than your bracket allows.

But earned income and *taxable income* are different, regardless of the source of that income. A number of things can have an effect on that income, such as distributions from pension plans or a change in your deductions. Investment income, however, and at least for the next several years, is taxed at 15 percent, not your taxable income rate.

On the other hand, you need not worry if your bracket changes. It doesn't necessarily mean that you will suddenly be shelling out a sizable percentage more. It is a graduated system with incomes taxed at separate levels—the dollar amount that pushed you into the higher bracket is taxed at the higher rate while your income taxed at 25 percent is still taxed at that rate.

As I have mentioned before, keep your tax deductions at the amount that will show zero taxes owed. This may increase your withholding—which is not based on tax brackets and will give you as much money as possible each paycheck. To download the form for your employer, you can go to the IRS Web site (www.irs.gov/pub/irs-pdf/fw4.pdf).

And, last, some of us teeter on the edge of two tax brackets. This can have some serious consequences when determining future possible earnings from accounts. The slightest error can mean thousands of dollars less—or more!

I Don't Need to Save as Much as Everyone Says I Do

John Karl Scholz and Ananth Seshadri, both from the University of Wisconsin Madison and National Bureau of Economic Research and Surachia Khitatrakun of the Urban Institute, begin their contrarian paper with the following disclaimer: *We solve each household's optimal savings decisions using a life cycle model that incorporates uncertain lifetimes, uninsurable earnings, medical expenses, progressive taxation, government transfers, and pension and Social Security benefits.* The paper, titled "Are Americans Saving 'Optimally' for Retirement?" was met with a wave of skepticism when it was first released. How could you save too little?

You can't save too little, it seems, without lowering your life-after-work expectations. One of the ways they did this was to conclude that after-work expenses would drop and are therefore overestimated when trying to calculate how much your post-work living expenses will be. But the authors make the claim with a caution.

People who are in the ages bracketed by 50 to 65 suggest that this group has saved enough to get by without too much worry. To do so, they would need to draw all of the equity from their current home, downsize their living arrangements, remained married—singles, divorcees, or widow(er)s tended to save too little in this group and in fact undersaved—use some of the equity they received from the sale of their property to help offset the potential for medical emergencies and spend between 75 percent to 86 percent of their preretirement income.

What is replacement rate? This is terminology for preretirement compared to postretirement income. Withdrawing 75 percent of your preretirement income after you stop working to provide you with an annual income is referred to as replacement income. But that should be based on another rate, the spend-down rate. That 75 percent rate you are using to target a retirement income should not tap more than 4 to 4.5 percent of your assets.

The second caution offered by the authors concerns the savings rate of younger generations. The push to leave something to their heirs, the estimated reduction in Social Security benefits and the possibly that economic conditions such as inflation and taxes might not be easily estimated, concerns them as they suggest that Americans are indeed saving enough.

The full paper can be found here: www.ssc.wisc.edu/~scholz/Research/Optimality.pdf

The most troublesome issue facing retirees is the fate of women. Statistically, they tend to work fewer years than men and because of that, tend to be able to draw less than their male counterparts for retirement savings and from Social Security. Couple that with lower earnings over the lifetime of work and you have a recipe for disaster. They live longer (85 years versus 82 for a man) and that makes them vulnerable to facing retirement single—statistically bad. With fewer than 35 percent of women entering into retirement with a pension, sharing their husband's retirement becomes a matter of getting by or barely existing. Once a husband dies, the pension benefit from a private employer might be reduced—by simply choosing a joint survivor annuity at the time they began distributions from the fund, married couples could avoid this late-in-life tragedy. Inflation takes it toll on women as well and doubly so if they see any reduction in benefits when their husbands die. Key to offsetting some of these problems comes with how you structure your pension payout (choosing the joint-annuity might create a smaller income when it is initially tapped, but it will last a lifetime), waiting to collect Social Security benefits and even working for several additional years would be best, participating in your employer's defined contribution plan and opening an IRA outside of work will add to the overall savings for women. Right now, the average retired woman has $100,700 saved; the average retired man has nearly twice that.

Now that we have discussed numerous preconceived notions about retirement and, with any luck, got you thinking straight, the next section of the book will concern itself with generating that cash and that nest egg. That's not to say we won't be uncovering numerous untruths along the way. The financial world is full of them, most disguised behind sales techniques. In this section, we will meet the Early Bird, a person just starting out; the Chaser, the poor soul who realizes that if he doesn't get going soon he will end with far less of a planned retirement than he would like; and the Relaxer, the person who can see the light at the end of the tunnel and has some very important investment decisions to make—more so than any other age group.

PART THREE
The Investor

◆▬◆▬◆▬◆▬◆▬◆▬◆▬◆▬◆▬◆▬◆▬◆▬◆▬◆▬◆▬◆▬◆▬◆

A Look Back

In truth, most of us don't like to look too far back in history, unless it is to prove a point. In the case of retirement planning, most of us look back on the changes that may have occurred then and how they work for or against us now. That almost always leads to a long look at the social program that changed the way we look at retirement: Social Security.

But retirement planning should not center around that sort of old age insurance. It should be more vibrant, self-controlled and yet it should be done in an atmosphere that allows you certain freedoms without completely cutting off the support you'll need in the future. If it sounds as if we should have it all, I make no apologies. We should.

Artisans in medieval Europe were faced with similar choices. They often worked until their last breath, toiling at their trades until they died. If they were successful, they were able to hire an apprentice to help. His guild would often step in and assist him if it could. His success even had a direct impact on his wife's retirement years.

He may have set up an annuity for her, providing her with a small income in her elder years. She could marry one of his journeymen, sort of staying in the business. Often, she took up another job. Much like her husband, her success in her later years was directly related to her ambition.

Her husband's designation as master kept both of them out of the downward spiral towards poverty. Those who failed to attain a certain level of skill were often left to fend for themselves without the help of guilds or savings.

In some ways, that doesn't seem all than much different that what faces us now. We have to have a certain ambition. We need to stay focused on where we would like to be in a future that is guaranteed to be wholly different than the present we live in. How hard is that?

Ambition can creep as well as soar.—Edmund Burke

Some people reading this book have never known a life without personal computers. And others may recall when dialing was actually a physical motion on a rotary phone. In the short span of our lifetimes, we have seen so many changes that developing a retirement plan requires only two things from you: the ability to be fluid and the ambition to keep at it.

CHAPTER 12

The Philosophy of Retirement

◆◆◆

D oes it all boil down to this simple graph? Does your level of risk determine your possible level of return? Is the tradeoff for low risk low return?

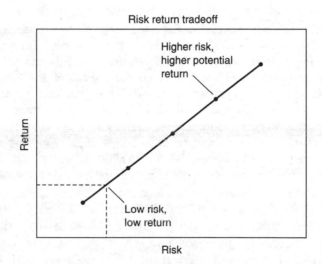

Risk return tradeoff

No conversation about retirement planning would be complete without a frank discussion about risk. Even that has changed, evolving into something akin to a walk down a dark alley rather than the simple choice on a pie chart. No longer can you simply feed your profile into a giant tumbler and come out with the perfect solution. Now, each investment is fraught with risk from sources you may not have even considered to be threatening just three or four years ago.

Granted, the tragedy of 9/11 changed a lot of things but, when it comes to finance, it just happened to be grouped in with so many other day/night differences in attitudes that, as a standalone event, it cannot be blamed. What we instead have is a shift in how we react.

It wasn't that long ago that reacting was usually the first and last thing you did in a retirement plan. You reacted to the external prompts of people like me and perhaps marched yourself into your personnel office and inquired about what was available. And the last reaction came when you signed up, picked a basket of funds from your company's planned offering, and forgot about it. Retirement planning in a nutshell, neat and tidy, and most important, done.

And then you found out that you would live longer. That there is a risk your money will not last as long as you might. You hadn't even thought about that one. You might need money for medical reasons, for taxes, for insurance, for home repair. Where is the extended vacation in that jumble of financial obligations? How do you plan for that?

What is the leading cause of financial anxiety? For most people, one doesn't describe the other; they are one and the same. In 1967 Thomas H. Holmes, MD, and Richard H. Rahe, MD, at the University of Washington School of Medicine, developed the Holmes and Rahe Social Readjustment Scale. They hoped to find a direct correlation between stress and health. Barron H. Lerner, MD, Department of Medicine, Columbia University wrote, "Although Holmes's work was rudimentary, his basic supposition may have been correct," adding that had he had access to modern scientific tools, his suggestion "that stress may lead to decreased immune function and thus to clinical disease" would have been proved. It is not coincidence that finances led the list of stresses.

Most investors, which are what I will refer to you as from this point until the end of the book, have a keen sense of who they are. They know how they feel about most of the every day confrontations we have with risk taking. They know how to create a layer of protection from what they fear most.

According to E. Thomas Garman, president of The Personal Finance Employee Education Foundation, Inc., a not-for-profit organization created in 2006, "Thirty million workers in America—one in four—are seriously financially distressed and dissatisfied with their personal financial situations." His organization believes that financial education rests with the employer. The group's focus is twofold. If you relieve the financial stress of the employee, you will increase productivity. And almost half of those employees report some sort of health related illness because of it.

Money creates a layer of protection. When that protection is threatened, it makes us anxious. It is this worry about our financial protection, especially when we know that had we had the money, that affects our day-to-day life. Our worries of a lack of future funding can cause the most damage to a retirement plan.

Our hard work, which if you will recall is called human capital, when we are young, turns into something that is very tangible. We know that money can purchase things. When we are older, we know how much financial capital we have amassed and understand that gathering it, sheltering it and even growing it, can help us when our human capital is on the wane.

But at what level we protect, shelter, and grow that financial capital makes all of the difference. We do daily battle with our own need to spend, something more than one psychologist refers to as "euphoric." If someone were to offer you a substantial amount of cash, not so large as to completely change your life, statistics have shown that you would first be inclined to create a laundry list of items you might like to purchase.

The emotional satisfaction is a very real response, so much so that you don't even need to actually have the money to tap those feelings. Who among us has not bought a lottery ticket and begun to strategize your next move *if* you win.

What the Experts Say

I figure you have the same chance of winning the lottery whether you play or not. —Fran Lebowitz

Sadly, the emotional response to "enough" is not part of our human make-up. If there is more, we would like to have it. If we cannot get more, we feel bad about not being able to get what we feel is "enough." Our approach to retirement planning hinges on our desire to want more. It is all in the hope that when we retire we will have enough.

So we have three basic problems to deal with: our emotional need to want more, our cautiousness, and our inability to see very far into the future when we are young and to see nothing but the future looming on the horizon when we are old.

Being wary and cautious is good when you are crossing the street. But when it comes to building a retirement, it can be hazardous to your financial health. Stepping lightly will make you much more prone to be indecisive when it comes to making good financial decisions. In the back of our minds, we doubt our abilities. And we owe that entire bag of mixed emotions to the "bubble."

Bubbles have now stepped to the forefront of financial anxiety and this anxiety has crippled far too many portfolios. Bubbles have some common features we are all familiar with and ones we are not.

Among the features of bubbles is the need for speculation. Speculators, by their nature and definition, are not in the business of investing for anything other than short-term gain. Their quest for quick or considerable profit is at the heart of what makes a bubble. But bubbles are not created on speculation alone.

In 1996, Jacob Freifeld suggested in his paper on behavioral decision making that "core phenomenon of the speculative bubble is one in which euphoric levels of valuation are validated by the market, and intelligence is measured only by profits, not reasoning and judgment. This is similar to the 'hot hand' maxim in basketball which says that players will predict with great confidence their ability to score again after scoring, despite statistical evidence to the contrary."

The second participant in the bubble is the fool. This person unknowingly becomes the "greater fool" when he believes that an asset can be bought and sold—hopefully for a higher price, because there exists a greater fool willing to buy it.

As each new fool enters into the picture, the bubble inflates. Meanwhile, the speculator waits until he feels as though the market has reached a predetermined point and sells his position. Worried, one fool sells as well. Then another. And the theoretical bubble bursts and whenever the inflated asset was reaches the point where it began.

The bursting bubble becomes newsworthy, as did the implosion of the stock market in 2000 and the currently deflating housing market of 2007. We watch in the beginning with rapt attention, trying to decipher what happened, whether it will have an effect on us and if we can learn something from it.

What we often take away from such events is not what we should. We withdraw and protect. This limits our exposure to risk and, even though we might be familiar with the old refrain, if you take away risk, you also take away the opportunity to gain.

Wall Street doesn't help. They encourage risk and at the same time encourage balance. We are allocating and shuffling portfolios to the point of absurdity. We begin to worry about being overweight or underweight, being exposed to too much volatility, or the performance of an individual stock or mutual fund as compared to the sector, the market, the portfolio of the guy sitting next to you. It's craziness. And it doesn't belong in a retirement plan.

Even more absurd than trying to avoid risk is the chance that we are actually inviting more by trying to prevent it.

The Birth of an Industry

The three words I hear the most when companies are trying to sell you on the idea that *they* hold the key to your future are "independence" and "financial security." What they should promise, but never do, is the freedom from worrying about whether your independence—however you define it—and your financial security are in jeopardy. The reason is relatively straightforward. They need you to worry.

Independence and financial security are ideals that few of us will ever experience. We have no concept of them while we are working towards them but we can imagine what they may feel like. We can envision ourselves in the warm wrap of those notions: no boss, no time clock, no alarm clock, just endless days filled with doing whatever you want to do. Are you sure you want to live life like you were four years old?

Part of the vitality of retirement lies in overcoming so many obstacles that a life with far fewer is actually more tempting than an existence devoid of any hassles. The first pensioners in the US were injured colonial combatants. Those pensions, funded by tax dollars, became the responsibility of these former soldiers, collected for their own retirement.

Much of the time between that moment and the Great Depression saw a gradual change in how the elderly were treated. From a secure farm household, where their contribution was equal to their ability to work, to the city, where the work was away from the home, the state of retirement was wholly based on the ability of your family to provide.

That's not to say that there were no retirement benefits to be had. Some companies, railroads, banks and utilities began offering pensions to their workers as early as 1875.

Because the labor market up until the mid-twentieth century was predominately male, statistics show how the creation of retirement affected the participation of the American labor force. By the time companies began offering pensions, nearly half the men who were considered retired lived in the households of relatives. By 2000, this number had fallen to less than 5 percent. In 1875, 78 percent of the workers aged over 65 were still in the workforce. By the year 2000, it had fallen to less than 18 percent.

But these pensions relied on the health of the company. Once the economic collapse that accompanied the stock market crash in 1929 unfolded, even families were unable to support themselves. If you were too old, you were unable to work.

President Franklin D. Roosevelt responded to this with the Social Security Act of 1935. In the tradition of a rural retirement, the people able to work helped support those that could no longer perform the job they once did. One percent of the first $3,000 a worker earned went to pay the retirees. The company added a matching one percent as well. Today, both the employee and the employer pay almost 7.65 percent each up to the first $97,500.

Social Security was not designed to be a program of last resort. Aside from the insurance aspect of the program, Social Security provides benefits to the disabled, a spouse or child of someone who gets Social Security, a spouse or child of a worker who died, or a dependent parent of a worker who died; the benefit offered in retirement is calculated to meet 40 percent of your postretirement needs.

Why can't I use Social Security in my retirement plan calculations? You could, at least in theory. Most younger people have begun to discount the viability of the program and have bought many of the stories about its eventual demise. I'm from the school of thought that believes that it will still be around when my children retire—however they happen to describe that word. Will the trust fund run out of money by 2041? Quite possibly. Will the benefits diminish as the population ages? Absolutely. The generation called the Boomers will put the same pressure on the program as a fat man in a bathtub. Smart money counts on Social Security as a supplemental income that will help with those ever-increasing health insurance and medical costs. If you approach it in this manner, you will be inclined to wait to begin benefits as long as possible.

Trying to Fix the Problem

According to the Heritage Foundation, a conservative think tank, there are only three possible solutions to fix the so-called looming problem facing Social Security funding: "raise taxes, reduce spending, or make the current payroll taxes work harder by investing them through some form of personal retirement account (PRA)."

While no self-declaring conservative would ever suggest we raise taxes and the debate over spending reduction looks to be off the table, at least in the near-term, privatizing the program seems, at least to this group, the only viable solution worth debating.

Behind Privatizing

The idea behind privatization seems simple on the surface. It would allow people to create private accounts that would be theirs alone, a pay-in-and-watch-it-grow program that would be much the same as a 401(k) plan and similar retirement programs sponsored by companies.

As we will learn later in the book, these types of plans have been successful for two reasons: One, they remove the burden of liability from the company and their profit and loss statement, and drop the responsibility squarely in the laps of its employees. Pensions are accounted for on the books when a company holds them privately.

In its most simplistic explanation, when a pension creates high returns on the underlying investment, the obligation to the pension is met and the rest of the money is accounted for as a profit. If the underlying investments in the pension portfolio do poorly, then the company is liable to make up the shortfall with money from another pool of profits. Not having to account for these plans was almost immediately embraced by all but a few companies in the three decades since these plans were created.

The second attractive part of these plans was the creation of a new investor class. Creating this new group of investors has not necessarily meant that the employee has done well. It is merely a shift in how companies take care of employees and their retirement.

Creating a new investor class the way this program has done has instead allowed companies to wash their hands of any retirement obligation. By forcing folks to explore their options, in many instances without any financial education or guidance from the company as to where to put their retirement savings, these programs have not been as successful for the employee.

Some of the former benevolence of the company sponsored pension plan has carried over into these plans as employers offered matching funds to encourage employees to take advantage of these programs. The problem was, these funds were mostly squandered as employees picked restrictive matching (i.e., when the company matches on company stock only) or failed to choose the right fund for their investment goals.

Many defined contribution plans offer a default fund if the employee fails to decide how to allocate their money. This is often a low yielding money market fund that could languish for years beneath the weight of current monetary policy.

What is monetary policy? The short explanation, always the best, gives the Federal Reserve Board the jurisdiction to raise or lower short-term overnight lending rates to the biggest borrowers—namely, the biggest banks. That rate, which also makes the news for its effect on stock and bond prices, is then passed on to other borrowers, with the few tenths or hundredths of a point added on. By the time businesses are allowed to borrow, the cost is higher and the possibility that they will not borrow and take that money to grow their businesses hinders growth. Additional factors play into the unfolding scenario—many of which we will discuss further along. That policy in effect acts like an accelerator or a brake for the economy, controlling inflation and growth.

Although some education gains have been made in correcting these investment mistakes, the average employee is still underinvested and largely misdirected when she finally does participate.

That is the downside of privatization. In President George W. Bush's plan, accounts similar to those offered by private industry will be created. These have been promised to somehow be better directed and offer more security. Don't count on it. There is a downside to adding security. It tends to increase risky behavior. I fear the same will occur here.

The stock markets have continued to fascinate us. We tune in to the goings on from Wall Street with either envy or confusion. For every report on the future of the markets and their cheerleaders, who see nothing but blue skies and sunshine ahead, there are those, like me, who seriously doubt the direction of the markets at any given moment.

But retirement planning is not about the *moment*. It is about a series of decisions all made with a single goal in mind—and, unlike the financial services companies trying to lure you in with boasts of past performance and promises to be one-to-one with you about your goals, retirement planning is an insurance policy. It can and will insure you against many of your greatest fears and anxieties, it can offset the inevitable had you not planned, and it can ensure that you will have money when you need it as long as you are alive. If that is your idea of independence and financial security, so be it.

Tying private accounts to the stock market is a risky business and the accounts may not even have the returns that are currently being touted. Citing historic returns in this era of soaring deficits, globalization and concerns over the economic disruptions resulting from terror, may not be the wisest approach to instilling confidence in the average worker, who may still see the Street as the den of robber barons.

You, the Account Manager

Privatization as it has been portrayed offers almost everyone an opportunity to manage their own accounts as they wish. Whether this will work, once again, depends on whom you listen to and whom you want to believe. The only group that did well when pensions were dismantled and shifted towards private accounts *was* the businesses that sponsored them and the industry that provides the investment services.

If the U.S. government decides to change its program, shifting the burden of retirement onto the worker, there is no one arguing the fact that not only will Wall Street benefit, but the government will benefit more than we will.

How much this shift will cost is still unknown. But, before I get to the cost of the programs such as Social Security, let's look at whom the change is proposed for and how it will affect us.

Without a doubt, some change is needed. Currently the Social Security system determines the benefits it pays and any increases in those benefits to the increases in the average wage paid nationwide. The reason the program has survived as well as it has is because of this wage-based accounting.

The changes in the amount of workers paying into the system has come down considerably since it inception in 1935. Because of all of those years of wage increases and payroll tax hikes, which are shared by both companies and employees equally, the system has permitted lawmakers adequate time to find solutions to the predicted problems that lie ahead.

From Social Safety Net to ...

The current Social Security plan is risk free. Politicians have been studying remedies to fix the program for over 20 years with little success. Many of their decisions, often reached because there were no viable solutions otherwise, simply put off any meaningful change by pushing the retirement age eligibility further into the future.

While this is a good idea, at least based on life expectancy and considering that there are so many convincing statistics pointing towards the same conclusion, any attempt by lawmakers at actuarialism often misses the point. What many fail to take into account are the middle and lower class workers' labor pains by the time they reach retirement age. Many simply cannot continue to work much past 65—if they can make it that far.

The mathematics department at the University of Michigan describes an actuary as: "a business professional who analyzes the financial consequences of risk. Actuaries use mathematics, statistics, and financial theory to study uncertain future events, especially those of concern to insurance and pension programs."

The risk in putting money into the markets is inherent. With a current return on Social Security investments at 3 percent and with the best long-term average for the stock and bond mix proposed in the change at 3.5 percent, it makes the change, accompanied by the cost of these new investments, hardly worth it. Many folks who work and actively invest in the markets all hesitate to make long-term predictions, often falling back on where they have been. That should raise a red flag.

Tallying Human Behavior

I'm no different than many of you. At age 25, the thought of retirement was not at the forefront of what was important to me. I did some investing but it was the hit and miss variety. At that time, Wall Street seemed like the bastion of greed. Much of my still-lingering skepticism was developed during that period. The late 1970s and early 1980s, a time when the investment world was portrayed as the land of Gordon Geckos, was also a time of high inflation.

The 1970s (1971–80)
    4 highest-inflation years 11.3%
    4 lowest-inflation years 5.4%
The 1980s (1980–89)
    4 highest-inflation years 6.4%
    4 lowest-inflation years 3.1%

At age 25, like many in my peer group, even if we had been given the opportunity to invest, I would not have done so if it had been voluntary. By the time I was 30, I was well into raising a family. By the time I was in my 40s, I realized that I needed to supplement my retirement, which was to be funded by a pension and Social Security. Had neither of those two been there, my working career would, without a doubt, need to be extended far beyond my ability to remain productive and viable in the work place.

David Ransom, writing for the *Concise Encyclopedia of Economics*, described inflation as "not simply the sum total of a collection of independent price changes, as the arithmetic of the CPI implies. It is the degree to which all of those prices move in concert." He continued, "Economists who view inflation as

Continued

a very serious problem point refer to what they call the inflation tax. By this they mean the reduction in the purchasing power of the cash balances held by the private sector—like a wealth tax. This tax is a drag on the economy—an efficiency loss—because it induces people and businesses to economize on cash balances, making it more difficult to participate in the money economy."

Poorer workers struggling in lower paying jobs have little incentive to divert much-needed funds to their future when their present demands so much. That is not a liberal patronization of the working poor. It is a reality that many of us have lived at one time or another and you knew what you were missing as every earned cent went to the family budget and not to some far off distant future.

Imagine for a moment, a sudden realization by American workers that retirement was nearing and they had done nothing to secure their futures. If young folks do not believe in the viability of the program now, there is little likelihood that they would possess the farsightedness needed to prepare for their future. While many of us had inflation to blame for our late start, what will the late-to-the-game investors, who are in their twenties and thirties now find 10 or 20 years down the road.

Social Security acts as a buffer against our own behavior, which can be incredibly shortsighted. In other words, it is doing what it was designed to do, keeping the elderly from poverty and, despite whatever fixes that the program might need, it will keep many of us who have failed to save enough from exactly that fate.

The Boomer Threat

You will have heard it called a tsunami (David Walker, Government Accountability Office), a speed bump in the road to economic growth (*The Economist*), or as a decrease in available workers, a decrease in growth of the GDP, a decrease in the growth rate of consumption, and a decrease in living standards (Ben Bernanke, Federal Reserve Chairman).

Depending on whom you listen to, and everyone seems to have their crystal ball polished and primed for predicting exactly what will happen in the next several years when the leading edge of the Baby Boomers turns 65, we are in for quite a lot of trouble—or not. Truth is, no one, not even the Boomers, can make any assumptions even as they approach yet another birthday. This leads to yet another moment of reckoning and decision-making. To retire or not to retire will remain the question on the minds of numerous aging workers and the investors that are trying to position themselves ahead of the rising tide. Personally, I think we are bracing for another Y2K.

From an investor's standpoint, the preretirement Boomer is signaling a shift in how the markets move rather than foreshadowing a sudden drop-off in market interest.

What is GDP? While there are numerous ways of measuring the health of the economy, the GDP, or gross domestic product, measures all of the products, services and goods a country makes within a specific time frame. In its simplest form, expressed as a math sentence it would read: Consumption + Investment + (government spending) + (exports − imports) = GDP. Consumption refers to personal expenditures for goods excluding new houses. Investment usually relates to what businesses do to create new or additional products—not the traditional way you and I might think of it. Government spending is exactly what it says it is. Because the government does not produce a product, it is a consumer of finished goods, and employer of public servants, and the financier of the military. Exports—Imports capture what we produce as a nation less what we import from other countries. These numbers are used as a backward looking prediction of future growth. If you are interested in the current GDP, it can be found at: http://www.bea.gov

The effect that Boomers will have on the GDP has been predicted to be any-where from zero to a significant drop-off of 1 percent or better. But who knows? Even the Fed cannot predict with any accuracy that the number reported in any given quarter is the *actual* number. How could they possibly make a prediction of how the economy will react 10 to 20 years from now?

You will find that government and, more specifically, GDP revisions can and do take place on a regular basis. The GDP number reported today, often with great stock and bond market anticipation, will, without a doubt, change by the next time the report is issued. According to the Federal Reserve Bank of

Minneapolis, this "fickleness" is attributed to the difficulty in pinpointing such a large economy at any one point in time. It takes time to tally those numbers and even as the Bureau of Economic Analysis publishes a number, the lagging indicators have yet to be added.

So why is this important to investors? How Boomers react to retirement or not could result in a shift in which companies will be the most prosperous. Reading these predictions and forecasts into the GDP has become quite the parlor game amongst legislators and businesses looking to position themselves for the onslaught. The act of simply trying to guess how it will play itself out is beginning to feed on itself.

Will these folks suddenly begin to spend rather than squirrel money away? Will they continue to save money and in doing so slow the economy by not buying goods produced here or abroad, or will their consumption of goods and services suddenly spike? Will they begin to make withdrawals on their savings, selling off their investments in the markets en masse or, will they realize that they have a good deal of time ahead of them to save even more?

Much like the daily activities of the stock market, it shouldn't matter. When we get to the actual investment plan you will see that, while you may make some allocation adjustments as you age, you will never be fully detached from the markets. While I will show how long it may take to spend an account to zero, I don't think, that with a plan, it is likely to happen.

Exploring the Scenarios

To understand how the Boomers might affect the GDP, you must first ask yourself, what would you do? If you no longer had to work, had saved a considerable nest egg, had it invested in the stock and bond market, and had made the decisions to "sell-down" your portfolio to provide you income, would you buy goods and services with abandon or do so conservatively? Would you think frugally or live life like you deserve the reward?

If you decided to spend money, the transfer from savings to spending would in fact increase the GDP and benefit the stock market. Selling shares from your portfolio would create a buying opportunity for those who are new or are currently investing. Your money, withdrawn as a distribution, would go back into the economy just the way it did when you were working. You would still have food, clothing, housing, and automobile needs. You would still portion a part of your retirement distribution for entertainment and leisure and you might reinvest some of that cash into a new business venture.

Yet, according to the Employee Benefits Research Institute, preretirees suggested that their spending would actually decrease compared to their working years and continue to drop after the initial years of retirement pass. That worries economists and investors alike.

The idea of creating a business would in fact add to the GDP if a considerable number of Boomers decided to pursue an entrepreneurial dream. This could add to the savings pool if you create employment opportunities as well as add to the export side of the tally sheet. The services you provide would further prompt those still employed to spend. (If you haven't already wrapped yourself around the notion, spending *is* much better for the economy than saving. Saving removes money from the economy, slows consumption, and limits growth.)

What the Experts Say Stocks are a safe bet, but only if you stay invested long enough to ride out the corrections. —Peter Lynch

Worries about a stock market crash are, for the most part, unfounded. Boomers have not saved nearly enough to impact the markets in a real way and certainly not enough to bring it to its knees. The rest of us are still building our savings and, as I mentioned before, as one Boomer taps her or his wealth, the pre-Boomer is there to pick up the baton.

Couple that information with the fact that over 90 percent of the stocks are owned by 10 percent of the investors—a fact you will need to keep in mind as we look at the different types of investments later on in this section—and you have a relatively stable growth pattern ahead. Will it be vibrant enough to maintain the seemingly endless climb that the markets have experienced? At this stage, it is hard to tell.

Below you will find a chart of the historic returns on the stock market from 1928 through 2006. It will also show you what the value of $100 invested would be, assuming all of the dividends were reinvested. (Dividends, as we will discuss later, relate to a portion of the profits a company returns to its shareholders. This number in terms of a percentage to share price has been dropping over the last several years, because stock prices have been rising more rapidly.)

Year	Annual returns	Stocks compounded value of $100 initial investment
1928	43.81%	$143.81
1940	10.67%	$107.37
1950	30.81%	$355.60
1960	0.34%	$1,614.37
1970	3.56%	$3,510.49
1980	31.74%	$7,934.26
1990	−3.06%	$28,895.11
2000	−9.03%	$142,482.69
2001	−11.85%	$125,598.83
2002	−21.98%	$97,996.61
2003	28.41%	$125,838.91
2004	10.70%	$139,308.83
2005	4.85%	$146,062.54
2006	15.63%	$168,886.53

Arithmetic average (stocks)

1928–2006	11.77%
1966–2006	11.61%
1966–2007	11.06%

Geometric average (stocks)

1928–2006	9.86%
1996–2006	9.56%

Social Security Projections

With good reason, Social Security has created its own projections for the Boomer demographic. Estimating the costs of retirement is an important and a necessary piece of information for lawmakers as well.

Surprisingly, SSA believes that Boomers will be less likely to retire married as compared to previous generations. They expect a higher degree of divorced and never-been-married retirees. They also expect that this group will be retiring earlier in larger numbers, be much more racially diverse than past numbers indicate and be better educated as well. To borrow a phrase for their dilemma, "past performance is not an indication of future results."

 It is better to have a permanent income than to be fascinating.—Oscar Wilde

If past statistics could be applied to the future, especially concerning health, we could be in real trouble. Of the current group of retirees more than half are women, most of the current group are white and two of five retirees are disabled. The poverty level is a real factor in the daily lives of 10 percent of the current crop of retirees.

And despite the fact the companies are encouraging older workers to retire earlier, be wary of such corporate benevolence. The average age of retirement at many companies is dropping at the same time benefits for employees who are still working are disappearing. This means that a worker who is eyeing early retirement should consider one primary thing: medical cost.

A worker contemplating early retirement will often calculate the tangible costs and how much replacement income will be needed, possibly the balance remaining on the mortgage, and how developed their marketable skills may be. What they often fail to add in to the equation is the cost of pre-Medicare medical coverage.

Fewer and fewer companies are offering any sort of benefits beyond your working years, according to the latest studies by the Employee Benefits Research Institute. That shortfall in coverage could set you back almost $100,000 if you retire at 50.

 According to a recent survey by the Employee Benefits Research Institute, the younger you are, the greater the chances you know what the current retirement age is. Most surprising about the confidence survey is the number of workers 55 and older who were unaware of the phase-in period between 65 and 67 to

Continued

receive full benefits (42 percent). Nineteen percent of this age group missed the correct answer by four years or more. Although the survey doesn't record the amount of people who actually opened the yearly statement mailed by the Social Security Administration, three-quarters of the respondents said they had received a statement. (Mailed out prior to your birthday every year, this statement should be examined not for the potential benefit you will receive but instead for the amount that was contributed from your payroll tax.) The survey also uncovered a general unease about the future of Social Security and Medicare benefits as compared to what current level of benefits retirees receive.

Slow Changes

Lawmakers in Washington have been met with committee resistance to changes in health insurance coverage for the all-important gap experienced by retirees who are too young to qualify for Medicare but no longer are employed or employable. A recent but failed attempt to allow retirees to buy into Medicare beginning at age 54, or to purchase the same coverage offered to federal workers, was introduced by Representative Pete Stark (D–CA) and summarily rejected.

As Chairman of the Ways and Means Health Subcommittee, Pete Stark delivered the opening statement at a hearing on Medicare Trustees Report. In it he said: "While the program faces undeniable demographic challenges in future years, the so-called 45 percent 'funding warning,' which has been triggered in this year's report, is little more than an arbitrary, hidden hatchet designed to eliminate Medicare's entitlement and continue the march toward privatization started in the 2003 Medicare law."

While it seems that Medicare keeps cropping up in the conversation we are having, the issue at hand is health. If you as an investor were to look at the true Boomer effect, you might see more opportunity than downside.

For instance, health providers and other ancillary businesses that will provide to the medical needs of this group should show surprising but not unexpected growth in the next decade. Technology, travel and leisure and the financial sector can all expect to see significant gains. While the last two might seem like natural places for Boomers to dominate and grow the sector, the technological advances in entertainment (flat screen televisions) and home improvement can expect to see a boost from this group as they spend what they have saved.

Two things will need to take place for the Boomers to have an impact. First, Boomers need to save more than they currently think they need. In order to maintain a consumer level comparable to their current spending habits, what is currently projected as retirement savings will need to double.

Households with incomes ranging in the middle class ($35,000 to $74,000) have a widespread belief that they will need only $250,000 in savings when they stop working. Twenty-four percent of those surveyed by the EBRI in April 2007 thought that twice that amount would be adequate, with almost 13 percent offering an answer of "no idea" when questioned.

Whether the stock market will fall as Boomers retire remains to be seen. Many market analysts predict that supply and demand will take over (more supply compared to diminished demand) moving the markets down. If Boomers begin cashing out their 401(k)s and other defined contribution plans, including IRAs, there will be, at least in theory, far more sellers than buyers. Pensions will also begin selling their holdings to accommodate the payouts needed.

Two things will thwart those predictions. One, Boomers, whose retirement horizon spans over 18 years, could hesitate to sell their portfolios if they see the markets declining. Who among us doesn't know someone who was forced back to work after she retired on the bull market of 2000 only to find the underlying assets in her plan worth far less than when she walked? If the value of their portfolios are dropping, Boomers may just wait a few additional years. This would be a good thing for everyone concerned.

What the Experts Say

It has been said that arguing against globalization is like arguing against the laws of gravity.—Kofi Annan

The second and probably most likely scenario relies on the globalization of economies. I mentioned earlier how just a few people control the majority of stocks. This is not likely to change once an arbitrary age such as 65 is hit. If that is the case, positioning your retirement portfolio in a larger percentage of international investments might be the best protection against any precipitous fall in the stock markets. (That last sentence is *not* a recommendation. In fact, later on in the book I will make the argument that, because so many companies are intricately intertwined in foreign economies, both for supplies and final products, that many US companies are in fact international entities.)

Much of what the investors over the next decade or two will be focused on is that first wave of retirees. Will they sell? Will they invest? A good deal of what we do from this point on depends on this simple assumption: Boomers will affect the markets much less than many academics predict.

As we move into the next chapter, we will discuss the investment options for our three groups of retirement planners based on that assumption. Beginning with the youngest group, the Early Birds, we will discuss the benefits of aggressive investing, the pitfalls of not paying attention and the merits of rebalancing in life cycle funds.

CHAPTER 13
Retirement Planning

◆◆◆◆◆◆◆◆◆◆◆◆◆◆◆◆◆◆◆◆◆◆◆◆◆◆◆◆◆◆

The Early Bird

 The profusion of drummers undermines the authority of the drum, softening each beat by multiplying it. With one drummer each beat is a decision. With 77 each beat can only be a suggestion; the underlying pulse is somewhere in the middle of that refracted thwack.—Kelefah Sanneh, reporting for the New York Times on the festival of 77 BoaDrum on July 7, 2007.

The celebration is built on a lie. Originally begun in Japan as a celebration of the Seven Evenings, or Tanabata, and held on July 7 every year, the story supporting this festival is a sad tale of deception, love, and punishment. Mikeran, a young farmer, found a robe belonging to Tanabata. When questioned by the goddess as to its whereabouts, he denied any knowledge. Enthralled by her beauty, he helped her look for the missing robe and, as all good love stories go, they fell in love.

But time would uncover his deceit when she found a portion of the robe years later. His punishment would absolve him of his lie; he would need to weave a thousand straw sandals. He never completed his penance.

The Japanese celebrate the holiday as a reason to make wishes, poetry, and elaborate decorations. In the US, 77 drummers gathered, formed a snake, and played in unison in a form of tympanic celebration. Ms. Sanneh's comment about the effect of this collaboration struck me as particularly poignant.

"With one drummer each beat is a decision. With 77, each beat can only be a suggestion." As we look at retirement planning for the group of investors just beginning their long journey through work and life, it is important to remember that "each beat is a decision." regardless of what the majority might be "suggesting."

If you have stayed with me through our discussions about what retirement is, you will understand that it is vitally important to build this structure piece by piece, with the right amount of thoughtfulness and the right amount of risk. If you have ventured through all of the misunderstandings described in Part Two, you will understand why a celebration of youth is in order.

The Best Opportunity

I mentioned earlier in this section about the hype built around three key buzz-words, repeated in any number of variations by the industry that caters to selling you a rock solid retirement: independence and (financial) security. The Early Bird, the investor who is just starting out, who has a first job, who has her or his first *real* paycheck, is the one group most likely to attain those lofty goals; the rest of us will, if we are fortunate and diligent, experience some degree of those ideals.

But, just as many opportunities present themselves, an equal number of self-deceptions lie in the path of the Early Bird. You might see yourself in a house. You might see yourself with a family. You might see yourself in the corner office. None of those are available to someone who is not completely honest with themselves about the expectations each one of those goals requires.

Time

As they say, it is on your side. Without a doubt, you have absolutely no idea what this means. You may have some concept about compounding but you do not have the experience to wrap your mind around those numbers. You are skeptical and you should be. The proof that anything I might say is correct is still many years away.

Compounding and all of its so-called magic is lost when three basic ingredients are not met. To begin, the Early Bird needs to take the first step: make the initial investment. The money you begin with does not need to be sizable. Compounding works with any amount. When the money is deposited, you will receive interest for your effort.

The second ingredient is regularity. To make compounding even more magical, periodic deposits need to be made. And the last and most important detail is the reinvestment of any gains. When you receive interest from your deposit, do not withdraw it. Instead, leave it in the account to gain additional interest. When the interest gained is added to the balance and the interest rate is calculated against the new balance, the magic will have begun. The key to making compounding work is to leave it alone to grow.

Understanding each concept relies on a cohesive understanding of how you will react. Will you see a growing account balance as spendable income, a windfall, or some sort of financial right? The rules of this "game" are simple. Compounding works in retirement planning because it widens the distance between assets and liabilities.

The Balance Sheet

Statistics show that the chance you will enter the workforce without any debt are slim to none. That first job will find your personal balance sheet with more liabilities than assets. Turning that equation around is what a good plan tries to accomplish. Liabilities can represent college tuition bills, car payments, rent, or worse, credit card debt. You may have all of these and more or you may have only several. No matter the number, getting yourself into positive territory as quickly as possible is the goal.

Breaking this down into balance sheet form (see the budget in Appendix A — Budgets) helps you see how these two items impact your income. Once you see them laid out in black and white, you can further break them down into appreciable assets and depreciable liabilities.

An appreciable asset is something that is designed to gain value over time. But not all assets qualify.

Houses are often grouped into this category, but, as we discovered in Part Two, they should not be. There is little likelihood you would consider selling your house to pay a debt.

Unless the house was *the* debt. Homes are and should be put on the liability side of the balance sheet. Understanding liabilities as a drain on your economic future is important when trying to build a plan with a solid base. Understandably, most of us will ignore the notion of a house as a liability, calling it instead a home. I'm okay with whatever you refer to it as, as long as you do not refer to your first home as an investment.

Retirement funds, savings, or other items that have value that *could* grow over time, depending on the markets for those items, also could be considered assets as well.

For the sake of this conversation, let's leave retirement accounts off the balance sheet altogether. You should never consider it a saleable asset; something you could sell to balance the difference between what you owe and what you own. In other words, an asset represents something with real cash value that, if you were forced to sell to satisfy a debt, you could.

You are, as I mentioned earlier, more likely to be acquainted with the debt side of the balance sheet. Cars with outstanding loans qualify. Nothing will depreciate faster than a new car. All of the credit cards in your possession with a balance that exceeds your weekly take home pay are liabilities. Student loan obligations also fit on that side of the ledger.

Testing the Difference

The easiest way to test the difference between what qualifies as an asset and what could fall in to the category of liabilities is in the answer to this question: Does whatever you consider an asset have the potential for interest, dividends, or capital gains?

Haha!, you might say. Houses have capital gains. You might even point out that I called any potential gain in the sale of a house as nothing more than a dividend. And you would be right—almost.

Assets can either appreciate in value or decrease in value depending on the market place where you might sell them. Liabilities represent debt and a negative financial drag on savings and saleable assets. Unearned cash comes as a result of interest, dividends, and capital gains on assets.

From a tax perspective, the money above and beyond what you owe is called equity. Equity is the degree of difference between a mortgage and the real market value. The farther apart those two numbers, whether it be because you have paid down the loan or the marketplace has placed a higher value on your home, you will probably not take into consideration any number of factors that reduce that price down to a more dividend-like level.

And as a dividend, it is not a profit from an asset unless you sell it. Unlike a share of stock, the dividend is paid to you regardless of whether you intend to sell the share or not. That is a major difference. The sell factor always enters the equation—not *if I sell it would be worth ...* but *I could sell this tomorrow for ...*

The First Step

As an Early Bird to this concept of retirement, I would probably be safe in the assumption that you are or have used your parents recently to bail you out of some sort of financially sticky situation, a corner that you no doubt painted yourself into. It has become the new hot topic of late. College graduates who live at home long after school ends. Parents who do more than subsidize their children but instead enable them to drift along waiting for opportunity to knock. Not just any opportunity, the right one.

You have to stop this. I am not speaking as a parent—although I am and I empathize with your difficulty in developing the discipline to tell your children, "no, move out, get your own life, stop by occasionally for dinner, call every day." But if you are holding this book and you are not yet on your own, you need to be.

Parents are there to help and in many cases they are more than willing. The financial ties that parents offer can extend well beyond the time you move out.

This was uncommon among the Boomer generation. We may have borrowed from our parents but we seldom used them to pay regular bills like cell phone charges or insurance premiums.

But your lack of independence, your unwillingness to take the financial risk of living on your own, jeopardizes their retirement planning goals more than it helps you out in the short term.

Once you understand the term "living within your means" actually means "living below the standard your parents may have provided," you will be better able to grasp the concept of generating long-term cash. It's a cruel world with numerous obstacles but, as the song suggests, it is the same as it ever was.

The Wealth Generators

Risk is key here. Once you understand that you generate real tangible wealth, that if left alone to grow can generate additional compounded dollars, you have almost won the battle. This means embracing risk even if you consider yourself risk adverse. Even if you are in your fourties, the time horizon that the Early Bird operates with is actually quite long.

For the youngest investors and those about midway through their careers, the essential element to developing a retirement plan with any bite is consistency. I have mentioned numerous times that plans, while on the surface appearing optimistic and hopeful, are at their core, pessimistic. They expect the worst.

Generating wealth requires you to build in some sort of emergency fund. Now numerous financial writers before and after me suggest this: it is nothing new. An emergency fund is the hand holding the seat of your bicycle as you peddle for the first time without training wheels.

An emergency fund needs to be built with the smallest possible sacrifice. And it needs to be done before you see a dime of take-home pay. Open a small savings account and sign up for a $25 a week payroll deduction. And then forget about it. Seriously.

It will, at that paltry pace, take well over four years to build the three months of emergency funds that is necessary to offset any sort of short-term disaster you might experience. What you will have built by doing this is a small in-road to consistency. You can, and should, check your balance when each statement arrives, whether it comes by snail mail or via the web. Examine it for errors and file it away.

You can move it to a better interest bearing account but never withdraw a dime. Moving some of the balance to a certificate of deposit can generate additional interest and under any other circumstance might be considered a wise move. It sort of defeats the idea of emergency cash, however. It does need to be available when you need it but not too easy to get to and certainly not locked into a one-year commitment.

In order to generate the three elements of wealth, you need to pick a time horizon. In the short-term, you might choose:

Savings accounts are often our first brush with generating wealth and one of the lowest paying, in terms of interest earned. Your bank will no doubt have other accounts that provide the same liquidity—a reference to the ease in which you might have accessing your cash, like in an emergency.

Some checking accounts and **money market accounts** require minimum balances along with some additional access privileges. The interest at the bank down on the corner is not likely to be too high. Online banking provides the best interest rates for these simple accounts.

Certificates of deposit, purchased with a fixed interest rate for a fixed period of time and **Treasury Bills**, purchased as short-term government securities with maturities ranging from a few days to 26 weeks, provide excellent short-term investments.

T-Bills are sold at a discount from their face value, which basically means that when you purchase one, you pay less than the face value. When the Bill reaches maturity, the full face value is redeemed. Keep this in mind: Unlike Notes, bonds or TIPS, Treasury Bills pay the interest due on maturity (because of the short term they do not offer coupons, an every-six-month payment feature found in notes and bonds with longer maturity dates). There are some tax advantages. The interest received is exempt for state and local taxes but the holder of the bill is taxed on a federal level.

Treasury Notes are securities with maturities ranging from two years to 10 years. Both the T-Bill and Treasury notes are sold in minimum $1,000 increments.

Building Beyond Three Months

Your first brush with investing may have come with your first job. You may have been offered an opportunity to participate in your company's defined contribution plan. You may have not known what that was and fearing some chance for loss, depending on when it was first introduced to you, you may have declined. Time passed; an opportunity squandered.

Sadly, Early Birds starting a little late can't recover those missing years, time that could have been generating wealth. No matter, it is not too late to get into the game.

Once you have begun your emergency fund, it is time to begin thinking about that tax bill of yours. Most of us look at that paycheck and wonder why we need to pay so many taxes. We think: we will never see a dime of Social Security yet they take 7.5 percent of my pay. We think: what does Medicare do for me? We think: I need something to change the way my taxes are calculated. And that's when we begin thinking about buying a house.

Think about that logic for just a moment. You are going to buy a house to take advantage of the tax deduction, a deduction on the single largest liability (debt) you will ever have. There is a much simpler way to offset those tax bills without going into debt with a house—which does not have as many tax advantages as you may think. Give the government less in taxes by lowering your taxable income. It won't change your SSA or Medicare deduction, but it will result in less income — income that is being saved—from being taxed.

We will discuss the nuts and bolts of this a little further along in the book, when we take a longer deeper look at the defined contribution plan offered at your workplace or the individual retirement account you can set up independent of your employer. Both of these plans have the advantage of lowering your taxable income by withdrawing the money before it is taxed.

 What to Ask? How much to I deduct? Most plans will allow you to deduct a percentage of your income or a fixed amount. Whatever you decide on, $15,500 a year is the limit. But the Early Bird is focused on take home pay. You know what your expenditures are—which include everything from rent and entertainment to debt servicing and how much you need to "get-by." Ask your

Continued

employer if they match the contribution. Many do in some shape or form. Some companies will match your contribution dollar for dollar up to a certain percentage of your gross pay while others match only if you but the company's stock in your plan. A match is free money. Early Birds should take the match no matter what. Learn to live on what is left. But if your employer doesn't match, begin with 5 percent of your take-home pay. If that increases your take-home pay, increase it another percentage point until you reach your prededuction pay. If 5 percent is too much, tweak it down a percentage point at a time. This whole process may take several weeks to a month to hone in on the exact percentage need to achieve a prededuction take home amount. How hard is that?

For now, let's concentrate on what that money can do to grow wealth.

Your First Brush with Investing

Let's take a look at some of the basics of investing. For those who have not yet begun to invest, this is a just teaser about what lies ahead.

Suppose, for the sake of our example, we make a $1,000 investment in an index fund that tracks the top 500 capitalized companies in the country. *Capitalization* refers to a company's worth, arrived at by dividing the number of shares that are available to trade or outstanding times the share price.

 A share represents your portion of ownership in a company. A share in a mutual fund represents a portion of numerous companies. Equity shares come with voting rights. When you own a share of a mutual fund, you make the mutual fund manager your proxy, allowing them to vote in your best interest.

If you have 1,000 shares of stock in your company being traded on the New York Stock Exchange and those shares were valued at $15, your company would have a market capitalization of $15,000.

1,000 shares × $15 a share = $15,000 (market capitalization)

The Standard & Poors Company issues one of the most popular indexes of just such stocks and is widely used by the industry as a benchmark. So we place our hypothetical $1,000 in a mutual fund that picks the same stocks as the S&P 500.

A mutual fund is basically a managed account where investors with a similar goal and risk tolerance hire a manager to invest their money. Because you are doing so as a group, you are able to buy large quantities of stock with a single purchase, owning a portion of everything in the fund. This spreads the risk over a basket of stocks rather than concentrating the risk in one or two companies. There will, I promise, be more on this a little further on as well.

What is a benchmark? The term originated as a chiseled mark, usually placed horizontally by surveyors. The bench refers to the metal rod placed inside a bracket. Once measured and found to be level, it could be used repeatedly with additional surveys. For investors, it refers to a standard by which other investments are judged. Find a similar benchmark to the investment to compare, such as a mutual fund that invests in large companies that would use the S&P 500 as a benchmark.

That $1,000 investment in an S&P 500 index fund will generate some very good wealth, but will do so over a long horizon. To keep our example simple, we will neither calculate the real rate of return for each year over the time span below nor will we add in the dividends the companies within the index might pay. (Almost two-thirds of the companies in the S&P 500 index do pay some sort of dividend with their investors, money that is channeled right back into the fund and your account to purchase more shares.)

Let's just say that the historic return on the S&P 500 is around 12.5 percent—which is not far off the historic average return. With that interest on our original investment compounding we can create a sizable amount of money.

Year	Original investment: Interest	$1,000.00 Running balance
1	$127.00	$1,127.00
5	$204.90	$1,818.10
10	$419.80	$3,725.30
20	$1,387.70	$12,314.10
30	$4,070.00	$36,117.50

That is only a rudimentary example of how compounding can work in your favor. Suppose you began investing in the S&P 500 in 1969. You opened an account with the same $1,000. Had you invested in the S&P 500 and allowed the interest and dividends to be reinvested, you would have had much different results than the example above.

Growth over 30 years without withdrawals

Year	S&P 500 ending value
12/31/70	$1,039.84
12/31/80	$2,326.56
12/31/90	$8,569.59
12/31/99	$47,123.13

By June 2007, the S&P 500 index had posted a 12-month gain of 20.59 percent. If that pace were to continue over a similar time period of 30 years, that original $1,000 would have grown to $342,424.

Early Bird Takes the Risk

Risk, when it refers to the stock market and other similar investments, is discussed most often when those markets are suffering losses or declines. Suddenly, everyone is talking about risk. How should they manage it? Did they assume too much?

What to Ask? In 1921, Frank Knight wrote "The Meaning of Risk and Uncertainty." Up until that time, economists had not clearly identified risk or its economic importance. Once this paper was written, numerous economic theorists lined up behind the notion that there was a certain amount of randomness necessary in order to use risk to your advantage. Knight linked profits, entrepreneurship and the very existence of the free enterprise system to risk and uncertainty. Without bogging you down in a lot of economic mumbo-jumbo, economists break risk down into two categories: deduction—using probabilities to predict certain outcomes and induction—and behavior.

Continued

> Using deduction, economists can predict with some accuracy how much the stock market might return to investors. It is mostly theoretical. Using induction, economists look at past performance for indications of future results.
>
> Frank A. Schmid, senior economist at the Federal Reserve Bank of St. Louis, wrote: "Risk and uncertainty are two concepts that emanate from randomness. Neither concept is fully understood. Although risk is quantifiable, uncertainty is not. Rather, uncertainty arises from imperfect knowledge about the way the world behaves. Most importantly, uncertainty relates to the questions of how to deal with the unprecedented, and whether the world will behave tomorrow the way it behaved in the past."
>
> For investors, not being able to distinguish between risk and uncertainty is hazardous to their financial health.

Risk provides the investor with innumerable opportunities. The problem is, we rely on the past to point the way. While someone may have blazed the path through the woods, there will always remain a certain amount of risk and uncertainty. Perhaps the risk might be the chance something random will happen and the uncertainty acting as the off chance that something may have changed since the path was last taken. Perhaps a tree may have fallen, blocking the way. The past would have little relevance with this sudden change of risk.

We often suggest that risk is for the youthful. Their tolerance for both risk and uncertainty is high. So we derive the belief that portfolios held by the Early Bird should be chasing the optimal amount of growth. I have given numerous examples of the probable outcome of an investment based purely on some mathematical assumption that the world will hum along, unchanged and predictable for the entire time frame of each example.

Phrases like "keeping your eye on the target" mean much more to our Relaxer investor, the one who can actually visualize how their investments have done over many years. For the Early Bird, the target is over the hill and down the valley, repeated again and again for 30, maybe even 40 years.

What the few bought for the right reason in 1925, the many bought for the wrong reason in 1929.—Warren Buffet

Most of what masquerades as good advice for the young investor suggests quite the opposite of what is logical. The markets have rewarded the buy and hold strategy of investing because of the reinvestment of dividends and capital gains. In fact, since 1925, the total stock market has marched forward at a rate of about 7.43 percent.

Without calculating inflation into that kind of growth, our $1,000 investment would have grown to $342,424 (add in inflation at 3 percent and you still have an astounding adjusted savings of $163,544). This is far better than any investment over the same time period.

But there is a certain amount of uncertainty that is predictable. For instance, we know that the stock market in the United States has experienced highs and lows. A high-risk market is one that offers very little in the way of dividend or capital gains reward for your effort. A low-risk would then represent the opposite, suggesting that the face value of a stock is not as great as the dividend and capital gain reward.

What the Experts Say

My goal in sailing isn't to be brilliant or flashy in individual races, just to be consistent over the long run. — Dennis Conner, four-time winner of the America's Cup

For the Early Bird investor, two very important concepts need to be emphasized: dollar-cost averaging and the reinvestment. One might seem, at least on the surface, to take care of the other, but the temptation to watch balances rise and fall has a psychological effect on the long-term investor.

There will be periods where the markets seem to be in the doldrums, which, over that 82-year period in the example above frequently happens. This presents the investor, even the most seasoned one, a problem. The lure of sitting on the sidelines is often overwhelming. We are told we can maximize our returns by doing one thing or another when, if we choose correctly from the beginning (and I will offer you some suggested portfolio ideas in the next section), all we had to do was sit back and wait.

Dollar-cost averaging is just another phrase for consistency. Keeping a steady stream of money headed into your portfolio will give you every competitive edge. Defined contribution plans such as 401(k)s rely on this method.

Once you sign up for the plan and work, the steady withdrawal of money from your paycheck is key to growing your future. Because it is done *before* taxes are levied on your gross income (some plans now offer a Roth option, taking the money out *after* taxes), you do not have the opportunity to direct the money elsewhere. This is the least painful method of retirement saving available.

The Chaser: I Know Who You Are

I know far more Chasers than I do Early Birds or Relaxers. This is my age group, my peers, and the ones who may have realized that they are behind the investment eight ball.

Chasers entered the workforce with debt and kept it. They rearranged it in every refinance of their home. They have been upside down in car loans and, with a fair amount of certainty, added those to their home loans as well. They have financed their children's education at a greater degree than they financed their own retirement. They have lost sleep over the bad habits they know they have and yet, if asked, they will tell you they are doing okay.

 Okay, here's my personal theory; 53 is the age of maximum financial anxiety.—Alan Murray, an assistant managing editor of the *Wall Street Journal*

Once a person realizes that they have under utilized their investments, made numerous wrong decisions and were unable to take advantage of all of the youthful opportunities with compounding, the tendency is to give up.

Thinking and Experience

Chasers have the added expectation of experience. Numerous studies have pointed to this "middle-age" as the time when investors bring their investment histories into perspective. How do you do that when you have had no luck or little history with investing aside from wishful thinking.

So let's focus on thinking. George Korniotis and Alok Kumar of the University of Notre Dame's Mendoza College of Business published a paper in July 2005 suggesting that older investors have more difficulty in generating a good rate of return—necessary to generate enough retirement wealth— because psychological evidence points to a number of roadblocks. These two researchers based their study on the end-of-the-month returns of what many now refer to as middle aged and slightly older.

Biology is working against us, they say. We aren't as quick cognitively as we were when we were squarely in the Early Bird group. Socioeconomic influences and demographics also affect us. How much education, where we live, our race and ethnicity, our choice of careers and the wealth/income we may have generated all are cited as having an influence on whether we can make good investment decisions as we age.

Economists have discovered that we tend to get suboptimal portfolio returns because we see a decreasing investment horizon and, with that, we lower our risk. Our investments they suggest become more *conservative* and *efficient.*

The Diversity Issue

If you were to ask any financial professional how to diversify the portfolio of a 50-year-old, they would, without a doubt, suggest that there be a certain allocation of bonds along with their stocks. I have done so myself by suggesting that the average investor hold, much in the same vein as Benjamin Graham, some sort of protection of capital once a person reaches a certain investment age.

But suppose you haven't gotten to the prerequisite beginning. Suppose you just realized that you haven't really done much in the way of investing. You never did much with that employer sponsored plan. You might take the minimum amount out of your paycheck, perhaps just enough to take advantage of the employer match. You may even still have the remnants of a stock portfolio, frozen by your losses when the stock market crashed at the beginning of this decade. In other words, what you call investments are a jumble of ideas, half-baked.

Or you may have a collection of IRAs, opened years ago and never fed the steady diet of pretax deposits so essential to smart investing. Or, you may have nothing to show for your years besides a mortgage and a wallet full of family pictures.

Aristotle wasn't speaking of investing when he said, "Of mankind in general, the parts are greater than the whole." But it is apt nonetheless. The key to any portfolio is diversity, making the parts add up so each can stand alone and contribute.

 What Orville and Wilbur Wright did on December 17, 1903, was reported as a successful test flight. What these two brothers were looking for was control. The understanding of the airfoil, a necessity if an airplane is to lift off the ground, was already known at the time of their flight. Control theory operates on the idea that if you take a reference point or output (they wanted to fly not just in the air but from point A to B) and added input (the invention of "three-axis control," which enabled the pilot to steer the aircraft effectively and to maintain its equilibrium) you could achieve the control needed to successfully fly. It was one thing to take to the air but it was a true achievement to go where you intended.

Seeking a Different Balance

For the Chaser, diversity means finding a balance between the distance to retirement and the necessary risk to come close to the goals we might have. Professional money investment managers offer hints on allocation (what is expected of a segment of the market at any given time) based on risk tolerance (or aversion—how much are you willing to lose to make money) and investment goals (an abstract term that sometimes means time frame, acceptable volatility, inflation expectations, etc.).

But how do you know whether you should have this allocation or that, your willingness to risk some of that late-to-the-game money for the opportunity of snagging a bigger brass ring, or even what your goals are? You don't. But there are ways of finding out.

The Risk Test

Do you know your own risk? This little exercise suggests that you have a basic knowledge of what an investment is. How you arrived at the purchase of any stock, bond, or mutual fund that holds both or either, should come with some degree of research. (I'll give you some hints on how to do that in the next section: The Investment.) Your answers will form the basis of our discussion in the coming pages.

1. If you make an investment that rises in price in a very short amount of time and it is something you have bought for the long-term, what would you do?

   Would you sell it immediately with the understanding that this gain is substantial enough to warrant taking that amount of money off the table, or would you hold onto it and keep with your long-range buy-and-hold plans? If you have done your research and nothing has changed, the fact that whatever you invested in has gone up is a reason to believe that it will still go higher.

   Or perhaps you might think buying more would be the best thing. If it rose this fast after you bought it, do you tell yourself that the chances are good it could go ever higher?

   In question number one we are faced with the temptation to take our profit and run or stick with the investment. Because the question doesn't specify what the investment is, we can make one of two assumptions. If it was an individual stock held outside of retirement portfolio, you should have set a price target to sell. That target should also include a downside target as well.

   But if it was a mutual fund in a retirement portfolio and you are already making regular contributions to the fund(s), don't do anything. Dollar-cost averaging will limit the amount of shares you can buy at this new high price but will still allow you to stay with the fund while it climbs. The nature of dollar-cost averaging enables you to buy more shares when an investment price is low and less when the price rises. It keeps you involved and keeps the emotion out of the equation.

   Investors in individual stocks should also take note. If you like a company and have done your research, you will recognize some gains as inevitable (good growth of earnings, new products or new markets for old ones) and some as unexpected (a shift in investor sentiment, a change in the economy or some other outside force exerting pressure). Regular and steady investments work just as well here, building discipline and removing that mental maniac that wants to take over and make rash decisions where a cool head is needed.

2. The Dow hit 14,000 recently. You buy in on the hype surrounding the market only to have some piece of news derail the run. Even though you

bought an investment with great fundamentals, in sympathy, it falls with the rest of the market as seller's panic. Do you sell as well or hold on? Perhaps you see a price reduction as a buying opportunity. In that case, would you purchase more of that investment?

I just made a reference to that "mental maniac" in your head. In *Investing for the Utterly Confused* I defined it as the voice that "wants to follow the markets with great intent; wants to be where the in-crowd is; wants to take huge risks in the face of reason; wants to sell low and buy high instead of vice versa."

When markets rise, risk increases. The opposite is true when markets decline. Think of it this way: a bull market, a term that describes a market as something that is surging forward, enthusiastic, and optimistic offers buyers a new high price each and every day. A bear market, on the other hand, a term that offers the investor a pessimistic outlook, should be considered a market "on sale." Once again, dollar-cost averaging rescues you from a bad decision, buying shares as they fall, with each new investment dollar buying more shares than the last.

3. At the heart of all 401(k) plans is the mutual fund. Almost every plan offers a basket of such funds in a variety of investment styles, ranging from almost no risk, such as a money market fund, to a fund that has a lot of risk and specializes in aggressive growth. When you examine the offerings and look at historical data, do you choose the safe bet to protect your hard earned investment or do you look at the reward for your risk and choose the fund with the most growth potential?

A great deal of the conversation in any investment book deals with risk. Risk as it relates to the Chaser needs to be measured based on time. Money market funds are often the default investment in a defined contribution plan offered by employers. Signing up for your company's 401(k) does not necessarily mean that you are signing on with the best opportunity for capital appreciation. This has been a cause for great concern among lawmakers as they increasingly shift the burden of your future to you.

Further along we will look at the wide variety of options this investment group should consider but, for the sake of this question, the conservative portion of your retirement portfolio should not have more than 5 percent of your money at any one time in cash (money market funds). Chances are your other (actively managed) mutual funds in your portfolio employ money market accounts to park some cash. Most index funds do not.

An aggressive mutual fund is usually one that is actively managed. The mutual fund manager picks a basket of stocks that are considered to have a high growth potential, usually newer, unproven and mostly small capitalized companies (worth less than between $250 million and $1 billion with micro-cap funds among the most aggressive – risky—investing in companies with a market value of less than $250 million).

For the Chaser portfolio, a small percentage should be committed to just such funds if your time horizon for investing extends at least 20 years.

4. Investing does require a certain gamble. It is unfortunate, but that is the way it works. You take an educated guess when you buy a stock that the company will continue to grow and prosper and reward you for your investment. While mutual funds tend to react less dramatically than an individual stock, thereby lessening the risk by spreading it across many stock and numerous investors, it still remains a risk.

And yet, you may realize that one of the key components of gambling is protection of the "nut." The "nut" refers to the smallest amount of money needed to pay your day-to-day existence, something true gamblers keep at a bare minimum. But you must protect it if you expect to play again in the future. So at what point, when it comes to investing, do you protect your original investment?

Suppose you had to choose between three envelopes. Each offered an ever-increasing amount of winnings with diminishing chances to win it. In other words, each envelope represents a greater risk that the other.

One has cash. One offers you a 50 percent chance of doubling your money while the last offers an opportunity to increase that cash prize tenfold but only a one in ten chance of doing so. What would you do?

Take the cash. What the intelligence investor needs, as described by the investment sage Benjamin Graham, "is a trait more of the character than the brain." The sure thing is always something that offers the investor more control. You can grow $1,000. The second choice with the 50-50 chance relates to the chances you might receive with a coin toss. Heads will eventually pop up, even if it takes 100 attempts. But each try diminishes the potential while increasing the risk. A one in ten chance to increase that $1,000, while tempting, is far too aggressive for a person trying to play catch-up. The Chaser will need to take a more measured and calculated approach to attaining her/his goals.

5. Some of the best investment information can come based on the advice of a trusted friend. They may be known for their attention to detail and have a

history of previous successes with investments that you may have secretly envied. She has approached you because of a business opportunity that has crossed her investment radar. The company is still forming but she assures you that this is a great time to get in on the bottom level.

She makes no promises that this investment will be your rainmaker—a reference to the ability of an investment or a person to generate huge amounts of profits. But, she warns, nothing is a sure thing and there are some regulatory hurdles, product development issues and, so far, no real profits.

Although she doesn't say so specifically, she implies that this could be the opportunity of a lifetime. Would you pass knowing that your money could get 5 percent in a good online banking account? Or would you commit a week's or even a month's salary in the hopes of a payday sometime in the future, even when you know the risk potential is high?

This represents yet another question about your risk tolerance. But it also suggests that, based on someone's expertise, you might be swayed to take a risk, while in the previous question you relied solely on your own intuition.

That mental maniac I mentioned earlier is much harder to control than you might imagine. So, rather than deny what is clearly a human characteristic, contain it within reason. Invest on your friends advice only if you have done the following things: you have built your emergency fund or are in the process of doing so, you have developed a long range strategy for removing as much debt from your balance sheet as possible, you are participating in a defined contribution plan, whether it be an IRA or a 401(k) type account, and you have created a taxable account for investing (there are certain types of funds that belong outside of your regular retirement accounts).

The investment money should come from a mad money account. This account refers to a term first coined by Graham as a pacifier for that maniac. You deposit a fixed amount of money, possibly from a windfall of some sort and never add to the account again. Ever. This money can be used for whatever aggressive venture comes along. If you gain, keep the money in the account. If you lose, however, take your losses with the knowledge that you gambled with money you did not need.

6. Many investors consider what they do as a skill. Numerous television talk show personalities boast of past performance records that make them seem superintuitive, able to predict where the market is going, almost as if they had transcended normal logic. And, worse, many refer to their successes as winnings.

Do you regard a $100,000 lottery prize on a $1 ticket as more rewarding than that same amount of cash coming from an unexpected inheritance? Or would you consider an investment you bought for $1,000 several years back that, because you have reinvested dividends and capital gains, used a dollar-cost averaging approach, and held on to it for numerous market changes, both up and down, as even more rewarding when it hits a $100,000 plateau.

The odds of winning a $100,000 lottery depends on the number of players involved in the game. Powerball, the multi-state lottery, pays $100,000 for five numbers from a field of 49 choices not including the PowerBall, and offers one chance in 1,953,393,366. The chance your relative will gift you $100,000 upon their death depends on several things, including how well you were regarded by that relative and the fact that they have to die.

Far more satisfying is the achievement of a goal. While $100,000 is a great one, it is only a milestone on the road to enough.

The Relaxer: The Feel of Proximity

I have only sparingly referred to each of our investor categories by their age. An Early Bird could be as old as 30; Chasers could begin their pursuit as late as age 50. What I prefer is time horizon. By doing so, you take a stab at your future retirement age by suggesting that you will, if all things are equal, continue to work until a certain point in time.

The Early Bird should have a 30 to 40 year time horizon. The Chaser should be eyeing retirement in 20 to 30 years. But at what stage do either of these two groups, one starting out and one playing catch-up, turn into people who can restructure their portfolios to protect all that they have gained over the years in preparation for the money in time when they will begin to spend-down those investments?

What the Experts Say

The proximity of a desirable thing tempts one to overindulgence. On that path lies danger. — Frank Herbert (1920 1986)

If you begin as an Early Bird, you will want to turn into a Relaxer within 10 years of your retirement goal. If, on the other hand, you are a Chaser, you may not make the shift until you actually retire.

What to Do with Less Debt

A Relaxer is someone who has built a portfolio based on all of the tenets we have discussed. They have some sort of financial capital at the end of a career that began with human capital, the starting position for the Early Bird. As a Relaxer, you have diminished your debt-to-income ratio to less than 20 percent and you have been able to increase your savings to both pretax and aftertax accounts, with each percentage point in debt you have eliminated.

What is a debt-to-income ratio? If you have ever purchased a home, your lender has inquired about your debt-to-income ratio, or DTI. For our example, a Relaxer's DTI should include the front ratio and the back ratio. The front ratio only expresses the amount of money that is used to pay for your mortgage. Back ratio includes not only the mortgage but also all of the other costs associated with the house, including taxes and insurances but any other recurring debt such as credit cards. I have chosen 20 percent as an equitable amount of debt to carry towards retirement. Much more and you will need to make some adjustments to your plan. Debt makes every portfolio more defensive in an attempt to protect what you have from the drain debt servicing places on your income. Too much debt, and the Relaxer is actually a Chaser.

Because debt plays a major role in retirement planning, there is no good debt/bad debt equation. It is all debt. It detracts from every effort you make but is unavoidable in any successful plan. You can have a mortgage when you retire, as long as it is manageable and falls into the 20 percent DTI range. You can have cars as well as long as they also fall into those same parameters.

As the Relaxer moves closer to their retirement goals, each downward shift in debt should see that money redirected towards retirement savings. This is the percentage of protected cash you should direct towards the safest investment possible.

Assuming that you have invested primarily in stock funds across a broad spectrum (more on what this means just a little further along), moving to a more conservative approach is prudent. But this doesn't mean selling your shares in funds that are actively involved in the markets. Instead, it simply means moving to a more conservative approach with a fund that isn't chasing growth. Capital preservation is now the goal, not capital appreciation.

What it means is much less invasive. As you begin to pay down debt, you will need to shift any debt repayment to a conservative investment such as a money market account (if it is paying more than 5 percent), an I-Bond (which protects against the ravages of inflation), or, if you choose, a bond fund. Keep this account outside your tax-deferred investments. This keeps the other portion of your portfolio growing while protecting accessible assets.

As you will find out, making use of balanced or life style funds as a portion of your portfolio lessens your exposure to risk as you age and approach retirement. These funds keep your money growing, albeit less aggressively, and this allows for a percentage of your portfolio to be actively involved. These can also be used to preserve money as you free it up. It also provides some protection but they should also be kept outside of your tax-deferred accounts. Pay the taxman on these investments.

What's Next ▶ With any luck, you now have a relatively good idea where you are and more importantly, who you are. The discussion about risk will continue in the next section as we look at some of the investment options available for the groups we just defined. Also, in the coming chapters we will look at health savings accounts, annuities, and taxes. This is the portion of the book where we take all of the things we have learned so far and put them into practice.

PART FOUR
The Investment

◆◆◆◆◆◆◆◆◆◆◆◆◆◆◆◆◆◆◆◆◆◆◆◆◆◆◆◆◆◆◆◆◆◆◆

Looking Back, Forward, Sideways ...

We are all familiar with the term *déjà vu*. The phrase, first coined by French psychic researcher Émile Boirac, was defined as an experience laced with familiarity, a feeling that something had happened before and was re-experienced.

In his classic novel *Catch-22*, Joseph Heller wrote: "There were terrifying, sudden moments when objects, concepts and even people that the chaplain lived with almost all of his life inexplicably took on an unfamiliar and irregular aspect that he had never seen before and which made them seem totally strange: *jamais vu*." He continued, "And there were other moments when he almost saw absolute truth in brilliant flashes of clarity that almost came to him: *presque vu*."

CHAPTER 14
The Balancing Act

If you are new to retirement planning, this chapter on balancing your portfolio may take on some aspect of *presque vu*. If you have followed along as we systematically dismantled some of your preconceived notions about what retirement is and how much it is really going to cost, those "brilliant flashes of clarity" may have been somewhat unsettling.

We want to go to sleep at night comfortable knowing that the decisions that we have made were the right ones, that the choice of investments we have chosen will result in enough to get us where we *think* we would like to go. We have discussed some of the financial aspects of how those end-of-work days will look and whether they will actually be the end of work. We have, perhaps unwittingly, changed our perspective about what lies ahead.

The portfolio I have mentioned numerous times in the preceding pages is the cornerstone for everything that lies ahead. While getting your head on straight, coming to grips with your everyday debt, and taking a look at the way retirement is evolving in the public and political debate, merely feather the nest for that often referred to egg. It can be all for naught if you have failed to build your dream on solid ground. It is all about location.

What the Experts Say

I make money using my brains and lose money listening to my heart. But in the long run my books balance pretty well.—Kate Seredy

Shaky Ground

Balancing requires two things: a sense of equilibrium and some sort of solid surface. Mutual funds, the cornerstone of our discussion about retirement, exist with the sole purpose of providing the inexperienced investor with the opportunity to make their money work with less risk that you might have had you purchased individual stocks.

The way they work is simple but the pitfall of not understanding how they work can cost you money that you could have had working for you for the long-term. Mutual funds provide you with a basket of stocks, a manager who has published her or his thoughts about investing and how she or he hopes to get to those goals, and a fee structure that seems, at least on the surface, as something that is straightforward and easy to understand.

That manager may or may not be a real person. Some funds offer a technological substitute for real people that adhere to technical analysis and metrics based on quantitative research, hence the name: Quantitative Mutual Funds. This is an idea that has been batted around the halls of investment philosophy since the early 1970s. The creation of exchange traded funds, mutual funds that can be traded actively like stocks, helped quantitative strategies to gain acceptance. The cold, hard fact about these funds: they care little about the business of the stock, focusing instead on the mathematical attractiveness of the stock. This idea, which now accounts for almost 20 percent of the available funds, is returning slightly better returns for investors than funds that are actively managed.

But, like all things financial, there are some worrisome traits you need to know. Those machines have human programmers who may offer some biases. Keeping their trading methods secret takes away from the transparency other mutual funds offer. And despite lower fees, these funds are not that easy to understand. But that will change as more investors see the possibilities and make demands to know how these products work.

This may at first seem like *déjà vu*. But you would be somewhat incorrect.

Mutual funds have the unique ability to remove that "mental maniac" that often makes bad decisions. By spreading the investment over a basket of stocks managed by a professional, you remove the erratic behavior often associated with an individual stock picker.

On any given day, the news can give the individual investor that restless urge to buy or sell. Mutual funds take the day-to-day events out of your hands and let the manager decide whether the fundamentals of the market have changed enough to warrant a move. And yet, most people still don't understand how they work.

Mutual funds were designed for the long-term investor. Their fee structure makes staying invested easier. They provide diversity in a relatively inexpensive format. And, lastly, they are much easier on the brain, leaving you with more time to worry about or plan for some of the other obstacles we have talked about so far.

 It's amazing how fast later comes when you buy now.—Milton Berle

They became the perfect fit for the inside of those defined contribution plans for all of the reasons I have mentioned. Even the least experienced among us can pick a fund based on three basic criteria: how much it costs *(for 401(k) and similar types of plans where your deposit is removed from your paycheck, either pretax or posttax, the initial minimum investment usually required for funds outside these plans, is waived),* who is running it *(the fund manager(s) or, in some instances, the cold calculation of a computer's ability to attract new investors and keep old ones based on performance over a number of years),* and what are the objectives *(beyond the obvious, growing your money as quickly and safely as possible, funds often pick a particular area of expertise or, in the case of index funds, a particular sector).*

How You Pay

One of the attractions of the 401(k) plan for employers was the shift in who was paying for the investment. When Ted Benna uncovered that line in the tax code over three decades ago, he unleashed a series of changes that brought the employee to the forefront, forcing them to make the decisions about their investments and by default, making them pay for it. It was unintended. He had hoped it would provide another opportunity for the employee, not a nearly complete disintegration of the pension system.

Before we delve into the workings of this type of retirement planning, let's take a closer look at *the* tool of the trade: the mutual fund.

Mutual funds come with costs, all of which are passed onto the investor. They sometimes come with the transaction — front loaded funds charge a fee when the investor joins, taking a percentage of the asset deposited right off the top while closed end funds charge you a fee as you exit the fund. No-load mutual funds, the kind that are often recommended by folks like me, cost nothing to join but come with certain fee structures that do not exist in the other two types of funds. This is how they break down.

There are some dramatic differences between front-end, closed end and no-load mutual funds. Each of these types of funds is distinguished by the industry in terms of letters: A, B, or C.

Class A shares represent the front-load type fund, charging you a percentage of your initial deposit when you join the fund. On the surface, this seems like a bad idea. Deposit a $1,000 and they snatch 5 percent right off the top before they even invest a dime. It appears at first glance that you are actually starting the process with less money [$1,000–($1,000 × 0.05) = $950] but the fee structure is different than the other two types of funds.

What to Ask? What are breakpoints? Class A funds offer "breakpoints," a sort of discount based on the amount of money you invest. The more you deposit, the lower the fee that you are initially charged. Pledging to make additional investments in the fund, usually over a certain agreed upon period, can also trigger breakpoints. Class A shares are similar to buying in bulk; the price goes down when you buy a larger than average package.

Class B shares work in the opposite manner, charging you an exit fee. People who buy Class A shares normally do so because the large amount of money they wish to deposit can actually make the investment far more profitable because of the lower overall costs of maintaining the fund. Class B fund buyers usually have less money to invest initially but understand that, if they stay for the long term, the so-called exit fee can be waived. That back-end fee, referred to in the industry as a contingent deferred sales charge (CDSC) will diminish over time. When that predetermined waiting period expires, your Class B shares convert to Class A shares, with no exit fees and lower fees in general.

How does a CDSC work? The deal the fund makes with you is based on the length of time you stay with the fund. For instance, if you leave within a year, you will be charged the full closed-end fee on the assets you own. For example, if you deposit that same $1,000 in a Class B fund charging a closed-end fee of 5 percent and the fund performs relatively well in the first year, you might actually pay more than if you had bought a Class A fund instead. Suppose the fund you bought had a 12.5 percent return in the first year. Your costs for exiting would be $56.25 or $6.25 more than if you had paid the fee upfront. ($1,000 x .125 (the return) = $1,125 x 0.05 (the CDSC) = $56.25). But hold the fund for a predetermined period of time, usually six to eight years, and the CDSC goes away.

Class C shares of a mutual fund are often referred to as no-load. They charge nothing to join and levy almost no penalties if you decide to leave early. A CDSC is charged, however, if you leave the fund before the initial 12-month period expires. But this is no free lunch. The fees are generally higher than Class A funds and generally do not decrease over time. There are also no discounts for large initial purchases.

What kind of fees does a no-load fund charge? Many of the same fees are charged by each fund, no matter which class of shares they offer. Among those fees are payment for the manager's involvement, the costs of buying and selling shares or transaction costs and 12b-1 fees. The difference is the rate at which these fees are charged against the assets in your account. The 12b-1 fee refers to a rule in the Investment Company Act of 1940. Designed to cover marketing and distribution expenses—which cannot exceed 0.75 percent of the fund's average assets in a given year, it also compensates for services and sales professionals—which is not usually more than an additional quarter of a percent of the assets under management. It is sort of an installment payment plan for services rendered throughout the time you own the fund. They can be reduced however, should the fund close (this happens when the fund becomes too large or the focus of the fund is so narrow that investment opportunities diminish, forcing the fund managers to "close the doors" to new investors).

All of these fees are lumped into one expense referred to at the expense ratio. For the no-load fund buyer, this can give you a glimpse into how much the fund will charge compared to other funds of a similar ilk.

Numerous websites, including Morningstar and finance.yahoo.com, offer a general overview of funds and their expenses. The prospectus is another place where this is listed for the investor. A **prospectus** is the largely unread document that details the fund's objectives, the historical returns, the number of shares in each fund, along with their percentage of overall weight and worth and the fee table. That document often adds to the overall cost of the fund and, because of its complexity, does little to clarify the simplest information. For this reason, people often choose an index fund, a passively managed fund that mimics certain portions (or in some instances, all of) the markets.

The Cost of Doing Business

Surveys indicate 80 percent of investors are not aware of the fees they pay.—Brad M. Barber, Professor of Finance at the University of California, Davis

Something happened when the calendar turned in 2007. Mutual fund companies rejoiced. No longer would their five year returns, often referred to as a gauge of how well a fund performed, reflect the year 2001, a year when the markets hit a historic bottom. That simple change of date made so many funds appear so much better than they may have seemed otherwise—had that disastrous year been included.

As numerous investors watched their funds drop through the floor, some actually losing the initial investment that many investors had made, the subsequent revolt that followed seemed inevitable. Many of those investors did not have a long investment history and because of that, they had not calculated the downside possibilities of any investment.

Adding to their anger over losing what they perceived to be a sure thing, the fees the funds charged remained the same. Ruffled by the thought that their fund manager(s) had spent the year at the movies, investors began to question the nature of many of the expense ratios being charged by their funds.

The expense ratio is broken down into two categories, shareholder fees and annual fund operating expenses. (This is detailed in your mutual fund's prospectus in the fee table.) It is designed to provide you with information for easy comparisons of costs between funds. It will look something like this:

Shareholder Fees

A maximum sales charge (load) imposed on
purchases (as a percentage of offering price)   4.5%

This fee is charged to the investor in a front-loaded fund and cannot, by law, exceed 8.5 percent.

B Maximum deferred sales
charge (load)   None

This fee is charged to the investor in a back-end or closed-end loaded fund and generally diminishes over time. This fee is referred to as a CDSC.

C Maximum sales charge (load)
on reinvested dividends   None

This fee is no longer allowed by law but may still be added to funds that were opened prior to 2000. It charges a reinvestment fee when dividends are reinvested.

D Redemption fee   None

This fee is charged to the investor when they sell their investment in the fund. Unlike the CDSC, this charge goes directly to the fund to cover transaction costs and is often listed as a flat price or a percentage of the shares redeemed. Redemptions can create havoc for a fund and its managers.

When a fund is chartered to have 100 percent of its money invested, a redemption forces the sale of shares or redirects money that would have bought more shares to the exiting investor. When the markets suffer a downturn, redemptions can soar, putting pressure on the fund to cover those investors and diminishing the returns of those who stay.

E Exchange fee   None

This fee is charged to the investor for movement of funds within the fund family. If you decide that one fund is better suited for your changing investment needs, this fee covers the switch. It is often charged in the short term but waived after a certain period. It is designed to prevent some kinds of market timing.

F Annual account maintenance fee   None

This fee is charged to the investor if the amount invested falls below a certain amount. There are numerous reasons this fee is applied, none of which is good. If your fund charges this fee, look for another that does not.

Annual fund operating expenses
G Management fee   0.52%

This fee is charged to the investor in payment for the fund manager's services. Her/his advice is key to the portfolio's success and worth the cost in an actively managed fund. Actively managed, as we will discuss later, refers to a fund that picks stocks, as opposed to a passively managed fund, which mimics a sector or all of the markets. In the latter, this fee should be almost nonexistent.

H Distribution (12b-1) fee   0.25%

This fee is charged to the investor and cannot, by law, exceed 1 percent.

I   Other expenses   0.20%

This fee is charged to the investor for a basket of services that can range from printing and mailing to website services. This fee is probably the most objectionable of these fees because the company that owns the fund, not the shareholders in the fund, should pay for these operational services.

Total annual fund operating
J   Expenses (expense ratio)   0.97%

This fee is the total of all the above-mentioned fees on the operational side of the fund.

K   Example of how the fees affect returns

This is a requirement of the Securities and Exchange Commission and is used as an at-a-glance tool for investors to see how these expenses and potential annual returns, assumed at 5 percent, affect your investment. The text that accompanies this portion of the fee table explains how it works.

The following example is intended to help an investor compare the cost of investing in different funds. The example assumes a $10,000 investment in the fund for one, three, five, and 10 years and then a redemption of all fund shares at the end of those periods. The example also assumes that an investment returns 5 percent each year and that the fund's operating expenses remain the same. Although actual costs may be higher or lower, based on these assumptions an investor's estimated expenses would be:

1 year	$547
3 years	$754
5 years	$977
10 years	$1,617

There is a calculator on the SEC Web site that can help make generalized assumptions of how much your fund will charge you in fees (www.sec.gov/mfcc/mfcc-int.htm).

What to Ask? Who provides oversight to my mutual fund? Oversight of the fund's operations and fee structure is a board of directors, usually independent of the fund's adviser. These directors act as advocates for the shareholders in the fund—not the company that owns the fund—and concern themselves with how much and how those fees are levied. This board, on an annual basis, approves the Rule 12b-1 fees.

Additional sources of information on how your fund operates can be found by visiting or contacting:

U.S. Securities and Exchange Commission
Office of Investor Education and Assistance
450 Fifth Street, NW
Washington, DC 20549
202/942-7040 or 800/SEC-0330
www.sec.gov

SEC Online Publications for Investors
www.sec.gov/investor/pubs.shtml

SEC Investor Education and Assistance
www.sec.gov/investor.shtml

The Department of Labor publishes information about how fees affect your 401(k) investment. The document is available online at:
www.dol.gov/ebsa/publications/401k_employee.html

The NASD—National Association of Securities Dealers—has a fund comparison tool available for side-by-side comparisons of up to three mutual funds. It can be found at:

http://apps.nasd.com/Investor_Information/EA/1/mfetf.aspx

The Future of Fees

Rule 12b-1 fees have not been well received by investors. Many do not see the purpose for charging what seems to be a veiled attempt at bilking an extra one percent from investors, many of which are unaware of how they work. Christopher Cox, the SEC chairman, thinks that these fees have strayed away from their original purpose.

The Securities Industry and Financial Market Association, or SIFMA, an organization of financial professionals that was formed when the the Securities Industry Association and the Bond Market Association joined forces, objects to the notion that 12b-1 fees have outlived their usefulness.

 What to Say!

SIFMA promotes numerous objectives in its goal to get as many people invested as possible. According to their Web site, the organization's goals include efforts to increase and "ensure the public's trust in the securities industry and financial markets, encourage retirement savings and investment, promote effective and efficient regulation and facilitate more open, competitive and efficient global capital markets." They also take an active role in promoting investing and financial literacy in schools by sponsoring the Stock Market Game, InvestWrite and Path to Investing.

SIFMA answers those accusations with the following comment: "Rule 12b-1 has been a success; curtailing or withdrawing the rule would harm investors and competition in the marketplace. Similarly, other fee arrangements have fostered innovation and supported higher levels of services. It may be appropriate to improve disclosures for the benefit of investors and fund boards, but it would be a major mistake for the SEC to withdraw or substantially curtail Rule 12b-1, or otherwise to restrict the fee arrangements that have fostered innovation, flexibility, and investor choice."

SIFMA also provides a long-range look at the history of the 12b-1 fee, something it calls, "one of the critical events in the facilitating diversity in fund products." The file can be downloaded at: http://www.sifma.org/regulatory/pdf/12b-1MFWhitePaper6-13-07.pdf

Fees Versus Performance

It remains to be seen how history will treat Barry Bonds, left fielder for the San Francisco Giants, now commonly referred to as the human asterisk. His accusers suggest that the only reason he has surpassed Hank Aaron as the all-time home run leader was due to his artificial performance enhancement.

While mutual funds tend to *juice* their performance in a number of ways, many of which we will get to shortly, investors have wondered if the fees charged by a fund have any effect on its performance. The SEC did a study and found that, yes, they do, and in a negative way.

The math is rather simple. There are basically only two types of mutual fund investors: active and passive. A passive investor chooses an index fund, which reflects the performance of a sector (much like an S&P 500 index fund reflects the performance of the top 500 capitalized companies). These funds allow the investor to buy a large segment of the market that is only changed when the index rebalances.

What happens when an index rebalances? The act of rebalancing has had questionable results, both in performance of a long-term buy-and-hold portfolio and the risk of the underlying stocks. Jie (Jay) Cai of the Drexel University LeBow College of Business and Todd Houge of the University of Iowa Henry B. Tippie College of Business asked that question in a paper they published in March of 2007. They looked at the rebalancing that took place in the Russell 2000 Small-Cap index from a period of 1974–2004 and discovered that the annual rebalancing of this index had negative effects on the person who indexed and the investor who held onto the stocks that were deleted. They did suggest that the reasons for index rebalancing and the expulsion of those stocks created a greater risk for the investor but, generally, those stocks outperformed the rebalanced index by 17.29 percent over a five year span.

The reasons for rebalancing an index vary. Because the market is not a static place, the composition of an index, which is supposed to reflect the companies in it, changes because of merger and acquisitions, bankruptcies, spin-offs, IPOs (initial public offerings) and delistings (usually caused by failing to file the correct paperwork or not doing so on time), to name but a few of the reasons.

The authors of that paper, "Index Rebalancing and Long-Term Portfolio Performance," suggest that index funds are not as passive as they seem. Annual rebalancing changes what the index was designed to do: provide investors with a wide swath of the market, based on certain criteria, and give active mutual fund managers a relative benchmark to compare their performance in order to entice new shareholders to join their ranks and to grow the capital of the ones currently on board.

What the authors concluded was this: the smaller the index, the greater the chances are the rebalancing works in a negative way as compared to holding the same stocks prior to the change in index holdings. The S&P 500 never removes the best performing stocks and because of that, creates the possibility of better returns over the course of five years. Other indexes could not boast the same conclusions. Their worry: "that index construction methodology may provide a structural incentive for portfolio managers to drift or deviate from their benchmark styles."

Beating the Benchmarks

Social historian Daniel J. Boorstin once said, "The traveler was active; he went strenuously in search of people, of adventure, of experience. The tourist is passive; he expects interesting things to happen to him. He goes *sightseeing*." Yet, when it comes to mutual funds, indexed ones outperform those that actively invest almost four out of five times. So why would investors bother with actively managed funds when the benchmarks are consistently beating them?

The Wall Street equivalent of that warning on the side of tobacco products reads, "Past performance is no guarantee of future results." Although they are loath to warn you about this they understand that the chance, the opportunity of gaining on a benchmark and the bragging rights that go along with it, is enough to entice investors into the attempt.

More than 40 years ago, Michael Jensen pointed this simple fact out to investors. Several years later, AG Becker and Company published the "Green Book," filled with comparisons to prove just such a point.

 Michael Jensen of the Harvard Business School wrote in a paper titled "The Performance of Mutual Funds in the Period 1945–1964" that "The evidence on mutual fund performance indicates not only that these 115

Continued

mutual funds were on average not able to predict security prices well enough to outperform a buy-the-market-and-hold policy, but also that there is very little evidence that any individual fund was able to do significantly better than that which we expected from mere random chance."

There are several reasons for the failure of active funds to beat indexed benchmarks. Because active funds do not necessarily carry the same amount of underlying stocks in a portfolio, they tend to trade more often trying to hit just the right basket of companies that will outperform. This creates additional fees that are in turn passed onto shareholders, diminishing whatever returns they may have mustered.

Actively managed mutual funds suffer from manager turnover. The attraction (and pay package) of hedge funds has lured some of the best fund managers away from this highly regulated business. Each time that happens, a new manager is likely to step in and make her or his own adjustments to the portfolio. Standard advice for buying an actively managed fund suggests buying one that has a manager with tenure of five years or more. That is becoming increasingly difficult.

In many fund houses, internal stock picking has become a groupthink endeavor. Consultants are brought in to help. Shadow funds are created to test theories. The hedge fund industry has created a new kind of risk, adding further pressure to strategies.

The best way to determine the success of a mutual fund remains as simple as cost. If the fund has the lowest cost while chasing the lowest risk factor, you will probably do better than if your money was in an actively managed fund.

Taxes and Funds

We are going to discuss taxes and your funds only briefly. It is a complicated subject best handled by a tax professional. Tax related events occur inside your fund all the time. If it occurs inside a tax-deferred account, the taxes on gains and losses are passed down to you to be paid at a later date. If the fund is outside of your retirement account, you will receive a statement of how those events impacted your fund.

Before we get to how taxes work inside the fund, it is important to note that early withdrawals from your IRAs are not only taxed as income but an added excise tax of 10 percent is added on as well. There is a loophole in that law. You may withdraw money to pay for deductible medical expenses or to pay for medical insurance premiums *if* you have been unemployed for at least 12 weeks.

Mutual funds are not taxed. The shareholder is. As a shareholder in a mutual fund, you will pay taxes on earnings. Earnings are generated from dividends (a portion of a company's profits paid to its shareholders) and interest earned. This is referred to as "ordinary income." Ordinary income is what the fund's shareholders get *after* the fund deducts its expenses. This is why the fees I mentioned above are not deductible.

When you sell shares you incur capital gains tax. When a mutual fund sells shares, the tax is passed down to the shareholders as well. The tax doesn't go away when you reinvest dividends, interest, and income distributed by the fund when it is held in a tax-deferred account, payment is simply put off until sometime in the future. Funds held outside that type of account will issue a report to you so that you can pay the taxes in that calendar year.

What is cost basis? According to the Mutual Fund Education Association, cost basis works like this: "Cost basis is the amount of money you have invested in your shares. It includes any sales charges or redemption fees you paid for the shares upon purchase or sale. It also includes any reinvested dividend or capital gain distributions that you used to purchase more shares." Your tax professional can help you with this and probably should, largely because you would need to calculate the following in order to arrive at your taxable income.

According the MFEA, you will need to give that tax pro the following information:

The date of each purchase, sale or exchange
The number of shares bought or sold each time
The price at which shares are bought or sold
Total dollar amount of each transaction
Any sales charges or redemption fees paid

You will also pay taxes if you sell shares in the fund at a profit.

Another reason to exercise investment caution revolves around the distribution date. Buying a fund right before it distributes its earnings to shareholders forces you to pay taxes on earnings that were earned by other shareholders. Avoid buying funds at the close of the quarter and right before the year ends.

How does a fund make a distribution? When a fund receives income (dividends, interest, capital gains) it increases the Net Asset Value (or NAV, the amount in the fund divided by average amount of shares owned in the fund). It might add $0.05 to the share's value. If the fund pays quarterly distributions, that $0.05 is taken out of the fund, lowering the NAV by $0.05. Multiply this number by the number of shares you own, and you have your taxable liability—at least roughly. If you buy into a fund right before this happens, you pay the higher price for the share and then, once the distribution is made to the shareholders of record, you pay the tax and are left with shares worth $0.05 less. The number of shares doesn't change, the balance in the account or the NAV does. Reinvesting, if it were an actual physical action rather than an automatic one done by the fund, would have you mailing the distribution check back to the fund to buy more shares.

One final note about taxes before we move on to the next chapter. If you have deferred your taxes in a retirement account, be careful about the timing of your distribution. If you are fortunate enough to have funds that you do not need until you are 70½, it is important to understand that those funds have continued to grow while you waited to withdraw them. Now, your required distribution may throw you into a higher tax bracket—the one you were trying to avoid by deferring the taxes in the first place. This is something you need to discuss with a professional tax preparer when you reach the beginning of retirement age (59½).

Now that we have taken a long and somewhat skeptical look at the mutual fund, it is time to put that information to work, bundling everything we have learned into something cohesive. In other words, it is time to put all of these pieces together into an investment plan. Time to peer inside the 401(k), the IRA and its variations, the 403(b) and their unfortunate mainstay, the annuity, as well as the

Continued

Health Savings Accounts that are cropping up at various companies across the country.

But first we will take a look at some of the pressures surrounding those plans, efforts by Wall Street to help you save more and why they are trying so hard. We will also take a look at taxes and how they impact your portfolio and what you should keep inside a taxable account, the account held outside your tax-deferred or Roth.

CHAPTER 15

Your Retirement Plan

◆▬◆▬◆▬◆▬◆▬◆▬◆▬◆▬◆▬◆▬◆▬◆▬◆▬◆▬◆▬◆▬◆▬◆

Had you been born in the late eighteenth or early nineteenth century in the village of Nantucket, you would have witnessed one of the greatest moments in whaling history. It was a time when an industry was born out of happenstance.

Towns created ordinances requiring two residents of the town take shore patrol in search of washed-up whales. When fate, predetermined by the effect that some storms had on hapless whales, proved inadequate to keep up with demand for the free oil these behemoth's provided, these colonists put to sea in search of this valuable commodity.

First, they fished these massive beasts close to shore, a vast improvement over the previous system that relied on luck. Eventually, as marketplaces often do, the demand for this resource outstripped the supply. These hearty men (and the occasional disguised woman) would set sail in search of these valuable leviathans. Months were spent at sea until the holds of these ships were filled with whale oil and bone.

The skill of the captain was key for the success of the crew. These brave mariners are a precursor to those fishermen who are glamorized on the Discovery Channel as they set off in search of crabs in the cold of the North Pacific.

Each crew member received a lay, or a portion of the proceeds, to take home. A lay, often one-one hundred and seventy fifth (1/175) of the take, was generally enough to keep the whaler in cash for six months or more.

The Lay of the Land

Your retirement plan is not so vastly different. You set sail, trusting your investment horizon will be bright and the sea will be calm. You trust that your captain will be able to net you an income for your risk and the reward will make your life more comfortable.

Had you been one of these mariners, you may have relied on your own skill once onboard one of these wooden ships. But it is ultimately the skill of the captain that determines your fortune—or not. This is not so different from the arrangement you have with your mutual fund manager(s). You rely on them for their insights where you have little or no expertise. You rely on them to plough through the vast and deep ocean of information, analysis, and research available to them about stocks and bonds and come up with a viable plan for your hard earned money.

You often do this with only the history of past performance as a guide to future successes, which we have found out, is a crapshoot at best in many cases. Although much of the investment world has been charted, the seas can get rough, the catch can be nimble and sometimes scarce and, worst of all, the world can be awfully unpredictable.

Benefit or Contribution Defined

What could be better: Guaranteed retirement income and the security of knowing that, for the rest of your life, and in many case for the rest of your spouse's, little or no risk, adjustments for the ever-increasing cost of living, and no dependence on you to grow the plan? This is the nature of the defined benefit. Retirement with a salary.

So who thought that dropping the whole future of your retirement into your lap was a good idea? With just over half of the working people in this country actively involved in saving for their own future and industry average of only 66 percent participation in the plans that *are* available to workers at their place of employment, the simple answer would be not everyone.

The advantages of saving in a tax-deferred environment, the ability to direct as much or little of your pay towards it using payroll deductions, the opportunity to position yourself for increased market upside, and despite the fact the participation is wholly reliant on the knowledge you bring to the effort, are all touted as better than a predetermined benefit.

With the investment risk now on your shoulders and the disadvantage you might have if you are forced to begin this journey late in life, the defined contribution plan requires you to be much more diligent, much more aware, and much more savvy than your predecessors. You must have evolved financially. The alternatives to this are not so appealing.

 The man least dependent upon the morrow goes to meet the morrow most cheerfully.—Epicurus (BC 341–270)

Pensions, for all they provide, seem to fly in the face of the American spirit of freedom. Yet, at the same time, the income these plans provide to retired workers and the companies who once offered them to keep good employees for a lifetime, offers a kind of independence that has no parallel. So why have they been disappearing for a more self-directed approach?

In a side-by-side comparison, and this is not to make you pine for those days of yesteryear, the pension plan has some distinct advantages.

Pension plans (employee benefits)	**Defined Contribution Plans (employees)**
Little or no investment risk	Retirement income depends on market performance
Pension formulas that reward high pay	
Pension plans (corporate benefits)	Death and disability insurance
Allows for income replacement goals	No guaranteed income security
Benefits from good investments	Depends on employee's ability to save
Cost-effective	No-cost of living increases
Easily budgeted using actuarial tables	No insurance coverage
	Defined Contribution Plan (corporations)
	Employees retire later
	Additional cost for education
	Higher administrative cost—often passed on to participant

The best of both worlds has begun cropping up in some industries that still have pensions. The defined contribution plan, often without the match that employers offer their salaried employees, is an advantage that pensioned employees should not pass up. This is a double-dip and can only shore-up your future.

A good example of just such a plan exists at Lucent Technologies. The voluntary 401(k) plan (holding over $7 billion in assets) exists alongside a defined benefit plan with assets in excess of $34 billion. Lucent believed that their participation rate in the 401(k) is not high enough—currently 90 percent of its employees contribute to the plan; the industry average is 66 percent—and sought ways to improve how their employees approached this self-directed plan.

What they found upon inspecting employee use of the 401(k) reflected what they perceived to be far too many bad habits, indicative of what has crept into these plans since their inception. Employees did not revisit their holding periodically nor did they rebalance them according to how some industry experts suggest. Far too many employees held one single investment. While their solution may not be one I necessarily endorse—they turned to what are known as commingled funds—the change came with better access to their funds, professional advice and a lower fee structure.

What is a commingled fund? A commingled fund or pooled fund combines numerous assets into one. This takes advantage of what is known as economies of scale—a microeconomic term that is often used when a corporation buys in quantity in order to keep production costs down. In Lucent's case, commingled funds created the much needed diversification it sought, better investor education and lower overall costs.

Companies like Dell and Intel took a different path in the ongoing battle to get their employees to take better control over these plans. This was achieved with offering additional choices to their employees, including more mutual funds, distinct asset classes from which to choose, and lifestyle funds.

As Opportunity Presents Itself

C. Wright Mills was an American sociologist who attacked the post-WWII institutions for their lack of consideration, their failure to inspire, and their inability to interact with the populace. Those of a certain age may remember that these accusations were greeted with name-calling and comparisons to Karl Marx. He did not deserve either form of criticism or comparison.

He once said: "Freedom is not merely the opportunity to do as one pleases; neither is it merely the opportunity to choose between set alternatives. Freedom is, first of all, the chance to formulate the available choices, to argue over them—and then, the opportunity to choose." As we approach the inside of your defined contribution plan, we do so with a healthy skepticism.

The questions are simply: How do you make your 401(k) as safe as your pension used to be? You do not have the ability to replace any downside market years with money from your corporate profits. You are not a corporation with profits; you are an individual with a paycheck.

How do you keep the costs down? Administration costs are now, in many ways, costs of your own. This dips into the potential for growth by subtracting from your returns. Hidden fees, redundant charges and unfit investments can seriously impact your plan.

How do you tailor it to your temperament for risk?

More or Less: How to Pick the Right Combination

Employees who sign up for their company 401(k) face an array of choices—or not. In some plans, hundreds of options are presented to workers/investors who have little or no experience picking the right fund for their goals—which they might lump into a single requirement: "I want to retire with all the money I'll ever need," their risks, "I sure as heck don't want to lose money," and their time frame, "I want to retire early."

In other plans, only a couple of options are offered—five or six index funds, a couple of overseas offerings, and the company stock. Most plans offer some sort of employer match, a term that refers to a dollar for dollar contribution, up to a predetermined limit, that employer offers as incentive. You invest a dollar and they do the same.

Before we get to the choices for our Early Bird, Chaser, and Relaxer, let's take a quick look at some of the problems facing *you* about *you*.

Statistics have shown that people are not taking advantage of the free gift the employer makes when it offers to match your savings contribution. There are no laws requiring this type of incentive. Yet there ought to be law requiring every employee to take advantage of what is offered. The average corporate match is 50 percent on up to 6 percent of what you contribute to the plan. This is free money, folks, and amounts to a 3 percent increase in your savings.

The choices you make inside those plans are often done based on public opinion, peer suggestion, or by employing a throw-the-dart method. Diversity is not so simple when the choices are limited and the default pick, often the most conservative choice or the one with the least tax advantage, are often facing the employee joining for the first time.

 Princeton University Professor Burton G. Malkiel first popularized the dart throwing option for picking stocks. He suggested in his book *A Random Walk Down Wall Street* that "A blindfolded monkey throwing darts at a newspaper's financial pages could select a portfolio that would do just as well as one carefully selected by experts."

Even those who come to the 401(k) with a modicum of investor knowledge often make similar mistakes when it comes to diversity. They may choose a higher percentage of company stock than would be advisable (some employees are forced into this decision when the company offers a match only upon the purchase of the company' shares) or own funds that have what is known as redundancy (similar stocks in a number of different mutual funds expose you to additional risk should anything unsavory happen).

You make other mistakes as well. You look at your account balance as a source of income by borrowing from it or, worse, when you change jobs, failing to roll the funds in it, which have been accumulating in tax deferred, into another account that is also postponing your obligation to the IRS. Early withdrawals are not only met with the tax penalty (everything not paid is owed to the IRS but the plan also penalizes you with a 10 percent excise tax deducted from those assets upon early withdrawal).

Aside from those problems you are not likely to see this as a long-term arrangement and, if you do, you may not have made the best beneficiary decisions to protect your efforts.

Most of us fail to think of what becomes of our IRA or 401(k) when we die. We are too busy thinking about all of the other aspects of the plan: what to buy, how much to allocate, etc. But that one move made right at the beginning of your enrollment can have long-term effects tax-wise on how that retirement plan is treated after you pass.

You may think this is handled in your will—a separate subject which we will talk about towards the end of the book. Naming a contingent beneficiary allows them to take advantage of the IRS's Single Life Expectancy table. Suppose you die at age 65 and your spouse, who is 60 years old, survives you as your retirement plan's beneficiary.

According to the IRS table, you would have a life expectancy of 32.5 years. Because of this, you leave the account alone until you are 70½ years old before you begin taking distributions (this is done once you roll it over into your account; you can also take it as lump sum as well). Once you reach that age, you may take graduated distributions over the remaining years.

Here's an example of how this might work (your tax professional might have a different option based on your specific set of circumstances). Assuming you died at age 65 with $300,000 in an IRA that is conservatively returning 6 percent. Your surviving spouse would be eligible for the following distributions:

Beneficiary age	Remaining life expectancy	Minimum distribution	Balance
70	27.4	$14,652	$410,904
71	26.5	$15,506	$420,052
72	25.6	$16,408	$428,847
73	24.7	$17,362	$437,215
74	23.8	$18,370	$445,078
75	22.9	$19,436	$452,347
76	22.0	$20,561	$458,927
77	21.2	$21,647	$464,815
78	20.3	$22,897	$469,806
79	19.5	$24,093	$473,902
80	18.7	$25,342	$476,994

What to Say!

Beneficiary age	Remaining life expectancy	Minimum distribution	Balance
81	17.9	$26,648	$478,966
82	17.1	$28,010	$479,694
83	16.3	$29,429	$479,047
84	15.5	$30,906	$476,883

Had you left that IRA to a grandchild aged 12, they could keep the portfolio in a tax-deferred account until they were eligible for withdrawal or wait until the last possible moment. Their withdrawal table in the first year of mandatory dispersals at age 70 would look like this (based on the same conservative portfolio return):

Beneficiary age	Remaining life expectancy	Minimum distribution	Balance
71	26.5	$352,307	$9,544,000

Helping the Irrational Investor Invest

Wall Street has every right to assume, based on some of the things we just discussed, failure to diversify, under investment and lack of participation in a meaningful way, to believe that you need help. Lobbying to come to the rescue of the investor led to the signing of the Pension Protection Act of 2006. While it did little to protect pensions—in fact it actually opened the door to closing many of them—it did allow a more active role in defined contribution plans.

The act requires employers to explain, at the onset, the importance of retirement savings. It also allows the employers to help the employees that have failed to help themselves by assigning your responsibility to a third party.

The PPA gives employers the right to save pretax income that may have been given to the employee as a pay increase prior to its enactment. Although it remains to be seen how this will impact the employee/employer relationship, it does give the employer the opportunity of lowering the incentives currently on offer (i.e., matching contributions).

There may be higher costs associated with investor education, a cost that was previously borne by the company. There is also the false sense of security that the initial 3 percent the first year, 4 percent the second, and up to 6 percent deducted will be adequate to fund a retirement plan.

Here are some highlights (and lowlights) of the Pension Protection Act of 2006:

What it does: The new law provides that federal law (ERISA) preempts such State laws to allow employers in all States to automatically deduct 401(k) contributions from employee's paychecks.

The legislation directs Department of Labor to issue regulations specifying certain default investments that won't deprive employers of the fiduciary protection for employee-elected investments. These would be "default investments that include a mix of asset classes consistent with capital preservation or long-term capital appreciation." These are generally understood to include balanced funds, life cycle funds and managed accounts.

The nondiscrimination exemption is conditioned on auto enrollment of not only new hires but also existing employees, except those existing employees who were eligible to participate before the employer adopted the automatic contribution arrangement and who made an affirmative/explicit election (either to participate or to refrain from participating).

The new nondiscrimination exemption is conditioned on automatic annual 1 percent increases in the rate of employee contributions up to 6 percent of pay.

Makes the Saver's Credit permanent. The Saver's Credit levels the playing field for moderate- and lower-income households in lower tax brackets by basing the incentive on the amount saved (a credit) rather than giving larger tax benefits to those in higher tax brackets (the deductions and exclusions that comprise other pension tax preferences). It is still nonrefundable and only acts as a deduction against tax liability.

What it doesn't do: The new exemption from nondiscrimination standards breaks the usual linkage between the amount of tax-preferred saving allowed for executives and the amount saved by most workers. Executive's 401(k) benefits would no longer depend on how much most workers save. The new exemption from the nondiscrimination standards is conditioned on auto enrollment at 3 percent of pay (at least), escalating 1 percent a year up to 6 percent, and an

Continued

employer offer of matching contributions conditioned on employee contributions (100 percent of first 1 percent of pay, 50 percent of next 5 percent of pay, vesting after two years). Under the new exemption, even if most employees don't participate or save very little, that will not affect how much executives can put away on a tax-favored basis.

On February 7, 2007, Vanguard Chairman and CEO John J. Brennan discussed what the PPA means to future of the US retirement system. The speech was given at the Investment Company Institute Pension Protection Act Developments Conference in Washington, DC. He said, "the era of defined benefit plans is drawing to a close, and the future rests on the success of the participant-directed defined contribution plan." What he does not say to his peer group, "This will be very good for our industry."

 Accuracy of observation is the equivalent of accuracy of thinking.
—Wallace Stevens

He continues on by making the point that "the median payout to a retiree from a private defined benefit plan is $6,800 per year" by citing a Congressional Research Service statistic from a January 29, 2007, report on the fate of mill workers. But that report, also debating the differences between defined benefit and defined contribution plans, bemoaned that number as the median retirement balance.

He is correct, however, in his assessment as to why these retirement accounts are so under funded. He suggested the retirement outlook for those with defined benefit plans was poor because: "They change jobs, they are laid off, their employer can't afford to be very generous."

He may have missed mentioning some nefarious business shenanigans that also sounded the death knell for many of these plans. Mergers and acquisitions, bankruptcies and reliance on the Pension Benefit Guaranty Corporation to bail out failed companies with outstanding pension promises (which caused the PBGC, which acts as an insurer, to raise its rates for participation higher for those businesses in good standing) are all sending repercussions throughout the retirement world—for those that are planning, about to, or who are currently retired.

What Taxes We Avoid

In a shameless plug for the previous book in this series, *Investing for the Utterly Confused*, the investor is asked to keep numerous accounts, each built one at a time based upon the completion of the previous one. Much as I encouraged you in the beginning of the book (and will take the opportunity to restate again) debt of all kinds, whether you think of it as good or bad, has an impact on your efforts to save. But understanding that we, or at least the majority of us, will never be free of it, debt is always lingering in the background, just out of focus in the shadows, while we instead concentrate on the brightest spot in our retirement picture, Chiaroscuro.

But once that speed bump on the road to retirement planning is accounted for, the focus both then and now is on building a retirement portfolio. My thinking in that book was simple. Once your future was insured, you could invest as you pleased. But building that retirement account needs to take into consideration the best tax advantage.

Current tax law on capital gains is set at 15 percent, at least in the near-term. If that should become permanent, it will have an effect on how your build you portfolio. The money kept inside of your 401(k) and traditional IRA is treated as money that is tax deferred. Those plans optimistically hope that taxes will be lower when you retire because your income will be lower as well.

 What the Experts Say An optimist stays up until midnight to see the new year in. A pessimist stays up to make sure the old year leaves.—Bill Vaughan

I'm not so sure that this kind of thinking is a safe assumption. If you consider your current tax bracket and how much you think you would like to retire with, you may find that the tax treatment for your 401(K) or IRA might be miscalculating some savings. When funds are eventually dispersed, they will be treated like income, not capital gains. If that is the case, tax friendly investments held inside a 401(k) or IRA will be better kept outside your retirement or held in a Roth account.

We will look at what life cycle or life style funds and balanced funds are in-depth just a little further along, but if this is the choice that Wall Street wants you to make inside a tax deferred retirement account, I would question their thinking—once again.

Let's talk about those indexes first. Not only are they among the most fee-efficient types of funds, they are also among the most tax efficient. Because the fund is usually locked into a fixed holding period, once the underlying portfolio is purchased and weighted properly, there are no sales of any one company until the firm that indexes those stocks rebalances the portfolio.

How closely does an index fund mimic the index it tracks? An index fund can actually beat the index it tracks with the right proportion of stocks based upon how each company is capitalized. When Standard & Poors releases the names and number of shares in this hypothetical portfolio, mutual fund companies who try to copy the portfolio but seek to offer their investors a better return will weight their indexes differently.

Weight refers to the proportion of shares in the portfolio and is usually based on the impact the total dollar amount has on the total portfolio. One company might be worth twice what another is. An index might see that as a sign that the market likes that particular company more because it has valued their shares at a much higher level. Because many of the indexes then base the number of shares on that criteria, an index might consist of a higher dollar amount of one company in the top ten holdings as opposed to your exposure to a bottom 10 holding in the index. This often referred to as market efficiency.

Any index fund on any given day could beat the index it copies simply by overcoming the cost of running the fund—low expenses because there is very little trading down aside from purchasing new shares for reinvested and incoming shareholders—and balancing the portfolio is such a way as to best the index.

Once a trade is initiated by the mutual fund, one of two things happens. There is either a profit or a loss. Often, in the rebalancing process there is a little of both, with the loser coming off the bottom and the incoming issues, the companies being added, have the potential of new interest and some upside gains in share price. But what the S&P 500 companies tend to do is pay dividends.

These are taxed at 15 percent. This is something you should pay now. This can only be done by changing what you are invested in within your tax-deferred account or by rolling the funds into a Roth.

The act of rolling-over cannot be emphasized enough. Because the 401(k) is by nature a traditional IRA trapped inside a corporate plan, transferring the contents of a 401(k) into a traditional IRA is rather seamless. But should you decide to make the move to a Roth IRA, you need to remember one very important rule: a 401(k) must first stop in a traditional IRA account before it can journey on to a Roth. The penalties are quite severe and could come somewhere down the road when you least expect them.

There are a couple of basic steps to make the transition. But, first, I should explain what a Roth IRA is and why it so attractive to some investors, so much so that it is beginning to sprout up in a variety of 401(k) plans.

The Roth IRA has been available since 1998, born into existence with the signing of the Taxpayer Relief Act of 1997. Money deposited in a Roth has already been taxed, giving the investor no income tax deduction. If you meet the requirements, all of the earnings in the Roth IRA are tax-free. This adds significant leverage to how you plan your retirement savings. Granted, the money invested has had the taxes paid by your current tax rate (sometimes lowered due to deductions and pre-tax contributions from your 401(k) type plan) but those earnings, falling prey to the effects of compounding and reinvestment of dividends and capital gains, can create some significant and enviable wealth that, even in retirement, cannot be taxed.

What are the advantages of owning a Roth IRA compared to a traditional IRA?

Here's a seemingly attractive list of pros followed by an interesting list of cons:

The pros:

1. What you contribute is yours to withdraw at any time. Although any contribution to a retirement account should be left there; in a Roth, the money is yours to use as you see fit).

Continued

2. After a so-called "seasoning period," about five years, a converted traditional IRA (to a Roth), the money is yours and you can begin qualified earnings withdrawals at 59½ or at the time of a disability. Qualified earnings are "qualified after five years."

3. The beneficiary of a Roth can roll it over into their Roth without penalty.

4. There are no forced distributions. In other words, if you don't need the money in a Roth IRA, it can stay there to continue to grow until you do need it.

The cons:

1. No tax deduction. If you have underfunded your IRA, this might work out to your advantage—tax-wise at least.

2. While it is not a good idea to withdraw early from your IRA, Roth or otherwise, tapping the earnings in a Roth is treated harshly.

3. The real tax benefit in a Roth only comes if you outlive the account. Your estate might need those tax benefits should you not live to use the account or die before its assets are fully dissipated. And, as long as we are on the subject of taxes, there is never a guarantee that that tax-free pool will be left untouched by future generations of legislators.

There are eligibility requirements as well. Contributions for the tax year are limited to $5,000 in 2008 for both IRAs and Roth IRAs.

Your ability to make those contributions have IRS mandated income limits. A Roth IRA investor who is single, head of household, married filing separately or did not live with their spouse for a year can earn up to $101,000–$116,000 (Adjusted Gross Income or AGI) a year in 2008 to qualify for a full contribution before phase outs begin. AGI represents, interest income, capital gains, dividend income, income from certain retirement accounts, alimony received, rental income, royalty income, farm income, unemployment compensation, and certain other kinds of income. Joint filers can have taxable earnings of $159,000–$169,000 in 2008 in order to qualify for a full contribution. Conversions to a Roth IRA from a traditional IRA however are limited to $100,000 for the years prior to 2010.

Those who contribute to a traditional IRA have slightly different AGI levels. Contributions are fully deductible for those not covered by an employer retirement plan (an exception applies for a non-covered spouse who files a joint return if AGI exceeds $156,000 for 2007; $159,000 for 2008 or if covered below a certain AGI (in 2007: $83,000 joint or $52,000 single; in 2008: $85,000 joint or $53,000 single)). If you are covered by an employer plan or you are unsure whether you qualify, check with your tax advisor.

Year	Traditional/Roth	Traditional/Roth catch up	401(k) 403(b)	401(k) 403(b) catch up
2006	$4,000	$5,000	$15,000	$20,000
2007	$4,000	$5,000	$15,500	$20,500
2008	$5,000	$6,000	–	–
2009	$5,000	$6,000	–	–

After 2008, the contribution limit will be annually indexed in $500 increments, adjusted for the cost-of-living (COLA).

Americans who have reached the age of 50 have the ability to contribute more to their retirement account under the "catch up" provisions as part of the Economic Growth and Tax relief Reconciliation Act of 2002.

Short of the Rollover

Your tax-deferred account should hold a basket of growth stocks in almost every instance. This flies in the face of what Wall Street would like. It upsets the balance that life cycle funds offer and keeps the investment in bonds found in a balanced account where they should be: outside of a tax-deferred account.

But, first, we need to build that retirement portfolio.

What's Next In the next chapter we will revisit our Early Bird and make a plan for the group best suited to start early but most likely to not follow through for the long-term, the Chaser, who, for want of a better term, has been blindsided by life and realizes, almost suddenly, that they are going to fall short if something isn't done right away, and the Relaxer, the fortunate soul who is most likely to underestimate the growth potential in their current portfolio and will, in all likelihood, be investing far too conservatively.

CHAPTER 16

Where, When and Why

N athan Lee, film critic for the *Village Voice,* bemoaned the role of the reviewer and the net effects of giving away the ending. He worried about his audience and their expectations. He wondered whether readers understood his role in making the artwork understandable and close, highlighting the good and the bad and trying to do so without giving away the ending, the spoiler.

He wrote in a *New York Times* op-ed piece on July 21, 2007, that "the integrity of the critic doesn't revolve around whether or not they're willing to spoil"—a reference to giving away the ending despite attempting not to do so— "but *why* they chose to do so."

We have reached the spoiler. Although we haven't quite finished filling in the final blanks in your retirement plan, we have reached the investment end of the book. Now I'll tell you where, when and why.

The Early Bird

We have discussed risk and fees, balance and diversity, how the industry views you, and the role the government plays in thwarting your best intended attempts, the costs and the composition of the investment of choice inside your retirement plan, the mutual fund, the managers of these funds, and the subtle but important difference between retirement investing.

One of the few topics we did not cover in the preceding chapters was volatility. Although most people would group this under the header "risk," it is probably the only real statistic revealed in the "past performance, future returns" disclaimer. How your mutual fund has done in the past as it weathers storms and sunny days does lend you some insight into how the fund will react to similar events in the future.

Provided the manager of the fund you may be looking at was the manager of the fund whose record you are examining—going back five years or more— you will have a relatively good indication of whether their philosophy works. Managing a fund is no easy task, although managing a hedge fund is. And this is the primary reason so many take flight and why you may have some difficulty finding good long-term investments based on a single manager's performance.

In the next century it will be the early mechanical bird which gets the first plastic worm out of the artificial grass.—William E. (Bill) Vaughan

The number of hedge funds actively managing portfolios has ballooned in the last several years. There are now over 8,000 of them with almost a trillion dollars under management. The pay structure that these funds offer their managers is often too enticing to pass up. The *2 and 20,* a reference to how the fund manager is compensated—2 percent of the assets under management and 20 percent, sometimes more, of the profits, presents a very attractive carrot to managers who operate in the highly regulated mutual fund arena.

By comparison, the world of hedge funds represents the financial equivalent of the Wild West. While it is not exactly lawless, the code of conduct is much less restricted by disclosures, filings and the seemingly innumerable regulations required by the SEC. The question left for mutual fund investors seems to be: Does this exodus of financial professionals have a negative effect on the mutual fund in general or did we just get rid of the cowboys and pioneers in favor of managers who are true to their skills?

Hedge funds have continued to grow since their inception in the early nineties. In those days, the 1 and 20 fee structure dominated the industry. But something shifted concerning how investors view these funds. Once focused on returns (or alpha as the industry likes to refer excess returns),

Continued

In the Real World... hedge funds are now advertising their strategies. Most hedge funds have added to their mystique by creating unbreakable lock-ups, early redemption penalties and substantially changed high water marks—a reference to a profit benchmark that, until recently, needed to be beaten year over year in order for the fund manager to be compensated. Unlike mutual funds, hedge funds can use arbitrage, this represents a statistical opportunity whether it be in stocks, bonds or the relationship between the two, derivatives, short-selling, options, futures, global and any other arcane and risky attempt at increasing manager and shareholder wealth. Time was, these were investor centric funds; now the emphasis is on who is running them and what new thinking they can bring.

Building the Nest, One Twig at a Time

There are five basic financial components or tools available to the average investor. They are *equities* (a reference to stocks, a portion of the company issued to raise money; gives the shareholder a right to profits; offers a vote), *fixed income* (or bonds, a loan to help companies finance various endeavors; investors receive no say in how the company is run; first in line though should the company liquidate), *real estate* (inside a retirement plan, these will be offered as REITs or Real Estate Investment Trusts; offers a portion of the profits on land, buildings, etc.; not usually taxed as dividends but as income with the fund required to distribute 90 percent of its annual taxable income while keeping 75 percent of its asset invested in one or all of the following— real estate, mortgage loans, shares in other REITs, cash, or government securities; economically sensitive; must have a least 100 shareholders with less than 50 percent of its outstanding shares controlled by five or fewer shareholders in the fund), *money markets* (the safe haven for cash; lower returns; not insured against loss: interest paid is economically sensitive) and *annuities* (an insurance product masquerading as an investment; additional information in the next chapter).

For the Early Bird, three of the five investments mentioned above should not be in your portfolio: money markets—best for that emergency fund you are building outside your retirement account, fixed income and annuities. REITs do have a place but it is equities that will make up the lion's share of your portfolio.

From Aesop, The Lion went once a-hunting along with the Fox, the Jackal, and the Wolf. They hunted and they hunted 'til at last they surprised a Stag, and soon took its life. Then came the question how the spoil should be divided.

"Quarter me this Stag," roared the Lion; so the other animals skinned it and cut it into four parts. Then the Lion took his stand in front of the carcass and pronounced judgment: The first quarter is for me in my capacity as King of Beasts; the second is mine as arbiter; another share comes to me for my part in the chase; and as for the fourth quarter, well, as for that, I should like to see which of you will dare to lay a paw upon it."

"Humph," grumbled the Fox as he walked away with his tail between his legs; but he spoke in a low growl. "You may share the labors of the great, but you will not share the spoil."

The Multifaceted Marketplace

The mutual funds I think these three investors should concentrate on break down into three basic categories: growth, value, and core—a combination of the two.

What's the difference between growth, value, and core mutual funds? Growth represents a type of investment that is meant to grow your money by purchasing potential in companies. Most businesses go through several distinct periods of development. They are created, with a widget or a notion or a service as their sole reason to exist. As they sell more products, introduce new lines, or explore new marketplaces, Wall Street considers them growth investments capable of increasing in value as they increase shareholder interest and, with any luck, their investor's wealth as well.

These periods can be rapid and volatile, filled with the potential for failure almost as much as for success. It is this allure, their mystique, their sexiness that attracts money and that is growth. Mutual funds pursue these opportunities if their chartered mission is to seek these types of companies. If they choose wisely, they can beat the indexes that mimic these companies.

Remember, with growth comes risk and reward and the smaller the company the greater that both will exist. This is where a skilled manager becomes worth his

Continued

paycheck—even if it isn't the size of a hedge fund manager's. Even large companies can have growth potential.

But time and markets and so many new competitors offering something newer with reactions more nimble than your own, have a tendency to slow a company down eventually. This is where leadership skills take hold and create investor value. There is a need for consistent profits and the chore of creating an ever-widening customer base sometimes shifts the focus from growth—although the term will never fall from the lips of analysts as they examine an enterprise's growth potential as a measure of continued health, these companies essentially transform into value investments.

Growth is sexy. Value is not quite the opposite but it is certainly less attractive, lacking flamboyance and pizzazz. Instead, value opts for staid and true. Value is how we can develop balance in a portfolio while still investing in equities for their capital appreciation.

Core funds for our discussion are a combination of growth stocks and value stocks—although many of the funds this size dedicate a certain percentage towards common stock and use the remaining available money to buy all sorts of things (foreign stocks, larger companies outside their charter, even some securities) to enhance the value of the fund. That's okay and often unavoidable.

Fund managers who oversee core or blended types of funds are not looking to shoot the lights out with their market performance. Instead, their focus is concentrated on steady-as-she-goes type growth with a nice, well-rounded allocation of assets. In other words, not too much of one thing and a market position designed to get as much juice as possible out of their underlying stocks without exposing anyone to too much risk—any more at least than is endemic to that sector.

Early Birds should hold all three of these funds. Chasers will build their nests with just two, growth and core type funds. I'll suggest the same number for the Relaxers, except in their case the two they will be holding will be the value and the core.

This sort of flies in the face of conventional wisdom, even some I've imparted in the past. But I have my reasons. The Early Bird is the most likely investor (ages for this group run up to and include the early 40s) to have accumulated the debt the fastest, made the most logical argument for why they have it, and live life with the attitude that, should they make a mistake, they have the better part of a lifetime to alter their course. What they fail to realize is the transition they make from Early Bird to Chaser.

Early Birds don't catch worms; they seize opportunities that are not available to older investors. Compounding aside, they are correct in the assumption that they do have a whole lifetime ahead of them. But taking years to recover from avoidable financial mistakes is a lot different than riding market highs and lows.

A Little of This and a Lot of That

One of the major pitfalls of mutual fund investing is redundancy. Far too many fund investors both in and outside of retirement plans have abnormal exposure to risk. This isn't because they have bet the farm on some hot IPO but because the funds they own have similar portfolios. A 5 percent exposure of one company in one fund might also be represented in another fund.

Early Birds can avoid this by concentrating on several subgroups of growth, value and core.

Earlier in the book I mentioned capitalization. This is a market reward for performance and is at the core of what is known as market efficiency. This means that other investors vote with their money and their feet. If they flock to stock, they raise the value of the shares and increase its market capitalization. The same thing happens in reverse should bad news surface about a stock. A lot of one equity results in a larger-than-needed loss for even the ever-young and resilient Early Bird.

Google is good example of how market efficiency prices a stock. The company does not have that many shares available for purchase, but what they do have has been deigned by the market as a worthwhile investment. And the share price times the outstanding number of shares available make it one of the largest companies on the planet with a market cap of $161 billion (07.23.07).

This redundancy flies in the face of diversification. One of the easiest ways to overcome it is keeping your three groups separate. The subgroups, small capitalized companies ($300 million to $2 billion), mid-cap ($2 billion to $10 billion), and large-caps ($10 to $200 billion) represent the best way to slice the marketplace. Three types of funds, growth, value and core investing in three different sized companies.

The Early Bird should have a basket of mutual funds inside a 401(k) that should look like this:

Growth funds 60 percent, Value funds 30 percent, Core funds 10 percent, and even further, those growth funds should be small caps/mid-caps, split evenly, large-cap value funds, and mid-cap core funds. Critics will quickly point out the flaw in this thinking as one of mechanics rather than potential.

Even Ben Graham would suggest some sort of protection be built in the event of a market downturn. I believe that as well but it should be outside of your retirement accounts, not in them. At first glance, it seems as if you are 100 percent invested in stocks and inside your retirement portfolio, you should be.

If it looks like a duck, and quacks like a duck, we have at least to consider the possibility that we have a small aquatic bird of the family anatidae on our hands.—Douglas Adams

By placing the majority of the mutual fund portfolio in small-cap and mid-cap growth, we create all the needed risk any investor should need to get a year over year return of 10 percent or better. The Russell Investment Group, publisher of small and mid-cap indexes, designs tools to improve investing. As they put it, their focus on small-caps has been profitable for investors: "Judging by figures from Ibbotson Associates, which date back to 1926, small-cap stocks historically have earned 12.4 percent a year against 10.7 percent annually for large-cap stocks."

The chart below shows how well the indexes published by Russell would have done in a hypothetical portfolio. Because there is a great deal of temptation to pick an index — hey look at those returns! — avoid it

Continued

if possible. Sometimes, though, the choices in a 401(k) can be kind of anemic. IRA investors have the full run of mutual funds to choose from as long as they focus on fees and expenses (this group tends to run higher on average than any other type of investment so expect to pay higher fees, but they should not exceed 1.75 percent). In the Early Bird portfolio (small-cap growth average here an expense ratio of 1.65 percent, mid-cap core at 1.42 percent, large-cap value at 1.33 percent), the manager of those funds should have some tenure, preferably three years or longer, and the funds should have done at least as good as its comparable index over the same period.

The Russell Index	1 yr	3 yrs	5 yrs	10 yrs
Small-cap Indexes				
Russell 2000® Index	16.43	13.45	13.88	9.06
Russell 2000® Growth Index	16.83	11.76	13.08	5.28
Russell 2000® Value Index	16.05	15.02	14.62	12.14
Mid-cap Indexes				
Russell Mid-cap® Index	20.83	17.16	16.39	11.86
Russell Mid-cap® Growth Index	19.73	14.48	15.45	8.66
Russell Mid-cap® Value Index	22.09	19.32	17.17	13.06

Those investing outside of a 401(k), or who have access to a much wider choice of funds, will find the fund screener at Yahoo! Finance helpful. You can enter a wide variety of criteria with which to narrow your search. But I would suggest you keep it relatively broad. Choose the category but not the fund family. Shoot for a top 10 percent return over a five-year period and little else. From there you can narrow it further by looking for a fund with a small entrance fee, usually lower when inside an IRA. This will allow you to take a thousand dollars in many instances and open one of each of the three funds groups needed to build an Early Bird portfolio.

Here are some top small cap growth funds as vetted out by that screener. These funds have acceptable fees, a low point of entry and a best of the bunch mentality. These are not recommendations; just examples of some long-term top performers.

	Ticker	Annual return
Small-cap growth		
Over the last five years		
Royce Value Plus Service	RYVPX	25.08%
William Blair Small-Cap Growth I	WBSIX	17.82%
Over the last three years		
Hartford Small Company HLS IA	HIASX	18.37%
Alger Small Cap Growth A	ALSAX	18.27%
Wells Fargo Advantage Small Cap Opp Adm	NVSOX	18.12%
Large-cap value		
Over the last five years		
Leuthold Select Industries	LSLTX	17.72%
RiverSource Diversified Equity Inc R4	IDQYX	17.27%
Over the last three years		
Amana Trust Income	AMANX	21.46%
BB&T Equity Income Instl	BEGIX	19.50%
Oppenheimer Select Value Y	OSVYX	19.25%
Mid-cap core		
Over the last five years		
Fidelity Advisor Leveraged Co Stk A	FLSAX	36.11%
Legg Mason Special Investment Instl	LMNSX	19.81%
Over the last three years		
CGM Capital Development	LOMCX	25.10%
Hennessy Focus 30	HFTFX	23.43%
Fidelity Advisor Leveraged Co Stk T	FLSTX	23.14%

The Early Bird should understand that any portfolio decision, even the buy and hold ones, are not meant to be buy-and-forget. You will get quarterly statements either online or in the mail or both. Take a moment to read them. I've given you some preliminary education on what to look for in a prospectus but there is more than just a statement by the fund manager and spreadsheet of fees.

Mutual fund managers are notorious for drifting. In the portfolio you have, the chances of that happening are slim but certainly not nonexistent. Look at the top holdings in each of your funds and find out if they are being held in any of your other funds. This could be a reason to move your money to another fund that doesn't present you with redundancy.

The key to the success of this portfolio is regular investing (Dollar Cost Averaging) and a 10 to 20 year horizon. By the time you are 40, it will be time for some realignment.

What about balancing? There is a great deal of emphasis placed on this but little of it is warranted. You will no doubt be all out of whack with that 60/30/10 ratio in no time. It is key to start with balance and let the market place maintain it. You are not going to do any real harm if your value funds out pace the performance of your growth and core investments. Dollar cost averaging will do the adjustments. One fund from each category to start and, if you can, add additional holdings in each category until you regain some balance.

The Chaser

A difference of opinion is what makes horse racing and missionaries.
—Will Rogers

For the Chaser, the basket of stock gets a little smaller. The Chaser should pursue risk in the mid-cap marketplace, which often drifts back and forth between the small- and large-cap growth space. Mid-cap growth funds should occupy 70 percent of the portfolio with Large-core funds making up the remaining 30 percent.

A portfolio like this would hold a sampling of mutual funds that would add risk and only a spattering of protection. Some of the large-cap core funds have and probably will in the future put money in securities and bonds. Once again, this is unavoidable and just a good use of the tools available to the fund manager. Also, once again, these funds were screened at Yahoo! Finance and are not recommendations.

And if I can add one more disclaimer; we held with our 1.75 percent maximum expenses (mid-cap growth averages 1.51 percent, large-cap core averages) and a small initial IRA investment amount ($1,000 sounds like a nice round number—that way, you can take the average tax return and start investing in two funds). Because we are going to hold onto these funds for longer than five years, the front-end load or deferred load charges are not really relevant. The emphasis on no-load funds is still a good idea if the fund company offers only that type. But if they offer a number of class shares, compare them for long-term expenses. You are building a buy-and-hold portfolio.

	Ticker	Annual return
Mid-cap growth		
Over the last five years		
Legg Mason Opportunity Institutional	LMNOX	21.98%
Baron Partners	BPTRX	19.23%
Over the last three years		
American Century Heritage Inst	ATHIX	23.44%
American Century Giftrust Inv	TWGTX	22.84%
Baron Partners	BPTRX	21.63%
large-cap Core		
Over the last five years		
Janus Contrarian	JSVAX	22.01%
USAA Capital Growth	USCGX	18.34%
Over the last three years		
Timothy Plan Large/Mid-Cap Value A	TLVAX	18.87%
Managers AMG FQ Tx-Mgd U.S. Eq Inst	MFQTX	18.83%
Jennison 20/20 Focus Z	PTWZX	18.43%

A Slightly Closer Look

A large-cap core fund such as the CGM Focus has been a consistent performer and, if you look at the numbers, it qualifies as a cornerstone type of fund. Billed as a 20 percent winner five years running in the large-cap blend category, the comfortable knowledge that it is a *large-cap core/blended* fund with those kinds of numbers and no-load too, almost makes you giddy that this kind of fund is going to fit nicely into the Chaser's investment objectives.

I had chosen it to be on the list of comparable funds for this investment category. And, ironically, I had also picked it to profile, by downloading the prospectus for a look inside, beyond the fund profile provided at some many sites. Let's take a look at their objectives stated in that document—just to make sure.

It reads in bold header: **Investment Objective**, followed by this statement:

"The Fund's investment objective is long-term growth of capital."

You will find most objectives stated very clearly in this portion of the report. But how will they achieve so noble a goal?

The Summary of Principal Investment Strategies offers the prospectus reader a peak into the methods behind their success. "The Fund," it begins, "is non-diversified and intends to pursue its objective by focusing on equity investments in a smaller number of companies, and/or in a more limited number of sectors (clusters of related industries), than diversified mutual funds.

I know what you are thinking. We are talking about a top performer in the large-cap core group. What about these investments in small caps? Good question because both MSN Money and Yahoo! Finance list it as a large-cap fund, with Marketwatch.com listing it very favorably as a mid-cap growth fund. So I called the company.

The gentleman I spoke with told me something entirely different. He portrayed the fund as being an "aggressive growth fund," so much so it has latitude to buy securities of between 20 to 100 companies at any one time," adding further down the prospectus that it "primarily invests in companies with market capitalizations of at least $100 million."

It adds that "The Fund is flexibly managed, with the ability to invest in equity, debt and fixed-income securities, in different industry sectors and in foreign issuers. The Fund may invest in companies regardless of the size of their market capitalization," as the agent who spoke with me at Capital Growth Management in Boston said, suggesting that those companies market cap can range all the way down to as little as $1,000,000.

"The investment manager invests both in companies that are attractively valued and that have the potential for growth," the report declares. It also told potential investors that "The Fund may invest in debt and fixed income securities of any maturity and any grade." If you would like to read more about this fund, you can find it at: http://wwww.cfmfunds.com/pdf/2007-05-01-focus-prospectus.pdf

This is why you read the prospectus.

The Relaxer

The portfolio, by virtue of its name, suggests a time in life where all of your hard work has finally paid off. In the same vein as the imagery, the nest is built, feathered and is now nursing the sizable nest egg. But that couldn't be farther from the truth if you are in your 50s and just getting started.

Life is full of financial pitfalls. Divorce, job loss or prolonged income interruption, possibly due to a disability, can set you back years, if not decades. Those prime growth years will have slipped away for good. Even the riskiness that is the Chaser portfolio might be more risk than you can handle.

But there is a way to provide some sanity to the process. You have to deal with your debt—I can never overemphasize that point for every level of investor. You can grow money while you deal with it, but you cannot outpace the steady fixation that indebtedness holds against those investment efforts.

Then you have to allow some more risk than you might have been told you should have. Popular investment wisdom has a portfolio full of bonds and only a slice of the equity market. The Relaxer is going to need a much more hefty exposure with a tempered amount of risk. Instead of the 60/30/10 (growth/value/core) of the Early Bird or the 70/30 (growth/core) of the middle aged Chaser, the Relaxer will need a 30/70 value to core mix.

We must believe in luck. For how else can we explain the success of those we don't like?—Jean Cocteau

The core mix of funds will be all large-cap offerings. See the table for large-cap core listed for the Chaser. The value funds will be mid-cap and, with any luck, add another layer of protection into the fund and can be found in the portfolio of the Early Bird.

There are some other aspects of retirement planning that need to be explained in detail. Among them: what investments are best kept in that outside account including life-cycle funds, lifestyle funds and a look at bonds, the growing popularity of Exchange Traded Funds, annuities—the backbone investment of the 403(b) crowd, and lastly, Health Savings Accounts. This will be followed by a look at your estate plan from wills to beneficiary designations.

CHAPTER 17
What Will They Think of Next?

◆▬◆▬◆▬◆▬◆▬◆▬◆▬◆▬◆▬◆▬◆▬◆▬◆▬◆▬◆▬◆

For almost 2,000 years, doctors believed in humours. For the entirety of that 1,000 year span, they were wrong. Sandwiched between Socrates and Aristotle was the ancient Greek philosopher Plato who, among the numerous scholarly achievements he was to be credited with, was the first to coin the phrase "elements." From there, he described Air, Fire, Earth, and Water. And although Aristotle wrote the "Categories" in 357 BCE, it was Hippocrates, the father of medicine, who further extended the thinking of Plato's elements to the human body.

The Four Humours represented the inner workings of the human body, providing balance and health. These physical elements: blood (which represented the air and spring gave us a feeling of amorousness and hope), yellow bile (which was assigned the element fire and the season of summer was largely associated with the proper workings of the gall bladder), black bile (which caused sleeplessness and overall irritability suggesting an affinity with the earth and autumn) and phlegm (which was recorded by Galen, who is blamed for all of this misunderstanding in the first place, tied water and winter to this calm and unemotional bodily element).

 What the Experts Say Yet when one of the two contraries is a constitutive property of the subject, as it is a constitutive property of fire to be hot, of snow to be white, it is necessary determinately that one of the two contraries, not one or the other, should be present in the subject; for fire cannot be cold, or snow black.— Aristotle, from "Categories"

Only when science replaced leaps of imagination did these medical foundations crumble. The world of high finance is always looking for new and interesting ways to attract the interest of the average investor. Often it is without good reason or benefit to the people it is designed to help. Just as doctors—right up until the middle of the 20th century they believed that the humours may be a cause of what ailed their patients, investors continue to ascribe to old wisdoms ignoring new opportunities for wealth.

Your Retirement Plan—on the Outside

I haven't exactly warned you away from life-cycle funds (or their similar but distinct counterpart, the lifestyle fund), but I certainly didn't suggest you give them much more of a passing glance. The reasons for this are simple and twofold. They create complacency and they may not do what they are intended to do.

The new pension law I mentioned earlier has made access to these types of funds increasingly easy. As many as 40 percent of the 401(k) plans now offer a basket of life-cycle funds to their participants.

They are usually listed by the year you plan on retiring. A 35 year old might choose a fund with a target date of 30 years out, labeled as a (year) 2040 fund. This kind of fund targets the auto-pilot set, giving them an "invest and go" opportunity.

Because they are a kind of fund full of funds, the underlying fees can actually be higher than had you invested in each fund separately. The category average, driven down by some front-end loaded funds, a good option for this type of investment is around 0.75 percent demands you do your shopping.

When kept outside of your retirement plan, this type of fund gives you the opportunity to pay the capital gains taxes at today's rate (15% until 2011 when it will convert back to 20%) while still growing the investment. Many funds in this category summarize their goals as high total return (which in financial jargon means conservative) and capital appreciation (which means some growth through the equities they are holding on an ever-diminishing basis). By the time you tap these funds, you might have as little as a 20–30 percent exposure to stocks. This is enough to satisfy the critics who think your retirement portfolio is *too* aggressive.

	Ticker	Annual return
Life-cycle funds		
Over the last five years		
Fidelity Freedom 2040	FFFFX	12.27%
Principal Inv LifeTime 2050 Instl	PPLIX	11.89%
Over the last three years		
T. Rowe Price Retirement 2040	TRRDX	14.44%
T. Rowe Price Retirement 2035	TRRJX	14.40%
T. Rowe Price Retirement 2030	TRRCX	14.36%

Lifestyle funds, often confused with life-cycle funds, act somewhat differently. They focus on a risk tolerance and build their underlying basket of investments based on that—much like we did in the preceding chapter with our Early Bird, Chaser, and Relaxer. In fact, they tend to be described as blended or core funds.

A Bonding Experience

Another key investment that should be kept outside your retirement plan but is key to its success is your bond account. I prefer to invest in this conservative investment using a bond fund. Bond funds provide the average investor with certain strategies that are hard to replicate.

Distrust and caution are the parents of security.— Benjamin Franklin

A bond manager, hired to protect your assets, can ladder your exposure to economic turbulence and take advantage of instances when the markets reward the conservative investor.

What is laddering? Laddering refers to a method of investing in fixed income securities, usually certificates of deposit (CD) or bonds. Because these investments come with varying maturity dates—a reference to when the

Continued

time period of the investment expires and you are due the interest, it is important to not have all of your money come due at the same time. Because these types of investments are interest rate and inflation sensitive, you may not get a good deal at the time of maturity and reinvestment because of some economic event. To protect yourself, you stagger your purchases or ladder them so, when one comes due, the rest of your money is still at work. Most of us lack the savvy to do this. Mutual funds specializing in bonds can achieve this at much lower cost.

Bond funds kept on the outside of a retirement plan can be helpful in avoiding inflation while conserving any wealth you may be accumulating in them.

Inflation, as we have found out in numerous examples so far, does not offer a friendly hand to any investment it encounters. Stocks may be beating inflation now, but when you begin to withdraw them to finance your retirement years, you will feel the pinch. In the back of everyone's mind, we should always be concerned with the potential of falling behind. While the focus is often on getting ahead, inflation works the same way debt does, against us.

Traditionally, inflation worries sent investors flocking toward gold and real estate. These seemed to be safe havens and, in some ways, still remain that way. And while we could talk for hours as to why those inflation-friendly investments may not be what they used to be, there are alternatives to winning the battle with this insidious economic force.

In the case of bonds, you run the risk of buying these paper financial instruments with money that is worth less when the bond matures. To this end, inflation indexed bonds or I-bonds offer a unique opportunity to protect against the continual erosion of the value of the bond.

The one upside to these bonds and the funds that use them (a short list appears below) is not only the fixed rate of interest, which can be less than high-yielding bonds, but the payment you received is adjusted for inflation. The downside: the inflation that is reported and ultimately used as the inflation adjuster may not be a true reflection of what your original investment is worth. But using them is better than taking your chances.

Can I buy I-Bonds individually, and how do they compare with series EE bonds?
Yes, you can buy I-Bonds from any US Treasury outlet. They earn interest for up to 30 years and come in a variety of extremely affordable denominations: $50, $75, $100, $200, $500, $1,000, $5,000, and $10,000. They must be held for at least a year, are free of state and local taxes and federal tax obligations do not kick in until you cash them. Individuals can purchase up to $30,000 worth of I-Bonds in a single year, per person. Because you buy them at face value, you can cash them whenever you need them. This makes them ideal for accounts designed to hedge against medical emergencies.

The main difference, aside from the built in inflation protection, is in the upfront cost. Series EE bonds are sold at half of their face value; I-Bonds are sold at face value.

Inflation protected bond funds are conservative by nature. They are designed to give the investor a total return that is worthwhile and do that while protecting the investor's capital. Expenses tend to be low, the category averages around 0.93 percent. One problem with these funds tends to be with the high, often outrageously so, initial investment outside of an IRA account. Because they are a buy-and-hold investment with good tax implications, using them in a Roth IRA often is best.

	Ticker	Annual return
Inflation protected bond funds		
Over the last five years		
FFTW US Inflation-Indexed Adv	FFIHX	6.37%
Vanguard Inflation-Protected Secs	VIPSX	5.88%
Over the last three years		
Western Asset Inflation Indxd Plus Bd	WAIIX	4.27%
Vanguard Inflation-Protected Secs Instl	VIPIX	3.75%
PIMCO Real Return Instl	PRRIX	3.64%

On a Foreign Soil

Proof that the world is getting smaller and our appetite for risk keeps increasing is the ever easy, and increasingly inexpensive, access we now have to marketplaces in other lands. While some portfolio managers sing the praises of expanding your risk horizons in a global way, I'm not so sure that international funds should be anywhere but in your mad money account—the one you set up with funds that never get replenished.

There is too much dilution in what would be considered domestic and what is referred to as foreign. Companies have spread themselves across the planet to take advantage of supply chains, cheaper manufacturing, and any other number of production enhancing tools. Is a company domestic if only its tax registration has a Delaware address but a global presence?

Much of the criticism of economic globalization has centered on factory labor abuses. But the majority of the world's poor are not employed in factories; they are self-employed—as peasant farmers, rural peddlers, urban hawkers, and small producers, usually involved in agriculture and small trade in the world's vast "informal" economy ('informal' because economists have difficulty measuring it).—David Bornstein

If you don't know the answer, it is "yes," and it is how you play globally while getting the protections that are currently in place in this country. Those regulations may be eroding as some forces in Washington attempt to lower regulatory standards to attract more foreign interest but, for now, they do what they were designed to do.

Because of the uncertainty in some parts of the world, the instability of stock exchanges in some emerging markets and the growing thirst for risk among hedge funds, global investing runs high on the scale for what is acceptable risk. Because some of that risk does not avail itself to the measure of "past performances," the investor, no matter how aggressive, should not expose their portfolio in foreign investments beyond 20 percent of the total. Once again, this type of fund should be kept in an account with limited crossover access. In other words, the temptation to feed an account that poses this much risk with cash from more conservative investments is something we battle as humans. Do what you can to battle that "mental maniac" by keeping them separate from your regular investments, or buy American. You probably are buying globally by default.

Here is a look at some of the global funds that are best kept in a separate account—away from your emergency funds, away from your tax-deferred retirement accounts, away from your conservative accounts kept outside your funds—the ones with bond funds and index funds. The expense ratio for these funds averages close to 1.58 percent (but expect upward of 2.5 percent for the best performers in the sector) and, almost ironically, these funds all tend to invest in US companies as well as global ventures.

	Ticker	Annual return
Global funds		
Over the last five years		
Evergreen Global Opportunities I	EKGYX	22.23%
AIM Global Aggressive Growth A	AGAAX	20.53%
Over the last three years		
Alger China US Growth	CHUSX	30.70%
Evergreen Global Opportunities I	EKGYX	27.76%
DWS Global Thematic A	SGQAX	26.98%

The Annuitized Retirement

Imagine what it must have been like for Antony van Leeuwenhoek, an everyman if there ever was one. He discovered, without the aid of any university degrees or higher education, bacteria, protists (a microscopic parasite that is classified by what it is not: plant, animal, or fungus), sperm cells, and blood cells.

Although van Leeuwenhoek did not invent the microscope, his observations allowed him to be given the moniker "father of observational microbiology." He was shocked at the "wee beasties" living in a drop of water.

... my work, which I've done for a long time, was not pursued in order to gain the praise I now enjoy, but chiefly from a craving after knowledge, which I notice resides in me more than in most other men. And therewithal, whenever I found out anything remarkable, I have thought it my duty to put down my discovery on paper, so that all ingenious people might be informed thereof.
—Antony van Leeuwenhoek

The Subtle Differences

Very few of the topics we have talked about so far have two sides. They all have their role in retirement planning and, for want of a better phrase, play a "what you see is what you get" role in the process. They have qualities that are clear and definable: it is either tax deferred or its not, it is risky or its not, it is a mistake or it is not. But annuities exist in a netherworld of possibilities, each with their own nagging query, "what if."

Fixed or variable? Deferred or immediate? Qualified or nonqualified? Single or flexible premium? Fixed period, fixed amount, or lifetime? Regulated or not? Investment or insurance?

I have referred to you as an investor for the whole of this section for good reason. Each step along the way dealt with real decisions about what to invest, where to put that money and why. But with a conversation about annuities, you are now the annuitant.

The simplest definition of this product is based upon how it pays you, the annuitant. Annuities are a contract with an insurance company. In the US, this contract is deferred until you annuitize it and begin taking regular monthly payments. In this regard, it has all of the characteristics of a pension.

The Rules of the Game

The Internal Revenue Service defines *annuities* in the US (European annuity buyers face a slightly different terminology and regulations) in publication 575 as a fully taxable payout (http://www.irs.gov/publications/p575/ar02.html#d0e402). States have jurisdiction over the product, falling under the regulatory eye of the insurance commissioner.

Because each state independently regulates the product, not all features are available in every state. The IRS cares only about the taxable treatment of the contract, not how it is structured. And while the IRS taxes your payout as income, it does not have any impact on the principal. That has already been taxed, in many cases, thereby leaving only the gains on the underlying investment subject to taxation.

Here's how they work—the simple version first. You receive a lump sum payment and, rather than taking the tax hit now, you purchase an annuity contract from an insurance company. At the time of purchase, you designate who will receive the periodic, usually monthly, payments for the life of the annuity. Often, the payments continue if there is a spouse involved and do so until one or both recipients die.

These structured payments can be fixed or can increase over time depending on the kind of contract you sign. A fixed annuity has a designated payout period. During that time, you or your heirs will receive a payment, usually monthly. Think of the lottery. If you were to win a $1,000,000 prize, unless you had chosen to get the money in a lump sum, you would have received what amounts to an annuitized payment over 20 years. The state buys an annuity with the winning money and gives you a yearly payment. Taxes are paid upon receipt of the money and are taxed as ordinary income.

Businesses do much the same when they offer you a pension. They determine how long you might live based on actuarial tables. They can then purchase an annuity guaranteeing you a steady stream of payout over the remaining portion of your life. Pension plans manage the money as an investment until the time you decide to draw on it and then your pension becomes, in many cases, an immediate fixed annuity.

Once you make the decision to annuitize your money, the agreement you make with the insurance company is quite simple. As long as you are alive, you will receive the agreed upon payment. When you die, there is nothing for your heirs and the payments stop. Insurance companies, employing actuarial tables, can pinpoint with uncanny accuracy when you will die. The resulting payout is then calculated based on that information.

Fixed or Variable

The attraction of annuities is based on two things: the first is your belief that you cannot adequately manage your money in retirement and want to protect the capital and, secondly, the hope that you outlive the annuity. Those two items can be addressed with a bond fund or laddered bonds held in a portfolio.

Bonds can give the investor liquidity—meaning that, should you have the need to, you may tap that capital for a medical emergency or a new car; you cannot do that once the money is tied up in an annuity. Bonds, on the other hand, particularly I-Bonds, which protect against inflation, can be cashed at any time once they are purchased, giving the owner full face value.

If you worry that you may not be able to manage that money yourself or worry that this might be a problem further down the road, a trust or a trustee can provide many of the same services an annuity offers while keeping your money liquid.

The **variable annuity,** on the other hand, has some additional features that might at first glance seem attractive. They act as an insurance policy *and* an investment, although when a marriage of opposites like these come together, the compromises can be substantial.

There is the tax-deferred nature of the earnings. This can also be had in a conservative mutual fund loaded with government bonds or balance towards capital preservation rather than capital appreciation.

A variable annuity, or VA, has an insurance component as well giving your beneficiaries the remaining balance upon your death. The underlying investment is placed in a mutual fund and treated just like an IRA. But that is where the two products part ways.

We have discussed the tax deductibility of an IRA at length. Annuities do not offer that feature. Annuities do not restrict how much you can deposit. IRAs have strict limits on the amount of money you may put away in a given year.

Because there are often investments involved in variable annuity contracts, whether they be bonds or stocks (in the form of mutual funds), the return is also calculated when determining the annual (or monthly) payout. For instance, a $100,000 annuity returning 6 percent —which seems modest, but these investments tied to annuities are not designed for growth or value but consistency of return and those returns are often further bogged down by higher than normal fees on the investment itself—would net the annuitant about $8,200 a year or $700 a month. Because this is an insurance product, those numbers will vary depending on how well you are doing healthwise. Fixed annuities also offer a rate of return, although it is often substantially lower.

For investors who fall into the Relaxer group and may have huge sums of money that cannot be put in a IRA or a 401(k) plan, variable annuities offer some interesting options. The insurance portion of the annuity is often the subject of criticism in these contracts. Because of it, you are paying additional and often unnecessary fees for a product that you do not need.

I had mentioned earlier that index funds should not be kept inside a tax-deferred retirement account. Because of the low turnover (a term that refers to the frequency in which the stock in the fund are traded — it is often expressed as a percentage, with actively managed funds turning over their portfolios as much as 100 percent in a given year), and the favorable tax environment for capital gains and dividends we currently enjoy, index funds are just better outside of those types of plans.

They are also a better option for people considering annuities. Taxes, among the most derisive effects of investing, are a consideration as well. In an annuity, you are taxed on all growth as income—and so are your heirs. An index fund does not have any tax implications for those inheriting the fund because of an asset treatment called "stepped up basis."

What is a stepped-up basis? According to Nolo.com, it is "a value that is used to determine profit or loss when property is sold." If someone inherits property that has increased in value since the deceased person acquired it, the tax basis of the new owner is "stepped-up" to the market value of the property at the time of death. The stepped-up basis means that, when the property is eventually sold, there will be less taxable gain." In your index fund, the IRS treats it as if you just purchased it at the time of inheritance, not the original balance at the time the fund was purchased. There will be more on this shortly when we discuss wills and estates.

The tax system also penalizes you should you decide to withdraw the annuity. The IRS will tax you on the full face value of the annuity until you bring it down to the original value of the purchase.

Also adding to the argument against these products, as if the shoddy tax treatment weren't enough reason to buy an index or bond fund instead, the fees charged to the underlying investment are substantially higher. Most index funds charge rock bottom fees. Although the industry average is 1.13 percent, most index funds charge far less and do so without loads.

The insurance product associated with annuities is not what it purports to be either. It only pays you if your investment falters significantly and falls below your original investment and you happen to die before you get a chance to annuitize the contract (determine the fixed monthly payout over X amount of years). If you feel as though you need insurance, buy a term policy. (But chances are, once you retire, you will not need to pay premiums to protect your loved ones. Drop your disability policy as well. This can add hundreds of dollars to your monthly income.)

Judging the Worth

The contracts associated with annuities are generally among the most complicated you will ever encounter. For this reason alone, someone interested should be wary. But because we are focused on what the contract offers, we tend to overlook what the contract will cost us.

Many people find out the hard way. They purchase annuity with all of the good intentions we bring to many of life's decisions. We hope for the best, control what we can, and trust that there is someone out there watching out for our wellbeing. The someone is not the agent selling you the contract.

People like to feel they are buying of their own good judgment as a result of the information the salesman has given them.—Paul Parker

While annuities do have a tax-deferred element, they are only as good as the rest of your plan. If you have access to a 401(k), take advantage of that first. Open an IRA if you do not have access to a 401(k) or similar plan at work and use a variable annuity as the investment of last choice if you are seeking tax-deferred status for your investment.

In many cases, agents will suggest and even point out the similarities between plans as they encourage you to roll your 401(k) or IRA into a

VA product. You will lose all of the flexibility you have with the other tax-deferred plans and, in return, you will get fees.

It is important to remember that one you initiate the annuitization process, you are essentially altering the contract. And to get your "lifetime income stream" you need to do exactly that.

Annuities give you a baffling array of options that pile fees on top of fees. The temptations of regular paychecks for life, you gambling against the insurance company in a slow crawl to the finish line, the chance at winning where few have won before, make the choices doubly difficult. You want an income stream—for life. The insurance company agrees but (and they don't come right out and tell you this), if you die during the annuitizing period (also known as the annuitization phase), the insurance company gets it all. The money you built up belongs to them not your heirs. That phase lasts until you die. So the annuity is yours until you die. Or you can buy a "term-certain annuity." That contract gives you and your spouse an income stream—for both for at least ten years—and if you both die before the term is over, the money in the annuity belongs to the insurer. Perhaps you want to do something better than that? Insurance companies, prying on that moment of future vision when you see all of your hard-earned money going to some corporate giant while your surviving spouse drifts into poverty, have developed a product for you: life income with term certain. This is basically a longer term certain contract and income stream for life—for just a few more fees.

In Sheep's Clothing

Variable annuities are many things offering numerous benefits, each with its own price tag. But what they are not is a mutual fund. They may have the components of a mutual fund: stock and bonds. If you held a mutual fund in a tax-deferred account such as an IRA, you would pay penalties and taxes for withdrawing your money before age 59½. If you held it outside a tax-deferred account, which I have suggested as an option to purchasing annuities in the first place, you would pay capital gains taxes only. With a VA, those taxes are at your current income tax rate plus, just for good measure, you will also pay a surrender charge.

A surrender charge is like a second thought penalty. You may, after buying the annuity, decide that you need the money or simply are disillusioned with the promised returns (more on that in just a bit) and you want out. If it happens in the first year, you will surrender 7 percent of the annuity. Each year after that, the penalty declines in one percent increments.

Even after all we have discussed in this book, I cannot keep you from worrying. You will worry about whether you made the right decision. You will also worry about whether your investments are performing adequately enough to meet your goals 10, 20, or 30 years down the road. It's not healthy but we tend to do it anyway.

Insurance companies understand this is as well. For another half of a percentage point in fees, you can be protected from poor market performance. If you were to put a price tag on that worry it would look like this: A $100,000 annuity × 0.5 (the cost of the fee to cover your concern)= $500.

Besides the cost of such a guarantee, known as a Guaranteed Minimum Income Benefit, the insurance company, like you, would be scrambling to cover its own losses. Long-term investors know that investments will take some dips along with the increases. It is what allows you to buy more with the same amount of money using dollar-cost averaging; less when the markets are sullen.

The insurance industry continues to evolve their product lines offering additional features with new annuities. In an effort to get you to move money from your old annuity to a new one, they may try to sell you on the tax-free exchange using a 1035. Unlike a 401(k) rollover, this is not as clearcut as it sounds. In other words, hidden fees.

What to Ask? What is a 1035 exchange? It is basically an offer to try an annuity that may have features your old contract does not. And while the new annuity might have a wider range of investment products (posing as mutual funds with higher fees) or better payout choices or even a heftier death benefit, the surrender charge renews itself, with the new contract enacting a new seven-year lock on any second thoughts you might have.

Before we move on to our next topic, I worry just like you. I worry that people will still see some redeeming value in an annuity. They will look past the fees that whittle away at their earnings, they will glaze over as they think of living to be a 100 years old and beating the insurer at their own game and, finally,

I worry that they won't read the whole contract, much of which is not readily understood even by many financial professionals. I worry that they won't see annuities as a snare. I worry that they haven't paid attention when I emphasized the need for liquidity, something virtually every other thing I mentioned in this book provides.

The 403(b) and 457 Plans

It is often suggested that a 403(b) and 457 plans are just like a 401(k), except for the fact that public employees, some nonprofits, and self-employed ministers, primarily use 403(b) plans. Okay, almost the same.

 What to Say! The Employee Retirement Income Security Act of 1974, often referred to by its acronym ERISA, is responsible for setting minimum standards for pension plans, 401(k) plans, 403(b) plans and 457 plans. It protects employee pensions, enforces vesting periods, regulates corporate behavior concerning pensions and was responsible for creating the Pension Benefit Guaranty Corporation (PBGC). It does not require employers to create plans for their employees but ensures that plans are capable of fulfilling the promises they may have made.

Positioning the conversation about 403(b) plans after annuities is no accident. Annuities have been the retirement vehicle for many of these plans throughout the years. Because 403(b) plans do not need to be qualified by the IRS the same way as 401(k) plans do, they generally have universal availability, making it easier for insurance companies to accommodate the need for some sort of tax-deferred product.

Let's do a side-by-side comparison of 401(k) plans with 403(b) plans.

401(k)	403(b)
Employer must set up and administer	Do not require employer involvement
Employees take their 401(k) funds	Employers allow funds to stay
Requires significant administration	Little employer administration
Vesting periods of up to 3 years	Vesting is automatic

Over 80 percent of the investors in 403(b) plans rely on annuities. Of that amount, one-third had some sort of VA product in use. With the high costs of maintaining VA accounts, many 403(b) plan users are at a significant disadvantage compared to their 401(k) counterparts. This is changing, however. With the addition of paragraph 7 by Congress in 1974, employers were allowed to do business with mutual fund companies. Unfortunately, the monetary incentives offered by insurers have kept their grasp on this group. New regulations have been created—the first in 40 years—bring the employer's fiduciary responsibility closer to that of the 401(k) administrator.

The 457 plan does have similar attributes to a 403(b), or at least one of them does. The 457(b), like the 403(b), allows you to save tax-deferred for your retirement. Unlike the 403(b), the money in the plan is not protected from creditors. This may come as shock to the rest of the retirement planners but a 457(b) plan can actually be held if your employer runs into financial difficulty. But you can have both plans taking advantage of the maximum deduction.

There is another type of 457 plan, the 457(f). This acts as a delayed compensation plan, allowing you to save an unlimited amount of pretax income. But once again, it is risky business if your employer is on shaky ground.

Health Savings Accounts

Recently legislated changes to Health Savings Accounts, or HSAs, have improved how these plans work. Designed in much the same way as your tax-deferred retirement plan, an HSA is an account where you can save money tax-deferred, with tax-free earnings, with tax-free distributions, and with the ability to take the account from job to job.

The funds in these accounts are exclusively for medical expenses. The contributions you make to this type of an account can grow until you need them. In the past, policyholders could not save any more in these accounts than their health insurance policy deductible. Now, single policyholders can save $2,850 per year in their accounts while families can save $5,650, starting in 2007.

My own prescription for health is less paperwork and more running barefoot through the gras.—Leslie Grimutter

These plans are available to anyone who wants to open one, with some exceptions. You must not be currently entitled to Medicare benefits, be under age 65, and/or in a qualified health plan.

The key to Health Savings Accounts was the use of high-deductible health plans. To open an account, your qualified health plans must include a deductible of at least $1,000 and a cap of no more than $5,100 on out-of-pocket expenses for individuals, and a deductible of at least $2,000 and a cap of no more than $10,200 on out-of-pocket expenses for families.

In 2006, Congress approved some very costly changes to these plans. Employers can now contribute more to these plans if their employees make less than $100,000. But the biggest and most expensive change comes with the treatment of IRA accounts.

There is now a one-time roll over exemption for IRA accounts into an HSA. This could be a potential win-win situation for a wealthy retiree. In many instances, an IRA, with it's ceiling on contributions, would have been taxed at a higher rate than less well-to-do retirees. Allowing these retirement plans to rollover tax free into a plan that can offset medical bills could cost taxpayers over $700 million over the next 10 years. Generally though, rollovers are only permitted when the funds come from other HSA accounts or from Medical Savings Accounts (MSA).

How do you invest the money in an HSA? HSAs offer many of the same investment options as other tax-deferred accounts. You may use stocks, bonds, mutual funds, or other types of investments such as fixed income accounts. The important thing to remember is that they must be used for medical expenses and only after the deductible is met.

The Employee Benefit Research Institute, along with a private research group, the Commonwealth Fund, reported recently that only 37 percent of the people who are eligible for such plans actually use them. Why, if so few people are using these kinds of plans, did Congress make changes to benefit so few?

Critics have been quick to point out that those enrolled tended to make poor decisions on when to use the plans, often deferring medical assistance until a later date. The high deductible is often cited as reason folks have avoided these plans and, as result, seem unwilling to use even basic services.

While the use of these plans is limited—currently only 7 percent of employers offer these consumer driven types of savings accounts for insurance, the belief that expanding these programs will widen the coverage of those currently uninsured is not well founded.

One last note about these plans. Do not get them confused with an FSA, or Flexible Spending Account. These accounts are employer funded and cannot accumulate a higher balance from year-to-year. Often referred to as the *use it or lose it* health account, the employee is given 12 months (with a 2½ month grace period at the end of that year) to use the money for medical purposes. If that money is not used, the employer does not add more in the next calendar year.

A much better idea for employer-funded plans is the Health Reimbursement Arrangement. Also unlike the HSA, these HRA plans do not involve any employee deduction although, and this is a big although, you may be able to exclude the amount of your employer's contribution from your gross income. Unused amounts can be carried forward and reimbursements may also be tax free for medical expenses.

The Windfall

 It is commonly observed that a sudden wealth, like a prize drawn in a lottery or a large bequest to a poor family, does not permanently enrich. They have served no apprenticeship to wealth, and with the rapid wealth come rapid claims which they do not know how to deny, and the treasure is quickly dissipated.
— Ralph Waldo Emerson

You may go through life without ever "coming into money." On the other hand, you may bump into a significant sum from the sale of house, a divorce or insurance settlement, a court award, lottery winnings, or from an inheritance. I would, if I may, like to offer a few words to explain the importance of this kind of (un)expected windfall.

We are worlds away from a time in history when wealth was merely a gifted state. There were many opportunities for inheritance depending on how you positioned yourself in line. *Vanity Fair*, William Thackeray's tale of social positioning, greed and idleness, deceit and hypocrisy, subtitled *A Novel without a Hero,* is often how we view life among the wealthy and the aristocratic.

Thackeray, acting as narrator, told his serialized story of consumed protagonist Becky Sharpe to enthralled nineteenth-century readers, many of whom had no chance of attaining sudden wealth. Her tale of jockeying for a better spot in financial line remains a fantasy to this day. Only these days, the line is at the lottery machine.

It may surprise you, but I have no problem with an occasional ticket here and there. It lends our overworked, under-vacationed minds a chance to take a flight of fancy. But what if we won? What if we came into some of the big jackpot, missing the multimillions by a single digit? What if we suddenly get a sizable chunk of money, not life changing but significant enough to make a difference?

Fortunately, most of us think about how that wealth will impact our families, setting up our own list of who we should give what to and how much. But this kind of windfall should be the shot-in-the-arm many of our retirement plans need.

If you have won/inherited/realized a sizable amount money, get a tax attorney and make a plan. If the sum is enough to pay down your debt and give you a clean slate, I highly suggest you do that—before re-entering the ranks of consumerism.

The Estate

Navigating the world of finance is difficult enough; but having experience in the world of law is another thing altogether. You count on legislators to work for you, although at times it seems as if it is the other way around. You count on the systems in place to protect you. But it is up to you to protect your wealth.

The easiest way to do that is by taking some simple steps that are surprisingly economical if you consider the amount of protection they provide compared to the dollars spent. Most of us are not leaving huge estates but, if we grew our retirement funds wisely, and we didn't outlive that nest egg, we will want to pass whatever remains in those accounts on to our heirs. And, even more important, we want to take the legal steps now to protect ourselves should our health fail unexpectedly.

We are going to discuss several ways to help those you love deal with the world you have created by navigating those legal waters and mapping a strategy. This is the last piece of your retirement plan.

Making a will without a doubt is the single most important document you can draft. It is a soul searching endeavor that many of us avoid until we feel as though we have something worth inheriting. If you have a life insurance policy, you have a need for a will.

Death is not the end. There remains the litigation over the estate.
—Ambrose Bierce

A will is a legal document that outlives our wishes about how we would like our property divided once we die, who gets what, who will execute those wishes, who will watch the kids and the property you bequeath them.

People still die without wills. In many cases, the property goes to a surviving spouse but in the event that transfer is not possible, the state is the entity left to make the decisions you could have easily made had you taken the time. If there are young children, the state will decide who will be responsible for their wellbeing. In the event you are living in a relationship, whether it be recognized as legal by the state you live in or not, a will can give direction. Without it, your domestic partner is not considered by the state as "in-line." Those laws are gradually changing and have done so in several states. A will takes the decision out of the judge's hands.

You do not need a lawyer to make a will, although the cost is relatively low and it can be your first contact with someone you might need to call on again in the future. If you do not hire an attorney, check with the number of witnesses your state requires to be present at the signing and whether their signatures need to be notarized.

What is a notary? By their full title they are Public Notary and are people who have been authorized to witness signatures (and oaths) by placing their embossed stamp recording the event.

Your witnesses will attest to the soundness of your mind should they be questioned or the will be challenged. If you hire an attorney, they will keep a copy of your will at their offices and give you a copy for safekeeping. (This document goes into your safe deposit box along with insurance papers, deeds, mortgages and any other valuable paperwork surrounding your life. You do have a safe deposit box?)

If you draft the will yourself, and many people with simple estates can do so without too much difficulty, be sure to name an executor to manage your wishes. And don't handwrite it! Holographic wills, as they are called, are often scrutinized in great detail by the probate judge examining the will. Best advice: get the lawyer to do it for you. Come prepared—time is money with these folks. Bring your lists and dispersal percentages with you.

In many states, intestacy laws apply where no will is present. Most states award the entire estate to the surviving spouse if there are no descendants. Wills simply streamline the process. Spouses cannot be disinherited. Many states have laws that provide for a spousal elective share of the estate even if the will states otherwise. Children, on the other hand, can be disinherited but only if the will specifically states your intentions to do so. But children who were born after you made the will, and were not specifically named in it, have a claim to a portion of the estate. Best advice: get a lawyer.

You should revisit the will every five years or so. My wife and I do it then and whenever we plan a trip overseas together. In many cases, it involves a simple shift in percentages (perhaps one child will need the financial boost more than another; a grandchild is born; a charity is named) or the addition of a piece of property requires you to direct who gets it or what you want done with it.

You should consider a **trust,** but only if you have someone who is need of special care. Giving money directly to someone can impact their ability to draw Social Security insurance or Medicaid benefits. The trust is actually the beneficiary, overseen by a trustee, and that legal arrangement keeps the money outside of that person's possession but under the guidance of the trustee. Best advice: get a lawyer.

One of the most overlooked documents you can create to protect your loved ones is a **health care directive**. This requires far more self-searching than a will does and is doubly important. We run a higher risk of facing a debilitating injury that leaves us unable to make pertinent health decisions than we do with dying.

This is not just for those approaching old age. It is for the young as well. The National Hospice and Palliative Care Organization offers a free link to connect you with your state's individual requirements (www.nhpco.org/). This important document should also be revisited every five years or so in the event that the person you have named in the directive is no longer available on short notice, or you change your mind about how you want the directive applied. Keep a copy with the person you have chosen or in a place where it can be found in an emergency.

The conversation we had about insurance earlier focused on your health. Life insurance plays a role in your retirement planning but only for a certain amount of years. As you build your retirement plan, insurance protects you from an unforeseen event that could derail that plan.

What the Experts Say

Another good thing about being poor is that when you are 70 your children will not have declared you legally insane in order to gain control of your estate.
— Woody Allen

For that reason, you should buy **term life insurance coverage** and not for much more than your balance on your mortgage, the average cost of your children's college education, and to cover any immediate needs your surviving spouse might have. The temptation is to set them up for life, but that is a costly waste of money. Social Security will provide your spouse and children with a monthly income. Your pensions and your retirement funds will be there as well.

The money you saved from overinsuring yourself can be directed to those retirement accounts where it will grow much faster and provide a better long-term benefit. The younger you are, the cheaper the policy and the greater the temptation to get more coverage than you need. The older you are, the temptation to leave your family a legacy amount of money will drain additional dollars from your real goal: saving as much as you can for retirement. In most cases, a $500,000 to $1 million policy is more than adequate.

Ignore the offers for whole life—a policy that creates a cash balance that can be used to pay premiums after a certain point, and variable life—a sort of hybrid between the two and, by all means, never make your term policy permanent. That money would be better spent on health care coverage, shoring up your daily expenses, and/or paying taxes.

If you own a business, chances are there is already insurance and possibly a provision in your will in place to cover any unforeseen tragedies. If not, now is a good time to do so. Best advice: get a lawyer.

And lastly, the tax question. Depending on how big your estate is—if it is valued in excess of $1 million —per spouse, you might consider developing a plan to thwart the IRS—legally of course. Current laws are changing. An individual can leave their heirs a tax-free amount up to $2 million in 2008 and up to $3.5 million in 2009. In 2010, it will supposedly be repealed altogether, putting it back down to $1 million.

Some Final Thoughts

I apologize if this has been a sobering journey. There are few ways to paint a rosy picture of what is ahead—especially when none of us has a clue exactly what our futures hold.

Much of what we consider our destiny is, now more than ever, in our own hands. This will, if trends continue, increase more as we get older.

You will notice that I made no mention of strategies for *after* your retire. That in itself is a book length discussion we may have in the near future.

Instead we focused on many of the obstacles in your path to that place. The strategies you develop will be and should be constantly discussed. My wife and I do it with great regularity as we age and the children leave the house. It is called dreaming. Retirement planning is your attempt at making those dreams tangible and real.

Best of luck!

Glossary of Investment Terms

Aggressive growth: Investment category seeking maximum capital appreciation by purchasing stocks believed to offer rapid growth potential or by employing risky trading strategies. These funds generally are high-risk and volatile.

Asset: Anything of value owned by a business or individual.

Asset allocation: Investment category seeking both income and capital appreciation by shifting assets between stocks, bonds, and cash to achieve the optimal return. Whereas a balanced fund (fixed allocation) maintains a fixed percentage of stocks to bonds, asset allocation funds are not tied to a specific asset ratio. Also called *flexible allocation*.

Assumed investment rate: Rate that must be assumed for the purpose of setting premiums and statutory reserves for a guaranteed minimum death benefit. The premiums are those which flow into a separate account.

Balanced fund: Mutual fund that strives for stability by maintaining a constant ratio of equity to debt securities, usually 60/40 percent. Also called *fixed allocation*.

Blue chip: Common stock of a large company with a record of stable growth and earnings over an extended period.

Breakpoint: Dollar-value where the sales charge percentage changes in a schedule of load-fees. Typically, a sales charge schedule contains five or six breakpoints with the commission declining as the dollars invested rise.

Broker: Person who buys and sells securities on behalf of others, receiving a commission for each exchange. *See also* Dealer.

Call: Tradable security derived from a prediction of a stock's price movement. A specialist on an options exchange can create a "call," or an option to buy a stock within a limited time frame and sell at a set, higher price (the "call price"). The call option can now can be traded and its value will fluctuate as the underlying stock moves. The opposite of a Call option is a Put. Option contracts and other derivatives may be used either for speculative or "hedging" purposes.

Capital: Material assets of a business, including plant and equipment, inventories, cash, receivables, etc.

Capital gains: Profits realized from the sale of securities that have appreciated while being held. Long-term capital gains are from securities held for more than one year; Short-term capital gains are from securities held one year or less.

Capital gains distribution: Payment to investment company shareholders from capital gains realized on shares held.

Capital gains tax rates: Under present law, all short-term capital gains are taxed as ordinary income. Although the maximum tax rate for individuals, estates and trusts can be as high as 39.6 percent, the tax on long-term capital gains is guaranteed by law not to exceed 15 percent through 2010. *See* Capital gains.

Capital growth: Increase in market value of securities.

Cash position: State of a company's fiscal situation comparing cash to total net assets.

Certificates of deposit: Bank or thrift note guaranteeing that a sum of money will be held by the bank for a fixed period of time and will earn a pre-arranged interest rate. CDs issued in euros can be purchased by foreign branches of US banks or foreign banks with branches in the United States.

Check-writing privilege: Ability to write a check and have the money drawn from an investment account, such as a money market. The holdings will continue to earn dividends until checks are cleared.

Closed-end investment company: Investment company that trades on the open market and holds a fixed number of shares in the form of investments as stated in its objective. The market value of the closed-end fund will usually differ from value of its holdings.

Closed-up fund: Open-end investment company that trades actively but does not accept deposits from new investors. It may continue to invest the money of current shareholders.

Common stock: Security representing partial ownership of a corporation and therefore normally carries voting rights. Should a company liquidate, the claims of a common stockholder rank below those of bond, debt, and preferred stockholders because the company's creditors receive compensation before the owners.

Common stock fund: Investment fund whose portfolio consists primarily of common stocks.

Contingent deferred sales charge (CDSC): A fee payable *when shares are* redeemed. *See* Load fee, Back-end load. Also called *trailers* or *redemption fee*.

Contractual plan: Type of accumulation plan under which the total intended investment amount and periodic payments to reach that amount are specified at the time of purchase. The sales charge corresponds to the total amount to be invested, and usually is deducted from the initial payments.

Contrarian: Investor who attempts to move against major market trends at any given time, searching for undiscovered opportunities.

Controlled affiliate: Company in which 25 percent or more of the outstanding voting securities are controlled by one source, as stipulated in the Investment Company Act of 1933.

Conversion privilege: *See* Exchange privilege.

Convertible securities: Preferred stocks or bonds that carry the right of exchange for given amounts of common stock before a prearranged date.

Conversion ratio: Specified rate of exchange from preferred stocks or bonds into common stocks, as determined when the convertible security is issued.

Corporate (master or prototype) retirement plan: Corporate or trust agreement which qualifies for special tax treatment because the company is investing for the benefit of its employees. Prototype plans typically take the form of pension or profit sharing plans. 401(k) plans are also offered.

Current liabilities: Obligations due within one year or less.

Custodian: Bank or trust company that holds all securities and cash owned by an investment company. In some cases, the custodian act as transfer agent and dividend disbursing agent, although it has no supervisory function in regard to portfolio policies.

Cyclical stock: Stock whose performance is closely tied to the strength of the economy. Examples are heating oil, air travel, and housing.

Death benefit: Contingent upon several factors, this is the amount guaranteed to the survivors or beneficiaries of the contract if the annuitant dies before the annuitization date.

Defined benefit pension plan: *See* Pension.

Defined contribution plan: A self-directed, company-sponsored retirement plan whereby the employee directs the size and amount of his contribution. Referred to by their tax code exemption: 401(k), 403(b), 457.

Depreciation: The loss of value of a security since its purchase.

Discount rate: Rate at which the Federal Reserve loans money to banks, which in turn guides commercial banks in establishing their loan rates for customers.

Diversification: Investment in a number of different security issues to insulate a portfolio from a painful drop in one market area. This risk-reducing strategy is akin to not "keeping all your eggs in one basket."

Diversified investment company: Fund that has not invested more than five percent of its total assets in any single company, and does not hold more than 10 percent of the outstanding voting securities of any company, as stipulated in the Investment Company Act.

Dividend: Payment of income from a share of common or preferred stock.

Dollar-cost averaging: Method of accumulating capital by investing equal amounts of money at regular intervals. This attempt to average or moderate for turbulence in the markets allows the purchase of more shares when the trading price is low, and fewer shares when prices rise. The collective shares are bought at an average price rather than at a particular moment when the market could be skewed, thus reducing the need to correctly time the market.

Dual-purpose fund: Type of closed-end investment company, originally developed in England and introduced in the US in 1967, designed to serve the needs of two distinct types of investors: (1) those interested only in income, and (2) those interested solely in capital growth. Two separate classes of shares are issued.

Duration: Gauge of price sensitivity to interest rates. Expressed in years, duration shows the weighted average time for an investor to realize the currently stated yield.

Earnings profit: Often expressed as earnings per share (EPS), which is profit divided by the number of outstanding shares of stock.

Emerging markets: Developing nations, usually defined by gross domestic product and various economic measures. Usually these new markets are in Latin America, Eastern Europe, and Asia (excluding Japan). Funds that invest in emerging markets can be high risk.

Equity: Money represented by stock holdings.

Equity-income: Investment category seeking income through investments in dividend producing stock.

Equity security: Technically, all securities other than debt, although it may be used to denote common stocks alone, or preferred stocks that behave like common stocks.

Exchange privilege: Right to exchange shares of one open-end fund for shares of another within the same family of funds, avoiding new sales charges.

Expense ratio: Proportion of total annual operating expenses to net assets.

Face-amount certificate: A promise by the issuer of a security to pay the certificate holder a stated amount at a future date. The security may be purchased in periodic payments (installment type) or as a single payment (fully paid).

Fair value: Value determined by the board of directors for those securities and assets that do not have a market quotation readily available, as stipulated in the Investment Company Act.

Federal funds rate: Rate which Federal Reserve member banks charge each other for overnight loans needed to meet reserve requirements.

Fiduciary: Person or entity with custody of assets for another.

Fixed income security: Preferred stock or debt security with a stated percentage or dollar income return.

Forward pricing: Pricing mutual fund shares for sale, repurchase or redemption at the price computed after the receipt of an order. Pricing is usually done once or twice a day.

Free partial withdrawal: Is expressed as a percentage of the investors' account values, earnings, premiums, or the greatest of some or all of these three, that investors are allowed to withdrawal free of surrender charges during a specific period of time.

Fully managed fund: Fund without restrictions on the securities which may be held, giving the portfolio manager maximum discretion in all investments.

Fund of funds: Investment company that invests in other investment companies.

Government agency: Issues debt securities issued by government-sponsored enterprises, Federal agencies and international institutions. These securities are not direct obligations of the Treasury, but involve government sponsorship or guarantees such as GNMAs or FNMAs.

Growth stock: Stock that has shown better-than-average growth in earnings, and is expected to continue to do so through discoveries of additional resources, development of new products or expanding markets.

Hedge: To offset, or a security that has offsetting qualities. For example, an "inflation hedge" would rise in value as inflation rises, counterbalancing the eroding qualities normally expected from inflation.

Hedge fund: Mutual fund type investment company which, as a regular policy, "hedges" its market commitments. It does this by holding securities it believes are likely to increase in value and at the same time shorts securities it believes are likely to decrease in value. This is an aggressive approach to capital appreciation with limited investors.

Incentive compensation: Fee paid to an investment company advisor based on fund performance relative to specified market indexes. Also called *fulcrum fee*.

Income: Money earned through dividends or interest (but not capital gains). Gross income is total money earned, while net income is the gross income minus expenses, fixed charges, and taxes. Also referred to as *net investment income*.

Income fund: Investment fund company whose primary objective is generating income.

Incubator fund: Investment fund company that operates as a private, closed fund before offering shares to the public.

Individual retirement account: Or IRA, tax-deferral retirement program for individuals, established under the Employee Retirement Security Act of 1974.

Inflation: Upward movement in the price level of goods and services, which results in a decline in the purchasing power of money.

Insured redemption value plan: Insurance program designed to protect investors against loss in long-term mutual fund investments.

Investment advisor: *See* Investment management company.

Investment category: Stated purpose or goal of an investment company.

Investment company: Corporation or trust through which investors pool their money to obtain supervision and diversification of their investments.

Investment Company Act of 1940: Federal statute enacted by Congress in 1940 for the registration and regulation of investment companies.

Investment management company: Organization employed by an investment company to advise and supervise the assets of the investment company (also called *investment advisor*).

Investment trust: *See* Investment company.

Issuer: With reference to investment company securities, the company itself.

Keogh Plan: Tax-saving retirement program for self-employed persons and their employees. Also known as HR, 10 Plans, or Self-employed Retirement Plan.

Large-cap: Fund that holds stocks with an average market capitalization greater than five billion dollars. Many of these stocks are considered blue chips.

Leverage: Borrowing money to invest in hopes of achieving greater returns on the new securities. This simultaneously adds debt and builds assets.

Leverage stock: Junior security of a multiple-capital-structure company; generally a common stock, but it may also apply to a warrant, or to a preferred stock established with loans.

Liquid: Easily convertible into cash or exchangeable for other values.

Living Trust: Trust instrument made effective during the lifetime of the creator, in contrast to a Testamentary Trust, which is created under a will.

Load fee: Sales charge. *Front-end load*—Sales charge imposed at time of purchase. *Back-end load*—Sales charge imposed at time of redemption. *Level-load*—Single front or back-end sales charges without breakpoints, or a 12b-1 fee greater than 1.25 percent imposed annually. *No-load*—No front, back, or level sales charges.

M&E (mortality and expense fee): Fee, expressed as an annual percentage of assets, that pays the insurance company for the mortality risk it incurs in guaranteeing to pay either a guaranteed death benefit or guaranteed lifetime income to annuitants.

Management company: See Investment management company.

Management fee: Fee paid by an investment company to a management company for portfolio supervision and advisory services. *See also* Incentive compensation.

Management record: Statistical measure of the performance of investment company. Management record as mentioned in chapter 16, refers to a number of different factors including tenure as a comparative measure.

Market capitalization: Market value of a fund or stock, calculated by multiplying the market value of each share and the number of shares.

Market price: Price at which an investor is willing to buy/sell a security on the open market. This is the offer (bid/ask) price for closed-end funds.

Maturity: Date when debt obligation will pay its face value.

Average maturity: Average time until maturity for all the securities held by a fund.

Micro cap: Fund that holds stocks with an average market capitalization less than $500 million. Considered a high-risk investment.

Mid-cap: Fund that holds stocks with an average market capitalization between one and five billion dollars.

Modern Portfolio Theory: MPT Statistical method of analyzing investments by comparing their return and risk characteristics to each other and to established benchmarks. Elements of MPT include Alpha, Beta, R2, and Standard Deviation.

Money market fund: Mutual fund that exclusively invests in short-term debt securities with the intent of maximizing liquidity, capital preservation, and current income. These funds typically maintain a stable NAV of $1.

Multi-sector bond: Fund that invests in a vast array of bonds, foreign or domestic, government or corporate, investment grade or high yield.

Mutual fund: *See* Open-end investment company.

National Association of Securities Dealers (NASD): Organization of brokers and dealers that regulates over-the-counter security markets to prevent fraud and to protect investors.

Net assets: Dollar amount of all resources at market value less current liabilities.

Net asset value (NAV): Market price of an open-end mutual fund; the value of all assets divided by the number of outstanding shares. For open-end funds, this is the daily price at which an investor can buy or sell shares.

Net cash inflow/outflow: Change in the amount of money entering or leaving a fund during a specific time period. If a fund has new investments totaling $1,000,000 (inflow) in March, and investors withdraw $300,000 (outflow) during the same period, the net cash inflow would be $700,000.

No-load fund: Fund that does not have sales charges. *See* Load fee.

Non-diversified investment company: *See* Diversified investment company.

Nonqualified plans: Retirement plans that do not meet the requirements of the Self-Employed Individuals Tax Retirement Act or the Internal Revenue Code Sections 401(a), 403(a) or 403(b).

Nontaxable dividend: Dividend paid by a tax-exempt bond, such as a municipal bond.

Objective: Goal of an investor or investment company, such as growth of capital, current income, stability of capital, or any combination of these.

Odd lot: Number of shares that is not a round lot, normally a bundle of 100 shares, and therefore may involve higher exchange costs than round lots. Not applicable to open-end investment companies.

Open account: Account where a shareholder has reinvestment privileges and the right to make additional purchases without a formal accumulation plan.

Open-end investment company: Investment company whose shares are redeemable at any time at approximate asset value. In most cases, new shares are offered for sale continuously.

Option: *See* Warrant; also Put; Call.

Optional distribution: Choice of a shareholder to receive distributions (capital gains or dividends) in cash or to have them reinvested to purchase more shares.

Par value: Amount an issuer promises to pay upon maturity of a bond issue. Also known as the face value or maturity value.

Payroll deduction plan: Arrangement between a fund, employer and employee to deduct a specified amount of money from the employee's salary to purchase shares in a fund.

Pension plan: Program established by an employer, union or other member-based organization to pay benefits to an employee/member upon retirement. Also called a *defined benefit plan*.

Pension portability: Ability of an employee to move accumulated assets from a pension plan to an Individual retirement account or other qualified retirement plan.

Pension rollover: Opportunity to take distributions from a qualified pension or profit-sharing plan, and within 60 days of the distribution, reinvest them in an Individual retirement account. Under current law, investors who do not transfer within 60 days to a qualified account will be assessed a 20 percent withholding tax plus a 10 percent fee for early withdrawal.

Performance fund: Generally, open-end investment companies which emphasize short-term results and have rapid turnover of portfolio holdings. May also refer to funds with outstanding records of capital growth, regardless of the policies which achieved those results.

Preferred stock: Equity security that generally carries a fixed dividend, and whose claim to earnings and assets ranks ahead of common stock but behind bonds.

Premium: Percentage above asset value at which shares of a stock or closed-end fund sells, or the percentage above conversion value at which a preferred stock sells. Regarding closed-end funds, it is the difference between the market price and the portfolio value.

Price/book ratio: Market price divided by stock equity. The ratio shows how much investors are willing to pay for each dollar of the company.

Price/earning ratio: Market price divided by profit. The ratio shows how much investors are willing to pay for each dollar of that company's earnings.

Profit-sharing retirement plan: Retirement program in which a company contributes a percentage of its annual gross profit to participating employees. In a Keogh plan, the earnings of the self-employed individual is substituted for gross profit.

Prospectus: Official document that describes investment policy, fees, risks, management, and other pertinent fund information as directed by the Securities and Exchange Commission. A prospectus must accompany any new offer to sell securities.

Proxy statement: Agreement allowing a stockholder to transfer voting rights to another person if the stockholder will not attend the stockholders' meeting.

Prudent man rule: Law limiting the investments in a fiduciary account to those which a "prudent" investor would make, thus checking the power of the trustee.

Qualified plans: Retirement plans that meet the requirements of Section 401(a), 403(a) or 403(b) of the Internal Revenue Code, or the Self-Employed Individuals Tax Retirement Act.

R2: R-squared measure of diversification that determines how closely a particular fund's performance parallels an appropriate market benchmark over a period. The market is understood to have an R2 of 100 percent. Therefore, a fund with an R2 of 85 percent contains 85 percent of the market's diversification and risk. The remaining 15 percent is unique to the fund manager's actions.

Realized: The appreciation or depreciation of a security after it has been redeemed. If a stock price increases by $50 to $100 and the shares are sold, the appreciation is realized and the investor receives his or her money. If the shares are not sold, the appreciation is unrealized because it exists only on paper. A security that loses value is said to have depreciated, and the loss may be realized or unrealized in the same manner.

Record date: Date by which a shareholder must be registered on an investment company's books in order to receive a dividend.

Redemption-in-kind: Redemption of investment company shares in forms other than cash, such as other securities. Permissible for many mutual funds and tax-free exchange funds.

Redemption price: Price at which an investor sells securities, i.e., redeems securities for cash. *See* bid price as applicable to open-end investment companies.

Registrar: Banking institution that maintains the list of the shareholders and the number of shares they hold.

Registration statement: Document detailing a security's vital information which must be filed with and approved by the Securities and Exchange Commission before sale to the public.

Registered investment company: An investment company that has filed a registration statement with the Securities and Exchange Commission under the requirements of the Investment Company Act of 1940.

Regulated investment company: Investment company that has elected to qualify for the special tax treatment provided by Subchapter M of the Internal Revenue Code; not to be confused with registration under Investment Company Act of 1940.

Reinvestment privilege: Service offered by most mutual funds and some closed-end investment companies in which distributions may be automatically reinvested for additional full and fractional shares.

Repurchase agreement: Temporary transfer of a security to another person, based on the understanding that ownership will revert at a future time and price. This "renting" of a debt security fixes the yield while held by the purchaser and insulates the return from market fluctuations during the temporary ownership.

Repurchases: In closed-end companies, the companies' voluntary open-market purchases of their own securities. For open-end companies, the stock taken back at approximate asset value.

Restricted security: Portfolio security not available to the public at large, which requires registration with the Securities and Exchange Commission before it may be sold publicly; frequently referred to as a private placement or letter stock.

Risk: A personal evaluation of market tolerance; the determining factor in how much (or little) reward will come from a particular investment or event.

Rollover: Movement of funds from one qualified retirement investment to another while avoiding tax liabilities. The investor receives money in hand and must move it to another qualified account within 60 days or be assessed a 20 percent withholding tax plus a 10 percent penalty for early withdrawal. If the investor does not touch the money but has it move from custodian to custodian, it is called a *direct transfer*. *See* Pension rollover; Qualified plan.

Round lot: Fixed unit of trading (usually 100 shares), which forms the basis for prevailing commission rates on a securities exchange.

Securities and Exchange Commission (SEC): Independent agency of the US government that administers securities transaction laws.

Selling charge or sales commission: Fee paid at the time of purchase to the broker or financial advisor for the service of selling the fund; generally stated as a percentage of the offering price. *See* Load.

Senior capital: *See* Senior securities.

Senior securities: Notes, bonds, debentures, or preferred stocks whose claim on earnings and assets ranks ahead of common stock. Should a company liquidate, the claims of senior security holders ranks above those of junior security holders because the company's creditors receive compensation before the owners.

Separate account: Account completely separated from the general account of the insurance company, since its assets are generally invested in common stocks.

Shareholder experience: Measure of the investment returns, usually expressed in terms of a hypothetical $10,000 investment and including sales charges.

Sharpe ratio: Sharpe is a measure of the portfolio returns compared to total risk. A higher value indicates greater return per unit of risk. Risk in this calculation is provided by the portfolio's standard deviation. Sharpe ratios cannot stand alone, and can only be effective when used in conjunction with other portfolios or securities.

Short sale: Sale of a security that is not owned in the hope that the price will go down so that it can be repurchased at a profit. The person making a short sale borrows stock in order to make delivery to the buyer, and must eventually repurchase the stock in order to return it to the lender.

Small-cap: Fund that holds stocks with an average market capitalization between $500 million and $1 billion. Considered a high-risk investment.

Special situation: Investments in distressed or undervalued securities, including restructuring firms, venture capital, mergers, reorganizations, etc.

Specialty or specialized fund: Investment company concentrating its holdings in specific industry groups, such as technology, natural resources, gold, etc.

Split funding: Arrangement that combines investment in mutual fund shares and purchase of life insurance contracts, such as under an individual Keogh Plan.

Standard deviation: Statistical measure of the month-to-month volatility of a fund's returns higher numbers indicate greater variation from a benchmark. If the standard deviation for Fund A and Fund B were 8.0 and 4.0, respectively, then Fund A has experienced twice as much variability as Fund B. Money market funds, which have stable asset values and low risk, have standard deviations near zero.

Standardized return: Return net of all fees that is calculated according to form N-4 as required by SEC rule 482.

Subchapter M: Section of the International Revenue Code that provides special tax treatment for regulated investment companies. (See Chapter VII.)

Surrender charge: Expressed as a percentage of assets, this is the charge that the insurance company assesses clients when they surrender all or part of their contract; is similar to a CDSC.

Swap fund: *See* Tax-free exchange fund.

Tax-free exchange fund: Investment company permitting investors with appreciated securities to exchange them for shares of the fund while avoiding capital gains taxes.

Total return: Investment category that strives for both capital appreciation and current income. Also, performance calculated assuming reinvestment of all income and capital gains distributions.

Trustee: Party with responsibility to delegate and administer assets for the benefit of others.

Turnover ratio: Measure of change in a portfolio holdings; extent to which an investment company's portfolio changes during a year. A rough calculation can be made by dividing the lesser of portfolio purchases or sales (to eliminate the effects of net sales or redemption of fund shares) by average assets.

12b-1 Fee: Fee covering marketing and distribution costs, named after the 1980 Securities and Exchange Commission rule that permits them.

Uncertified shares: Ownership of fund shares credited to a shareholder's account without the issuance of actual stock certificates.

Underwriter: Principal. *See* Distributor.

Unit trust: Investment company or contractual plan which has a fixed portfolio, as opposed to the changeable portfolio available in open-end or closed-end funds.

Valuation date: Day on which the value of a separate account is determined.

Value investing: Policy of an investor to buy securities believed to have a market price below their actual or potential worth.

Volatility: Price fluctuation of a security. This can be measured in various ways, most commonly by standard deviation and beta.

Voluntary: Plan accumulation without any stated duration or specific requirements as to total amount to be invested, although conditions may be set on the minimum amount invested at each instance. Sales charges are applicable to each purchase made.

Warrant: Option to buy a specified number of shares of the issuing company's stock at a specified price, often in the form of put or call options. Warrants become tradable securities with values determined by the performance of the underlying security.

Withdrawal: Plan option of an open-end shareholder to receive periodic payment from his or her account. The payment may be more or less than investment income during that time period and therefore may imply the selling of shares.

Yield: For stocks, the percentage income return, derived by comparing income dividends to market price and capital gains. For bonds, this is the interest rate. In bond investments, the yield moves in the opposite direction of the price.

Yield-to-maturity: Rate of return on a debt security held to maturity, including appreciation and interest.

Appendix A

The Budget

L ife is full of unexpected emergencies. These monetary bumps should not break a budget but should allow you to better absorb them. Budgets provide financial resiliency that would not exist without them.

Your budget projections: Now to a year from now

Budget income year	Budget house year	Budget taxes year	Budget insurance year	Budget debt year	Budget divided by 13
$50,000					$3,846
	$12,000				− 923
		$2,500			− 192
			$4,800		− 369
				$6,000	− 461

At the heart of many financial difficulties is a poor but widely practiced notion called "division of incoming revenue." This is kind of a fancy term for "what's mine is mine, what's left over is ours." The simplest solution and first on your list to fix this problem starts with this concept: *In a financial partnership, your paycheck is your contribution. Every dime of it.*

Couples that keep money separate from the budget always amaze me. If you have entered into a financial union (and every marriage is a legal and binding contract) why would someone undermine the integrity of that agreement by stashing money outside the budget?

If you are single but living together the arrangement can be quite different. If you have shared goals, then the same budgetary parameters for a married couple should be set. The financial agreement you have with your partner will force you to make many of the same decisions a married couple would need to make.

Every dime counts toward the goals you may have set, the hopes that the budget will fulfill any plans you may have made together.

If you are an unattached single, who has broken the financial ties and support your parents have provided, the budget becomes a measure of your financial acumen.

Next list all of your expenditures. An *expenditure* is basically a bill, a debt, and/or an obligation. This can be a loan, a car payment or a child support. If these total less than you earn, this is called a surplus. Your budget will begin to work its way toward your future faster. If your bills, debts, and obligations are more than what you earn, you have a deficit.

A *deficit* is by definition "an excess of expenditure over revenue." This is a problem that may have not been fully understood prior to this. It can be an eye-opener indeed.

After you have finished listing your income and expenditures, close the book and walk away. It is time to discuss what you have just done. It can be overwhelming. You have brought together in one place, in many instances for the first time, your whole financial present as well as your financial past.

Use this "walk away opportunity" to set up another time, preferably within the next day or so, and sit down and move on to the next step. The next step is to redefine your partnership or, if you are single, as a sole proprietorship—at least in business terms.

Your "annual budget meeting," as it will now be called, has a beginning, a starting point that either runs a surplus or a deficit from which you can take the next step. Now it is time to forecast for the future—much the same way a business does.

After you have added all of your income revenue and totaled it, divide the number by 13. For instance, $50,000 total household income divided by 13 equals $3,846. This is the figure you will use to express your budget in terms of income. Why 13? It is an accounting method often used by corporations to even out the year into equal parts, four week periods.

$$52 \text{ weeks} \div \text{ by } 13 = 4 \text{ weeks.}$$

Unfortunately, your obligations may or may not follow this schedule. This is where it gets complicated. To simplify this as much as possible, think of it this way: Your fiscal year starts on April 1 for example.

Your house payment may be due on the fifteenth of each month. On a 13-month calendar, the fifteenth actually moves. The next fiscal month begins on April 29, 28 days or four weeks later. The fifteenth of the month is now magically moved to May 13. The next fiscal month, 28 days after April 29, begins on May 26. By June 10, you have enough earned to pay a house payment that was normally due five days later.

In the example budget at the beginning of this section, the figures assumes that your taxes are paid in full from your paycheck Unfortunately, your property taxes are not deducted from your paycheck. This is something you must account for on your own.

The insurance figure (only an example) may not even be close to what you are paying for property, automotive, or health costs on a monthly basis. The credit card payment is based on an even split of the balance by 13 months, excluding any interest.

Once your obligations have been accounted for in this manner, it is somewhat easier to see what is left over. Hopefully, this number reflects a surplus. I say hopefully, because we haven't even accounted for food, clothing, incidentals for work, and the kids.

Many popular economists say that government runs best when it runs a deficit. Those same people also feel that if the government is running surpluses (bringing in more money than they need), then we are being taxed too much.

You, on the other hand, are not permitted to run your little household/ business with deficit spending. You need surpluses and a steady stream of month after month profits. And to do that, you need to identify your expenditures, recognize current deficits, predict your future ones, and adjust your family's spending habits.

The Rules

There was a time when debt was simple. You either had credit or you didn't. Credit was difficult to come by. For big purchases you had to save, scrimp, and do without to save enough money get what you wanted. Now all you need to do is throw down a little piece of plastic, sign on the dotted line, and you are out the door with whatever your heart desires.

This so-called "freedom" is why you need rules. Perhaps not rules so much as financial guidelines.

Rule Number One

It will take longer than you assume to create a working budget.

Necessity is the first reason to approach a budget. As much as we look forward to growing up and reveling in all those freedoms that grown-ups have, we often neglect to factor in the costs associated with those perks. We all have friends with nice cars, nice clothes, and a party lifestyle. We all have acquaintances that seem to live large while we struggle to get by. It is easy to become envious of their good fortune.

Mark Twain once said, "The lack of money is the root of all evil." He also said, "You can't reach old age by another man's road." These are basically good quotes about lack of money and the cost of envy.

Understanding that the Joneses are in all likelihood broke is a monumental breakthrough in financial thinking. As American consumers, we are inundated with offers and products. There is no escape from the parade of pleasures available to us. The first challenge to your budget will be ignoring those temptations.

Some of you already know how quickly you can bring down your financial house once you allow yourself to succumb to those impulses. It takes very little time to go from having money (a surplus) to totally broke to debt (a deficit) yet the distance back can be long and arduous.

Rule Number Two

You can do this. It is only a matter of perspective.

This whole idea of budgeting is a lot easier if you understand a few simple things. Money as you know, is something we earn. But few of us break down the everyday cost of the things we buy against our paycheck. Is a $12 haircut different than a $30 one? Based on the average hourly wage in this country, the answer is yes. With the average hourly wage of $17.38 in the US as based on a number generated from the Bureau of Labor Statistics from June 2007, you don't even need a calculator to see the impact of a something as minor as a haircut on an hour worked.

Our understanding of the direct relationship between the 20 bucks you just handed your teenage child and the time it took to earn it is usually the furthest thing from your mind, and theirs.

Rule number two breaks down this way. The more you understand about how you earn money, the more you are likely to be slower to part with it. This change of perspective is a sudden revelation for most. Once you can comprehend the relationship between your expenses and how long it took you to earn the money to pay for them, you will be ready for the gradual acceptance that you can break your free spending habits.

So far we have done what a financial planner would have done. We started with a little information gathering. We know how much money comes in and how much is going out. Now we will put it on paper.

Monthly Budget

Herbert Hoover once said, "The course of unbalanced budgets is the road to ruin." This little chart will keep that from happening.

1: Gross monthly, average total   _____

Payroll deductions:

2: Taxes (federal, state, etc.)   _____

3: Savings plan (401k, 403b, credit union)   _____

4: Other (medical, dental, etc.)   _____

Total payroll deductions   _____

Net income (gross minus deductions)   _____

Expenses:

5: Personal savings (pay yourselves first)   _____

6: Housing (rent or mortgage, etc.)   _____

7: Utilities   _____

8: Home maintenance

(laundry, toiletries, upkeep)   _____

9: Transportation

(purchase, lease, or public)   _____

10: Auto upkeep

(gas, insurance, license, etc.)   _____

11: Food (groceries + dining out)   _____

12: Clothes   _____

13: Books, periodicals, online services   _____

14: Entertainment

(TV, movies, CDs, vacation)   _____

15: Debt (credit card, school, etc.)   _____

16: Other expenses   _____

Total expenses   _____

17: INCOME, NET minus all expenses   _____

Line One

Gross monthly income

1: Gross monthly average (total yearly divided by 13)   _____

In the first part of our budget, we need to tally the entire household's income in what is called *gross* form. Gross income is what you earn before taxes and any other deduction you might have set up. Earlier in this section, I suggested that you divide the year into 13 parts. Each of these parts represents your monthly gross income, which represents your yearly gross income. Ask someone how much they earn and this is usually the figure they tell you.

Remember to be honest with yourself here. If you can count on certain yearly bonuses, alimony, child support, or other regular payments that the IRS might be interested in, your budget will be interested also. If scheduled raises due to some sort of evaluation or union contract are part of your income year, include them also. Child support, alimony, and trust payments should be added in as well. Some budgets suggest that you build in a cushion by using the smallest amount of income possible. This is a bad idea. It creates a false monthly surplus, which is mistaken as free money, which eventually leads to frivolous spending.

Lines 2 through 4

Everybody wants their piece of your money pie. Once you have determined your gross income, remove your tax obligations and enter them on **Line 2**. There are federal, sometimes state, sometimes local taxes that occur on a regular basis. One of the best guides is the tax return you filed last year. You will find the best approximation of what your tax bill is for this year in last year's numbers.

While we are on the subject of taxes, make sure your monthly deductions match what you actually owe. March yourself into your payroll or human resource office and change your deductible on your W-4 until you come as close to zero taxes owed on April 15 as possible (http://www.irs.gov/pub/irs-pdf/fw4.pdf)

I want to take minute a share a pet peeve. Every year I hear about folks who can't wait to file their taxes to get the refund they have coming. They have earmarked this overpaid tax money for any number of things from a vacation to paying off Christmas bills to simply splurging on some sort of shopping spree. How many people do you know who barely get to the end of the month financially? And yet, every year, they rush to their friendly tax preparer, file electronically, paying extra premium for the speed to get it sooner and then act as if they had received a gift from Uncle Sam.

I even know one guy who uses his father's tax preparation service. In complete disregard of his dad's advice and the test of his financial acumen, he will pay dear old Uncle Sam extra money all year long, swiped little by little from his much-needed paycheck. I know some people who receive as much as $3,000 back.

The average tax return has risen every year with 2007 filers receiving $2,548 according to Internal Revenue Service Commissioner Mark Everson. Every year. That's $49 a week that could have been saved, earned interest on, invested, or otherwise have been used to help to keep you out of debt. Don't overpay and, even more important, don't underpay. Use the W-4 form in your employer's office to calculate exactly the right amount of deductions needed to come out as close to zero owed, zero returned.

Using your pay stub, you can determine the approximate amount of money you paid to Social Security, disability, and Medicare.

Income Deductions

Payroll deductions:

2: Taxes (federal, state, etc.)   _____

3: Savings Plan (401k, 403b, credit union)   _____

4: Other (medical, dental, etc.)   _____

Total payroll deductions   _____

Use **Line 3** for the amount you contribute into your employer sponsored benefit plan. If you are saving in any other pretax or after tax plan, include this figure here.

Line 4 depends on your employer's health care plan. You might have some weekly dollar amount taken out to pay your premium. If so, enter that number. Better yet, be realistic and increase it by 15 percent.

Income minus deductions

Net income (gross minus deductions)   _____

At this point you can take a look at your financial picture with a somewhat clearer eye. Now for the expenses. Unfortunately, no matter how you try and master your personal finances, you will always have expenses.

Expenses

Expenses:

5: Personal savings (pay yourselves first)   _____

6: Housing (rent or mortgage, etc.)   _____

7: Utilities   _____

8: Home maintenance

    (laundry, toiletries, upkeep)   _____

9: Transportation

    (purchase, lease, or public)   _____

10: Auto upkeep

    (gas, insurance, license, etc.)   _____

11: Food (groceries + dining out)   _____

12: Clothes   _____

13: Books, periodicals, online Services   _____

14: Entertainment

    (TV, movies, CDs, vacation)   _____

15: Debt (credit card, school, etc.)   _____

16: Other expenses   _____

The primary question here is, can you be realistic in estimating these costs? These numbers are the first step in creating a reliable budget. Believe me when I tell you, this is the one section of the budget that is totally in your control.

Line 5 is the second time in the budget where savings is mentioned. This isn't accidental. Savings should be thought of as an expense. It is taken directly from money left after taxes. The old saying, "pay yourself first" is and always will be an excellent idea. Finding the right amount to pay yourself can be difficult if you have never done it.

This is a fine line. If your savings plan is too aggressive, if you are paying yourself too much, you might find yourself more likely to assume some debt. This is never a good idea, even in the short term. Remember in the previous step we discussed the negative effects that debt causes to savings. Debt costs money. You will need to adjust your goals by reducing your deductions. So save. It is important.

Lines 6 through **16** are the workable parts of a good budget. These are the parts of a budget that can be adjusted. These figures are less fixed and far more flexible. Taking a long hard look at these expenses, they can lead to some additional savings that you may have known existed.

The "workable" parts of this budget can be achieved by some common sense and good old-fashioned penny pinching. For instance, do you leave the heat on when you aren't home? Are there ways to curb your utility bills? Does the two-car garage need two cars in it? Can you really justify the added costs of upkeep, insurance, and gas? Many of these are also green solutions.

How often do you eat out? Is it because you can't cook or because you don't want to? When you shop for food at the grocery store, are name brands always better than store brands? Do you shop for clothes simply because they are on sale? Do you read all the magazines and newspapers you subscribe to? Do you avail yourself of online services that you don't need?

I think you get the drift of this. These questions need to be asked. Financial common sense begins with a series of questions just like the ones above. They are meant to help us understand that wanting and needing are two entirely different things.

Rule Number Three

*Stay with your plan.

You have considered a budget for a reason. Perhaps it is more than just finding a few extra bucks at the end of the month. Maybe your goals are loftier. Maybe you want to buy a home, or possibly pay off the one you own. It is important to know exactly where you stand financially before you start chasing your dreams. I'm trying to get you to free up even more money for that under-funded retirement plan.

Now for the real reason we use budgets. It is not because I want to see you calculate where you are or where you've been. I want you to determine, based on your budget, where you are going. In the past you had no difficulty identifying what you wanted. Impulses are short-term goals. Budgets create the ability to achieve long-term goals.

Budgets make you think about what it is that you want. Is it a house? Are those lazy afternoons watching the kids play on the front lawn while you sip something that makes the glass sweat all you can think about? Perhaps it is tinkering in the garage or working in the garden? Budgets are the only tool that will get you there.

Accountability or honesty in your budget is extremely important. You do not want to exclude some of those guilty pleasures that make life worthwhile. If you can't live without that $5 coffee in the morning, budget for it. If you want to see a movie every Saturday, or rent one or two for the weekend, budget for it. Too many people are missing the point when they begin a budget. You are no different from everyone else. You have different needs and wants; different goals and ambitions; different abilities and willpower. Your budget will reflect your individuality.

Your budget offers you an opportunity to understand exactly where you are at a given moment. It is an invaluable tool, opening up the financial conversation.

One final note: If you are single, find a financial mentor to help you. Someone you trust—parent, sibling, best friend; someone you can bounce financial ideas off of every now and again. This person can be as invaluable as a spouse or partner at keeping you true to your plan.

Appendix B

The Pursuit of Principles

Financial books like these are meant to be timeless, providing oversight to a shifting marketplace. But the news that affects these markets is not so static. And this can change not only how we view our investments but create a period where we question our strategy.

As I finished this book, the Dow Jones Industrial Average, the index that offers a cross section of all that is huge in the market, fell almost a thousand points from its lofty record setting height of 14,198. As many people will tell you, that number *is* only a number. But it represents a psychological milestone.

While some of us have been focusing on mortgage meltdowns, stock surges, credit crunches and inflation indicators, several of our distinguished financial leaders have been looking for ways to improve the American financial marketplace. The question is, does it need to be fixed?

Using the argument that rules tend to squash innovation and do little to lure the rest of the globe to our financial shores, the call for more principles and less regulation is quietly making its way out of the backroom and closer what may become reality. And if these folks have their way, much of the effort we have put into our retirement plan will be for naught.

The gap between a principles and rules is quite wide. Rules imply a lack of trust based on previous experiences where trust has failed -when no one was looking. And principles suggest that all of our corporate leaders are men and women of character who would never mislead shareholders or auditors with financial statements that were not really truthful. I always told my kids that character is what you have when no one is looking.

Until he more or less admitted on November 8th, 2007, that the economy was on somewhat shaky ground, due in part to what may turn out to be failed monetary policies, Federal Reserve Chairman Ben Bernanke had been focused on something other than mortgages, credit, and inflation. He joined the chorus expressing his concern over the strength of our financial marketplace and some of the rules that currently govern it.

That marketplace, if you were unaware, is at the heart of your retirement plan. The rules and regulations Mr. Bernanke is questioning, widely disdained by the businesses they regulate, have helped secure numerous retirement futures. Senator Paul Sarbanes (D-MD) and Representative Michael G. Oxley (R-OH) sponsored the regulation in question, The Sarbanes-Oxley Act of 2002 also known as the Public Company Accounting Reform and Investor Protection Act of 2002. These two officials wanted corporate accountability. The new standards had its critics who suggested the economic ramifications of this type of legislation would overshadow any perceived benefits.

The first attacks on Sarbanes-Oxley, were made several years ago in a report by R. Glenn Hubbard, the then Chairman of Council of Economic Advisers to President Bush and has continued adding critics, the latest of which include the Fed chairman, Treasury Secretary Henry Paulson, S.E.C. Chairman Christopher Cox, former S.E.C. head Arthur Levitt and former S.E.C. accountant Donald Nicolaisen.

Unfortunately, the wind of change may finally be blowing in the right direction for these financial leaders as the economy begins to slow down. The problems that may be facing the economy in the coming years are not the result of SarbOx. While the dollar may be in trouble, while the rising price of oil works its way into every corner of our financial plans in the very near future, and with the numerous deficits facing the country, which will need to be dealt with and with noticeable urgency, relaxing regulations will not solve any of the above problems.

There has been a seemingly endless advance in stock prices over the last five years. That may be coming to a close as this book goes to print. Corrections are a healthy part of the marketplace. Corrections such as the one that is long overdue play to our dollar cost averaging method of retirement saving.

The correction is not the problem. Even as the bull market surged, this esteemed group of economists and business people was making the claim that the financial markets were "in trouble." Why? Because the regulations that keep investors safe, are making the American financial markets less attractive to foreign companies.

At the heart of their crusade to alter the regulatory process is Sarbanes-Oxley. This legislation, signed on the heels of the debacle at Enron, Tyco, Global Crossing and WorldCom, has forced companies to own up to their financial statements or face penalties. These regulations are, they suggest, the reason why numerous IPO's are now making their way for less regulated and somewhat wilder frontiers overseas.

Sarbanes-Oxley or as it has been lovingly rechristened, SarbOx has been the focus of many unnecessary assaults including one by the former Federal Reserve Chairman Alan Greenspan, who was quoted as saying "Globalization is a critical determinant of economic activity. We're no longer a separate economy. Formerly, everything was here." No sooner did his eighteen-year stint at the Fed end than he was stumping for alterations in the law. There is no disagreement that the high initial cost of the regulation was prohibitive. But as is often the case with all costs associated when services utilize technology, they are dramatically decreasing.

Productivity, as Mr. Hubbard once suggested in report dated October 23, 2002 is determined by amount of the restraint regulation places on its growth. And while it is true that reducing regulations may in some instances increase productivity in many industries, in the field of business accounting and corporate audits, the cost goes down as time moves on.

The accounting industry has streamlined the processes required by the 2002 legislation incorporating many of the requirements into their software. This is a classic example of technology complimenting services. The accounting industry foresees those costs falling further.

So what has spurred the effort of late? Henry Paulson is the short answer. Believing that the financial health of the United States is at risk, he has pointed the finger at overregulation as the marketplace villain. Perhaps, the recent stock market volatility will bolster his efforts. I sincerely hope not.

SarbOx, to its credit, has forced over 464 restatements of earnings in the past three years. This is quite the shift from the previous ten years, which saw a combined average of 45 restatements a year. This is our *David* to their *Goliath*.

Several factors could be at play in this latest attack on the regulation. The cautious approach auditors have taken of late is worrisome to Mr. Paulson.

Unfortunately, the reason for the heighten caution is not due to SarbOx but because of the implied threat of litigation should those statements be less than factual. In effect, the regulation the SarbOx has created for many accounting firms has been overseen by the threat of shareholder action should they sign-off on phantom write-offs. Could the numerous big bank write-offs due to poor mortgage and lending practices be the real test for the law? The stock market's reaction may be telling us something but SarbOx will reveal what we need to know.

According to CFO.com, the reasons behind many of the restatements are almost always known to the companies and hidden from the audit process. "Improper revenue- recognition" is cited as a primary culprit in the restate-ment process followed by "improper inventory valuations and inadequate allowances for bad debt." Mr. Levitt is no stranger to this type of restatement calling it "accounting hocus-pocus."

What really worries this group is the crushing blow such accounting shenani-gans have on a company's share value. Restatements can cause a stock to plummet and this, Mr. Paulson believes is not very accommodative to overseas companies looking to tap the US financial system.

Unfortunately, many of the proposed changes are already taking shape. The S.E.C. is now in the process of slicing and dicing the best protection an investor might have. The simple fact that restatements have skyrocketed in recent years should be reason enough to believe that the regulation is doing exactly what it was designed to do.

Had principle ruled rather than regulation and had it been the guiding light for the 157 companies who restated in 2006 taking another look at their financial statements, we as shareholders would not have known that the house of cards constructed by these principle-less corporate heads was outside of generally accepted accounting practices. True, the value of these companies did drop on the open market, with good reason: the value in those businesses was misrepresented.

Changes in SarbOx will not increase competitiveness in the US market-place. The real reason for foreign companies to list overseas dates back to a pre-SarbOx era and a Congressional action that allowed shareholder litigation if any company, foreign or domestic misrepresented themselves to shareholders in our capital markets.

Demanding strict accounting allows our markets to thrive when principles are conveniently thrown to the wayside. Robert Pozen, chairman of MFS Investment Management suggested in a recent *Wall Street Journal* op-ed that "regulatory system needs a mix of general principles and detailed rules."

That is exactly what is in place now Mr. Paulson, Mr. Bernanke, et al and exactly what makes the financial markets in the US the preferred place to do business. Even if the economy needs to take a breather from some financially irresponsible activity, we will still be the envy of the free markets.

As we inch closer toward a global marketplace, the rules and regulations guiding the US markets should be adopted globally and not demoted in favor of a seemingly less lawful system.

Principles can stand taller than the regulations. But neither can standalone. Detailed rules protect all parties and create a transparency that will prove to be enviable to overseas exchanges. The risk may not be as attractive to foreign investors but the result will protect many risk-adverse investors here in the US.

Why is this important? You may use mutual funds as your default investment in your retirement plans but that doesn't let you off the hook. Not paying attention to what is taking place in Washington and on Wall Street can place the potential of those plans in jeopardy. Passive investing as we often do in our retirement accounts is no excuse for allowing those who represent us to undo the protections that favor the investor and keep the companies we invest in honest.

We are shareholder citizens with a vested interest in not only the fiscal health of the country but the profitability of the companies we invest our money in. We need to stay diligent. Demanding accountability from our government and from the businesses that employ us and with whom we invest does not weaken the financial markets. It strengthens them and by doing so, enables us to make those investments in our future through our retirement plans.

Index